Joseph Sanderson

The bow in the cloud

Words of comfort for those in bereavement, sickness, sorrow and the varied trials

of life

Joseph Sanderson

The bow in the cloud
Words of comfort for those in bereavement, sickness, sorrow and the varied trials of life

ISBN/EAN: 9783337268848

Printed in Europe, USA, Canada, Australia, Japan

Cover: Foto ©Andreas Hilbeck / pixelio.de

More available books at **www.hansebooks.com**

THE RAINBOW AROUND THE TOMB.

"The brightest bow is seen upon the darkest cloud."—*Havergal.*

THE

BOW IN THE CLOUD

OR

WORDS OF COMFORT

FOR THOSE IN BEREAVEMENT, SICKNESS, SORROW AND THE VARIED TRIALS OF LIFE.

EDITED BY J. SANDERSON, D.D.,
Editor of "Memorial Tributes," "The Pulpit Treasury," etc.

WITH AN INTRODUCTION
By WILLIAM M. TAYLOR, D.D., LL.D.

"Friend after friend departs; who hath not lost a friend?"—*Montgomery*.
"Earth has no sorrow that Heaven cannot heal."—*Moore*.

NEW YORK:
E. B. TREAT, 771 BROADWAY,
Office of the Pulpit Treasury.

Price in Cloth, $1.75.

"O, THINK OF THE FRIENDS OVER THERE."

With Sympathizing Regards of

PUBLISHER'S NOTE.

THE aim of this book is to console suffering and to comfort bereaved ones. It seeks to do this by directing them to look on their cloud of sorrows as spanned and beautified by the rainbow of God's promises; to consider the importance of having a hold upon eternal realities; to study the character and works of God who "knows our frame and remembers we are dust"; to commit their way to Him who was "a man of sorrows and acquainted with grief"; and by becoming a valuable assistant to any, who, by sending it to others, may, in this way, extend sympathy and consolation to the afflicted, and thus

>——tell, to sinners round,
>What a dear Saviour they have found.

For, it must not be forgotten, that God would say to many a suffering one now, as He said to His ancient people, "I have chosen thee in the furnace of affliction"; and the records of Christian biography testify that many of the purest souls have emerged from beneath the heaviest burdens, that many of the best characters have been seamed with scars, and that many have first seen the gates of heaven through their tears.

So long as the language of Solomon holds true: "Man is born unto trouble as the sparks to fly upward," so long will there be weeping eyes and aching hearts, and therefore demands upon our sympathies to alleviate their sorrows.

There is no anguish like that of the broken heart mourning for those that are not, and no sorrow like the memory of happier days with the loved of earth.

PUBLISHER'S NOTE.

The destroying angel knows no rest and takes captive from our homes one after another. The bleeding hearts of relatives, neighbors and friends have often touched the sympathetic cords of our nature and our inmost soul responds—would that we could go to them and tell them how deeply we feel for them and how gladly would we share, if possible, the grief they have been called to bear.

In such an hour of sore bereavement, it is not in human power to describe the full import of even a few stammering "words of comfort," a few lines of condolence, or a few sympathizing tears.

There are times when "silence is golden," and on such occasions we hesitatingly refrain from intruding upon the sacredness of the home, scarcely knowing how to approach its mourning inmates, what to write, what to say, or how to say it.

Under these circumstances this volume comes to our aid, not only in its personal ministrations of consolation, but may be addressed with "affectionate regards" (see presentation page), to the afflicted one, or bereaved family, as expressive of one's sympathy and love.

Its pages are laden with the best thoughts of the most eminent divines, who, by soul cheering and loving words, and rich experiences of the deep things of God, have done much to "bind up the broken hearted," by pointing to the source of all comfort in the belief that "earth has no sorrow that heaven cannot heal."

It would be impossible to acknowledge all the sources from which this volume is compiled; mention should be made that selections have been freely taken from "Words of Comfort for Bereaved Parents," published by J. Nisbet & Co., London.

INTRODUCTORY NOTE

Dear Mr. Treat:

I like exceedingly the idea of your volume "The Bow in the Cloud," and so far as a careful examination enables me to judge, I think you have very successfully carried it out.

Amid the manifold afflictions of life, the great solace is, and ever must be, the gospel of the Lord Jesus Christ, and the extracts which you have gathered together from so many quarters serve to show how its principles and promises have been brought to bear by different writers, upon their own trials. The book is pre-eminently a collection of individual testimonies to the efficacy of the consolation furnished by the Word of God to those who are in trouble. The writers have tried and proved it for themselves, and can therefore confidently commend it to others. Indeed the very rehearsal of their own experience is itself a comfort to those who are similarly afflicted, and so the book will be an appropriate gift to all who are in any trial; while at the same time it will be helpful to the Christian pastor in his visits to the house of mourning as suggesting to him words in season to those who are weary. By its publication you will become a true Barnabas, or son of consolation to many, and I trust it will have, as it deserves, a wide circulation.

I am glad that you have drawn so largely from my friend William Logan's "Words of Comfort for Parents bereaved of little Children." For more than twenty years I have been in the habit of putting that book into the hands of bereaved parents, and it has always been gratefully appreciated by them. But the loss of children is only one form of trial, and you have done well to widen your range so as to include most of the afflictions which go to swell "the still sad music of humanity."

Believe me, yours faithfully,

Wm. M. Taylor

PARSONAGE, BROADWAY TABERNACLE,
NEW YORK, NOV. 15, 1887.

The Bow in the Cloud.

I DO SET MY BOW IN THE CLOUD.—*Genesis* ix., 13.

ANGEL OF PEACE. KAULBACH.

CONTENTS

CONSOLATIONS FROM THE BIBLE.

	PAGE
Old Testament,	27
New Testament,	34

INTRODUCTORY.

The Common Grief,	David Russell, D.D.	43
Friend after Friend Departs,	James Montgomery.	46
Compare Your Afflictions with Those of Others,	J. Flavel.	47
How to Sympathize with Mourners,	C. J. Vaughan, D.D.	48
Comfort in Affliction,	Thomas Moore.	50
Uses of Chastisement,	Jas. W. Alexander, D.D.	51
The Necessity of Affliction,	John R. Macduff, D.D.	56
Calamity Resulting in Victory,	Theo. L. Cuyler, D.D.	62
God's Power to Comfort,	T. DeWitt Talmage, D.D.	63
Consolation Sought and Found,	John Bowring.	65
Prayer for Sanctification of Sorrow,	Archb'p Fenelon.	66
Benefits of Affliction,	Richard Baxter.	68
Calling His Children Home,	Theodore L. Cuyler, D.D.	69
We Are Going One by One,	Mrs. M. E. Carmichael.	70
The Ministry of Trouble,	T. DeWitt Talmage, D.D.	71
Uses of Affliction	R. Macduff, D.D.	73
"Jesus Wept,"	John Eadie D.D., LL.D.	74
The Sexton and His Little Graves,	David Rae.	77
Our Coming Life,	J. G. Whittier.	81

CONTENTS.

PAGE

Would You Call Them Back Again?	Rev. G. Whyte.	82
What Makes Heaven For Us,	D. L. Moody.	83
What Takes Place At Death?	Rev. Fergus Ferguson.	84

INFANT SALVATION. Articles and Selections from. 91

Wm. Alexander, D.D.,
James Morison, D.D.,
David Russell, D.D.,
Chas. Eliott, D.D., LL.D.,
Ralph Wardlaw, D.D.,
Alex. Macleod, D.D.,
Adam Thompson, D.D.,
Alex. Wallace, D.D.,
Robert Ferguson, D.D.,
J. Logan Aikman, D.D.,
Edward Steane, D.D.,
Wm. Cooke, D.D.,
John Macfarlane, D.D.,
Thos. Chalmers, D.D.,
R. W. Hamilton, D.D.

CONSOLATION FOR PARENTS BEREFT OF CHILDREN.

The Light that Radiates Around the Infant's Tomb,	Thomas Chalmers, D.D.	117
A Mother's First Grief,	Robert Smyth Chilton.	119
Bereaved Parents Comforted,	Wm. M. Taylor, D.D.	120
Parental Anxiety Removed by the Early Death of Children,	John Macfarlane, D.D.	123
Restoration of Children in Heaven,	John Brown, D.D.	126
The Lambs All Safely Folded,	Unknown.	128
Divine Beneficence in the Death of Children,	Thomas Binney, D.D.	132
"Is It Well With the Child?"	Rev. C. H. Spurgeon.	138
Happy Eva,	John G. Whittier.	143
The Faded Flower,	John James Methven.	144
The Mother's Blighted Hopes,	John Kitto, D.D.	145

CONTENTS.

		PAGE
A Little Child Shall Lead Them,	Rev. Wm. Blair, A.M.	146
The Charm of Childhood,	Rev. Geo. Gilfillan.	148
Address at the Death of a Child,	Rev. Joseph P. Chown.	151
God's Relationship to Children,	John Guthrie, D.D.	153
The Children Safely Folded,	Joseph Brown, D.D.	155
Safe with Christ,	Rev. Charles Garrett.	156
An Appeal to Parents,	Rev. Wm. Bathgate.	158
A Transplanted Flower,	Wm. B. Bradbury.	160
Purposes of Divine Mercy in Early Death,	Rev. J. Ker.	162
Parental Consolation,	John Guthrie, D.D.	170
Gone to Paradise,	Charles Wesley.	171
A Sweet Sorrow,	Philip Schaff, D.D.	172
Bereaved Parents Comforted,	D. Russell, D.D.	174
Germs of Immortality,	John Cumming, D.D.	175
The Flowers of Paradise,	Thomas Guthrie, D.D.	176
The Grave a Wardrobe,	Matthew Henry, D.D.	177
Christ Blessing Little Children,	John Brown, D.D.	178
A Mother Comforted,	John Morrison, D.D.	179
My Darling's Shoes,	Unknown.	180
Gone to Sleep,	Archbishop Leighton.	181
The Loss of Children,	John Flavel.	182
A Bud of Beauty,	Robert Hall, D.D.	183
Better to be with Christ,	Philip Doddridge, D.D.	184
Victory Without Conflict,	Rev. James Hervey.	185
The Flower Plucked by the Master,	Unknown.	186
The Crown of Life,	Rev. Richard Cecil.	187
The Child in Heaven,	Mary Hewitt.	188
Little Ones in Heaven,	Robert Ferguson, D.D.	190
The Infant Choir in Heaven,	James Montgomery.	192
Good Bye,	Unknown.	194

CONSOLATION FOR THE BEREAVED. Various Ages and Conditions Considered.

		PAGE
Mutual Recognition in Heaven,	G. Smith, D.D.	197
Grief Not Forgotten,	Rev. Wm. Blair, M.A.	199
Recompense,	Harriet E. Pritchard.	202
The Sympathy of Christ,	Prof. John Cairns, D.D.	203
The Day of Death Better Than The Day of Birth,	Principal J. Caird, D.D.	210
The Saviour's Sympathy With the Afflicted,	John Eadie, D.D.	215
Sorrow for the Dead,	John Tulloch, D.D.	217
How Are the Dead Raised Up and With What Body Do They Come?	Prof. I. Burns, D.D.	221
Blessed Are They That Mourn,	William Cullen Bryant.	226
A Lovely Life—Its Closing Scene,	Rev. Geo. Gilfillan.	227
The Believer's Confidence,	Rev. James Parsons.	231
Resignation,	H. W. Longfellow.	233
Heaven a Vast and Happy Society,	Wm. Morley Punshon, D.D.	235
Consolation Derived from the Hope of Immortality,	Robert Hall, D.D.	236
Oh, Where Shall Rest be Found,	James Montgomery.	238
The Hope of a Resurrection,	John Flavel.	239
Recognition After the Resurrection,	Wm. Anderson, D.D.	240
My First Household Grief,	Hugh Miller	242
For a Bereaved Mother,	Charles Sprague.	243
The Dying Mother and Her Child,	Rob't. Pollok, A.M.	244
Resigned in Hope,	William T. M'Auslane.	246
The Gathered Lilies,	Rev. Ebenezer Erskine.	247
From Shadow into Sunshine At Last,	R. C. Trench.	248

		PAGE
Home in Our Father's House,	Newman Hall, D.D.	249
The Rainbow of Promise, as Seen Through Tears,	Bishop Wm. Bacon Stevens, D.D.	253
Sorrow Succeeded by Joy,	Theo. L. Cuyler, D.D.	259
The Mount of Happiness,	Geo. Newell Lovejoy.	260
Christ a Man of Sorrow,	Edward Payson, D.D.	261
The Divine Sympathy,	John R. Macduff, D.D.	265
Comfort for the Poor,	James Smith, D.D.	270
To a Brother Departed,	Unknown.	271
Comfort for the Widow,	James Smith, D.D.	272
A Word of Warning to Mothers,	Wm. Anderson, D.D.	274
The Shadow,	Rev. J. S. Meissner,	275
Thy Will be Done,	Henry Alford, D.D.	275
A Word to Parents,	Henry Allon, D.D.	279
One Less at Home—One More in Heaven,	Unknown.	282
Beneficent Design of Affliction,	Rev. Robert French.	283
Our Evening Star in Heaven Afar,	"Christian Treasury."	287
The Mother's Comfort,	Miss Jessie Blevin.	288
Home Bereavements,	Henry Ward Beecher.	289
The Dead Are with Us,	S. Irenæus Prime, D.D.	293
One Link Gone,	Unknown.	294
Heaven Is Our Home,	E. L. Bulwer.	295
To a Father Bereft of a Son,	Ralph Erskine.	296
Weep not For Her,	D. M. Moir.	297
Consolation for the Lonely,	Mary Hewitt.	299
On the Death of a Young Girl,	William H. Burleigh.	300
On the Death of a Son,	Archbishop Fenelon.	302
Jesus is Drawing,	William Luff.	303
Death of the First Born,	Willis Gaylord Clark,	304

		PAGE
The Mourning Mother,	Bishop Doane.	305
The Departed Wife,	Rev. John Newton.	306
On the Death of a Son,	W. B. O. Peabody.	307
Mourn Not the Dead,	Eliza Cook.	308
Grief Was Sent Thee For Thy Good,	Rev. T. H. Bayley.	309
Comforted,	Rev. P. T. Pockman.	310
Friends Gone Before,	L. W. Ward.	314
The Silver Lining,	Unknown.	315
True Sympathy,	Unknown.	316
The Compensation of Life,	Rev. John Philip.	317
Our Sainted Dead: Living Epistles,	Alfred H. Moment, D.D.	324

CONSOLATION FOR VARIED AFFLICTIONS.

Temptations, the Trials of our Faith,	John Wesley.	329
Abiding in Jesus,	H. B. Stowe.	330
The Bible and Prayer in Affliction,	James Buchanan, D.D.	331
Love in Chastisement,	J. D. Burns, D.D.	335
God's Law of Compensation,	Theo. L. Cuyler, D.D.	336
The Pillar of Clouds,	E. Paxton Hood, D.D.	339
Needed Blessings,	William H. Burleigh.	340
Grace Proportionate to the Trial,	Rev. F. Whitfield.	341
Light on Dark Providences,	Robert F. Sample, D.D.	342
Joy After Sorrow. (Translated.)	Paul Gerhardt.	348
The Future Will Clear Up Many Mysteries,	T. L. Cuyler, D.D.	350
We Shall Know Hereafter,	Robert F. Sample, D.D.	351

CONTENTS.

		PAGE
Trust God in Trial,	Paul Gerhardt.	358
Blessings in Disguise	Unknown.	359
The Burden of Sorrow,	Rev. John Philip.	360
In Trial,	Sir Robert Grant.	362
Victory over Temptations,	Wm. S. Plummer, D.D.	364
Mystery Made Plain Hereafter,	F. C. Monfort, D.D.	367
Earth to Earth,	J. H. Gurney.	371
Immortality,	Philip Schaff, D.D.	372
Consolation and Warning,	James Smith, D.D.	380
The Light in the Clouds,	Theo. L. Cuyler, D.D.	383
Retrospection,	Anna Shipton.	386
Trials and Trouble the Lot of Mankind,	John R. Macduff, D.D.	387
The Sorrows of Care,	Rev. John Philip.	391
Patience Under Trial,	Wm. R. Williams, D.D.	393
Relief in Darkness,	Rev. E. C. Gordon.	395
Waiting for Day,	H. C. Brown.	398
The Burdens of Sympathy,	Henry Clay Trumbell, D.D.	399
Come Ye Disconsolate,	Thomas Moore.	402
When the Mists Have Cleared Away,	Annie Herbert.	403
Amen,	F. G. Browning.	404

CONSOLATION FOR THE AGED AND INFIRM.

I'm Growing Old,	John Godfrey Saxe.	407
Reverence the Aged,	Elihu Burritt.	409
Venerable Age: Its Trials and Consolations,	Wm. F. Morgan, D.D.	410
Why Mourn the Old?	Wm. Cullen Bryant.	421
Comfort for the Aged and Infirm,	James Smith, D.D.	422

CONTENTS.

		PAGE
A Few More Years Shall Roll,	H. Bonar, D.D.	424
The True Consoler,	Wm. Wordsworth.	425
The Burdens of Age,	Rev. John Philips.	426
The Better World,	George D. Prentice.	429
Time Bears Us Away,	Charles H. Spurgeon.	430
I Would Not Live Always,	Wm. A. Muhlenberg, D.D.	431
Desiring to Depart,	A. E. Kittridge, D.D.	433
The Sequel of Life,	Rev. John Philip.	438
Hopefully Waiting,	A. D. F. Randolph.	440
The Sunset of Life,	Bishop Wm. Bacon Stevens, D.D.	441
Beyond the Smiling and the Weeping	Horatius Bonar, D.D.	445
The Death Bed,	Thos. Hood.	446
Heaven and Earth,	F. W. Faber.	446
The Hour of Death,	Mrs. Felicia Hemans.	447
The Home Beyond the Grave,	Bishop R. S. Foster, D.D.	448
Shall We Meet Again,	George D. Prentice.	450
The Last of Earth,	Kate Putnam Osgood.	451
Review of Life,		452

CONSOLATION FROM THE BIBLE.

THUS SAITH THE LORD.—Exodus xix-16.

THE OLD TESTAMENT.

Genesis v. 24—And Enoch walked with God: and he was not; for God took him.

Exodus xxii. 22, 23—Ye shall not afflict any widow, or fatherless child. If thou afflict them in any wise, and they cry at all unto me, I will surely hear their cry.

Deuteronomy i. 39—Moreover your little ones, which ye said should be a prey, and your children, which in that day had no knowledge between good and evil, they shall go in thither, and unto them will I give it, and they shall possess it.

2 Samuel xii. 22, 23—And he said, While the child was yet alive, I fasted and wept: for I said, Who can tell whether God will be gracious to me, that the child may live? But now he is dead, wherefore should I fast? can I bring him back again? I shall go to him, but he shall not return to me.

—— **xxii. 28**—And the afflicted people thou wilt save.

2 Kings iv. 26—Is it well with thee? is it well with thy husband? Is it well with the child? And she answered, It is well.

Nehemiah viii. 10—The joy of the Lord is your strength.

Job i. 21—The Lord gave, and the Lord hath taken away; blessed be the name of the Lord.

—— **v. 17, 18, 19, 26**—Behold, happy is the man whom

God correcteth: therefore despise not thou the chastening of the Almighty: for he maketh sore, and bindeth up: he woundeth, and his hands make whole. He shall deliver thee in six troubles: yea, in seven there shall no evil touch thee.—Thou shalt come to thy grave in a full age, like as a shock of corn cometh in in his season.

Job xix. 25, 26—For I know that my Redeemer liveth, and that he shall stand at the latter day upon the earth: and though after my skin worms destroy this body, yet in my flesh shall I see God.

—— **xxxiv. 28**—He heareth the cry of the afflicted.

—— **xxxv. 10**—God, my maker, who giveth songs in the night.

—— **xxxvi. 15**—He delivereth the poor in his affliction.

Psalm vi. 8—The Lord hath heard the voice of my weeping.

—— **x. 14**—Thou art the helper of the fatherless.

—— **xvi. 11**—In thy presence is fulness of joy; at thy right hand there are pleasures for evermore.

—— **xviii. 6**—In my distress I called upon the Lord, and cried unto my God: he heard my voice out of his temple, and my cry came before him, even into his ears.

—— **xx. 1, 2**—The Lord hear thee in the day of trouble; the name of the God of Jacob defend thee; send thee help from the sanctuary, and strengthen thee out of Zion.

—— **xxiii. 1, 4**—The Lord is my shepherd; I shall not want. Yea, though I walk through the valley of the shadow of death, I will fear no evil: for thou art with me; thy rod and thy staff they comfort me.

—— **xxx. 5**—Weeping may endure for a night, but joy cometh in the morning.

—— **xxxiv. 19**—Many are the afflictions of the righteous: but the Lord delivereth him out of them all.

—— **xl. 1—3**—I waited patiently for the Lord; and he inclined unto me, and heard my cry. He brought me up also out of an horrible pit, out of the miry clay, and set my feet upon a rock, and established my goings. And he hath put a new song in my mouth, even praise unto our God: many shall see it, and fear, and shall trust in the Lord.

Psalm xli. 3—The Lord will strengthen him upon the bed of languishing: thou wilt make all his bed in his sickness.

—— xlii. 8—Yet the Lord will command his loving kindness in the daytime, and in the night his song shall be with me, and my prayer unto the God of my life.

—— xliii. 5—Why art thou cast down, O my soul? and why art thou disquieted within me? hope in God: for I shall yet praise him, who is the health of my countenance, and my God.

—— xlvi. 1—God is our refuge and strength, a very present help in trouble.

—— xlviii. 14—For this God is our God for ever and ever: he will be our guide even unto death.

—— xlix. 15—God will redeem my soul from the power of the grave: for he shall receive me.

—— l. 15—Call upon me in the day of trouble. I will deliver thee, and thou shalt glorify me.

—— lv. 6—Oh that I had wings like a dove! for then would I fly away, and be at rest.

—— lix. 16—I will sing of thy power; yea, I will sing aloud of thy mercy in the morning: for thou hast been my defence and refuge in the day of my trouble.

—— lxiii. 3—Because thy loving kindness is better than life, my lips shall praise thee.

—— lxviii. 5, 6—A father of the fatherless, and a judge of the widows, is God in his holy habitation. God setteth the solitary in families.

—— lxxiii. 25, 26—Whom have I in heaven but thee? and there is none upon earth that I desire beside thee. My flesh and my heart faileth: but God is the strength of my heart, and my portion for ever.

—— xc. 1, 2—Lord, thou hast been our dwelling-place

in all generations. Before the mountains were brought forth, or ever thou hadst formed the earth and the world, even from everlasting to everlasting, thou art God.

Psalm xci. 15—He shall call upon me, and I will answer him: I will be with him in trouble.

—— **xciv. 12**—Blessed is the man whom thou chastenest, O Lord.

—— **ciii. 13—17**—Like as a father pitieth his children, so the Lord pitieth them that fear him. For he knoweth our frame; he remembereth that we are dust. As for man, his days are as grass: as a flower of the field, so he flourisheth. For the wind passeth over it, and it is gone; and the place thereof shall know it no more. But the mercy of the Lord is from everlasting to everlasting upon them that fear him, and his righteousness unto children's children.

—— **cvii. 19**—Then they cry unto the Lord in their trouble, and he saveth them out of their distresses.

—— **cxvi. 6, 15**—I was brought low, and he helped me. Precious in the sight of the Lord is the death of his saints.

—— **cxviii. 5**—I called upon the Lord in distress: the Lord answered me, and set me in a large place.

—— **cxix. 50**—This is my comfort in my affliction: for thy word hath quickened me.

—— **cxix. 67, 71**—Before I was afflicted I went astray: but now have I kept thy word. It is good for me that I have been afflicted; that I might learn thy statutes.

—— **cxx. 1**—In my distress I cried unto the Lord, and he heard me.

—— **cxxxviii. 7**—Though I walk in the midst of trouble, thou wilt revive me.

—— **cxl. 12**—The Lord will maintain the cause of the afflicted.

—— **cxlv. 18**—The Lord is nigh unto all them that call upon him, to all that call upon him in truth.

—— **cxlvi. 9**—He relieveth the fatherless and widow.

Psalm cxlvii. 3—He healeth the broken in heart, and bindeth up their wounds.

Proverbs iii. 11, 12—My son, despise not the chastening of the Lord; neither be weary of his correction: for whom the Lord loveth he correcteth: even as a father the son in whom he delighteth.

—— **xviii. 54**—There is a friend that sticketh closer than a brother.

Ecclesiastes vii. 2—4—It is better to go to the house of mourning, than to go to the house of feasting: for that is the end of all men; and the living will lay it to his heart. Sorrow is better than laughter: for by the sadness of the countenance the heart is made better. The heart of the wise is in the house of mourning; but the heart of fools is in the house of mirth.

Isaiah xxv. 4—For thou hast been a strength to the poor, a strength to the needy in his distress, a refuge from the storm, a shadow from the heat, when the blast of the terrible ones is as a storm against the wall.

—— **xxxiii. 17, 24**—Thine eyes shall see the king in his beauty: they shall behold the land that is very far off. And the inhabitant shall not say, I am sick: the people that dwell therein shall be forgiven their iniquity.

—— **xxxv. 10**—And the ransomed of the Lord shall return, and come to Zion with songs and everlasting joy upon their heads: they shall obtain joy and gladness, and sorrow and sighing shall flee away.

—— **xl. 1, 11, 29—31**—Comfort ye, comfort ye my people, saith your God. He shall feed his flock like a shepherd; he shall gather the lambs with his arm, and carry them in his bosom, and shall gently lead those that are with young.—He giveth power to the faint; and to them that have no might he increaseth strength. Even the youths shall faint and be weary, and the young men shall utterly fall: but they that wait upon the Lord shall renew their strength; they shall mount up with wings as eagles; they shall run, and not be weary; and they shall walk, and not faint.

Isaiah li. 11, 12—The redeemed of the Lord shall return, and come with singing unto Zion; and everlasting joy shall be upon their head; they shall obtain gladness and joy; and sorrow and mourning shall flee away. I, even I, am he that comforteth you.

—— **xli. 10, 17**—Fear thou not; for I am with thee: be not dismayed; for I am thy God: I will strengthen thee; yea, I will help thee; yea, I will uphold thee with the right hand of my righteousness. When the poor and needy seek water, and there is none, and their tongue faileth for thirst, I the Lord will hear them, I the God of Israel will not forsake them.

—— **xliii. 1, 2**—But now thus saith the Lord that created thee, O Jacob, and he that formed thee, O Israel, Fear not: for I have redeemed thee, I have called thee by thy name; thou art mine. When thou passest through the waters, I will be with thee; and through the rivers, they shall not overflow thee: when thou walkest through the fire, thou shalt not be burned; neither shall the flame kindle upon thee.

—— **xlvi. 4**—Even to your old age I am he; and even to hoar hairs will I carry you: I have made, and I will bear; even I will carry, and will deliver you.

—— **liii. 4**—Surely he hath borne our griefs, and carried our sorrows.

—— **lix. 1**—Behold, the Lord's hand is not shortened, that it cannot save; neither his ear heavy, that it cannot hear.

—— **lxi. 1—3**—The Spirit of the Lord God is upon me; because the Lord hath anointed me to preach good tidings unto the meek; he hath sent me to bind up the broken hearted, to proclaim liberty to the captives, and the opening of the prison to them that are bound; to proclaim the acceptable year of the Lord, and the day of vengeance of our God; to comfort all that mourn: to appoint unto them that mourn in Zion, to give unto them beauty for ashes, the oil of joy for mourning, the garment of praise for the spirit of heaviness; that they might be called trees of righteousness, the planting of the Lord, that he might be glorified.

Isaiah lxvi. 13—As one whom his mother comforteth, so will I comfort you; and ye shall be comforted in Jerusalem.

Jeremiah xxxi. 15, 16—Thus saith the Lord; A voice was heard in Ramah, lamentation, and bitter weeping: Rachel weeping for her children refused to be comforted for her children, because they were not. Thus saith the Lord; Refrain thy voice from weeping, and thine eyes from tears: for thy work shall be rewarded, saith the Lord; and they shall come again from the land of the enemy.

—— **xlix. 11**—Leave thy fatherless children, I will preserve them alive; and let thy widows trust in me.

Lamentations iii. 32, 33—But though he cause grief, yet will he have compassion according to the multitude of his mercies. For he doth not afflict willingly nor grieve the children of men.

Hosea xiii. 14—I will ransom them from the power of the grave; I will redeem them from death: O death, I will be thy plagues; O grave, I will be thy destruction.

Jonah iv. 11—And should not I spare Nineveh, that great city, wherein are more than six score thousand persons that cannot discern between their right hand and their left hand?

Nahum i. 12—Though I have afflicted thee, I will afflict thee no more.

Malachi iii. 17—They shall be mine, saith the Lord of hosts, in that day when I make up my jewels; and I will spare them, as a man spareth his own son that serveth him.

—— **iv. 2**—Unto you that fear my name shall the Sun of Righteousness arise with healing in his wings.

Matthew v. 4—Blessed are they that mourn: for they shall be comforted.

—— **xi. 28—30**—Come unto me all ye that labor and are heavy laden, and I will give you rest. Take my yoke upon you, and learn of me; for I am meek and lowly in heart: and ye shall find rest unto your souls. For my yoke is easy, and my burden is light.

—— **xiv. 27**—Be of good cheer; it is I; be not afraid.

—— **xviii. 10**—Take heed that ye despise not one of these little ones; for I say unto you, That in heaven their angels do always behold the face of my Father which is in heaven.

—— **xix. 14, 29**—Jesus said, Suffer little children, and forbid them not to come unto me: for of such is the kingdom of heaven.—And every one that hath forsaken houses, or brethren, or sisters, or father, or mother, or wife, or children, or lands, for my name's sake, shall receive an hundredfold, and shall inherit everlasting life.

Mark ix. 36, 37—And he took a child, and set him in the midst of them: and when he had taken him in his arms, he said unto them, Whosoever shall receive one of such children in my name, receiveth me: and whosoever shall receive me, receiveth not me, but him that sent me.

—— **x. 13, 14**—And they brought young children to him, that he should touch them; and his disciples rebuked those that brought them. But when Jesus saw it, he was much displeased, and said unto them, Suffer the little children to come unto me, and forbid them not: for of such is the kingdom of God.

Luke ii. 29, 30—Lord, now lettest thou thy servant depart in peace, according to thy word: for mine eyes have seen thy salvation.

—— **viii. 52**—Weep not; she is not dead, but sleepeth.

—— **xviii. 16**—Jesus called them unto him, and said,

Suffer little children to come unto me, and forbid them not: for of such is the kingdom of God.

John xi. 11, 13, 24, 25, 35—Our friend Lazarus sleepeth. Jesus spake of his death. Martha saith unto him, I know that he shall rise again in the resurrection at the last day. Jesus said unto her, I am the resurrection, and the life: he that believeth in me, though he were dead, yet shall he live.—Jesus wept.

—— **xiv. 1, 2, 3, 18, 19**—Let not your heart be troubled: ye believe in God, believe also in me. In my Father's house are many mansions; if it were not so, I would have told you. I go to prepare a place for you. And if I go and prepare a place for you, I will come again, and receive you unto myself; that where I am, there ye may be also. I will not leave you comfortless: I will come to you. Because I live, ye shall live also.

Romans v. 3—5—We glory in tribulations also: knowing that tribulation worketh patience; and patience, experience; and experience, hope: and hope maketh not ashamed; because the love of God is shed abroad in our hearts by the Holy Ghost which is given unto us.

—— **v. 20, 21**—Moreover the law entered, that the offence might abound. But where sin abounded, grace did much more abound: that as sin hath reigned unto death, even so might grace reign through righteousness unto eternal life by Jesus Christ our Lord.

—— **viii. 11, 38, 39**—If the Spirit of him that raised up Jesus from the dead dwell in you, he that raised up Christ from the dead shall also quicken your mortal bodies by his Spirit that dwelleth in you. For I am persuaded, that neither death, nor life, nor angels, nor principalities, nor powers, nor things present, nor things to come, nor height, nor depth, nor any other creature, shall be able to separate us from the love of God, which is in Christ Jesus our Lord.

1 Corinthians xv. 22, 26, 42, 43, 53—57—For as in Adam all die, even so in Christ shall all be made alive.

The last enemy that shall be destroyed is death.—It is sown in corruption; it is raised in incorruption: It is sown in dishonour; it is raised in glory; it is sown in weakness; it is raised in power. For this corruptible must put on incorruption, and this mortal must put on immortality. So when this corruptible shall have put on incorruption, and this mortal shall have put on immortality, then shall be brought to pass the saying that is written, Death is swallowed up in victory. O death, where is thy sting? O grave, where is thy victory? The sting of death is sin; and the strength of sin is the law: But thanks be to God, which giveth us the victory through our Lord Jesus Christ.

2 Corinthians i. 3, 4—Blessed be God, even the Father of our Lord Jesus Christ, the Father of mercies, and the God of all comfort; who comforteth us in all our tribulation, that we may be able to comfort them which are in any trouble, by the comfort wherewith we ourselves are comforted of God.

—— iv. 17, 18—For our light affliction, which is but for a moment, worketh for us a far more exceeding and eternal weight of glory; while we look not at the things which are seen, but at the things which are not seen: for the things which are seen are temporal; but the things which are not seen are eternal.

—— v. 1, 4, 8—For we know that if our earthly house of this tabernacle were dissolved, we have a building of God, an house not made with hands, eternal in the heavens. For we that are in this tabernacle do groan, being burdened: not for that we would be unclothed, but clothed upon, that mortality might be swallowed up of life.—We are confident, I say, and willing rather to be absent from the body, and to be present with the Lord.

Philippians i. 21, 23—For to me to live is Christ, and to die is gain. For I am in a strait betwixt two, having a desire to depart, and to be with Christ, which is far better.

—— iii. 20, 21—For our conversation is in heaven;

from whence also we look for the Saviour, the Lord Jesus Christ: who shall change our vile body, that it may be fashioned like unto his glorious body, according to the working whereby he is able even to subdue all things unto himself.

Colossians iii. 4—When Christ, who is our life, shall appear, then shall ye also appear with him in glory.

1 Thessalonians iv. 13—18—But I would not have you to be ignorant, brethren, concerning them which are asleep, that ye sorrow not, even as others which have no hope. For if we believe that Jesus died and rose again, even so them also which sleep in Jesus will God bring with him. For this we say unto you by the word of the Lord, that we which are alive and remain unto the coming of the Lord shall not prevent them which are asleep. For the Lord himself shall descend from heaven with a shout, with the voice of the archangel, and with the trump of God: and the dead in Christ shall rise first: then we which are alive and remain shall be caught up together with them in the clouds, to meet the Lord in the air; and so shall we ever be with the Lord. Wherefore comfort one another with these words.

2 Timothy i. 10—Our Saviour Jesus Christ, who hath abolished death, and hath brought life and immortality to light through the gospel.

—— **iv. 8**—Henceforth there is laid up for me a crown of righteousness, which the Lord, the righteous judge, shall give me at that day: and not to me only, but unto all them also that love his appearing.

Hebrews ii. 18—For in that he himself hath suffered being tempted, he is able to succour them that are tempted.

—— **iv. 9, 15, 16**—There remaineth therefore a rest to the people of God.—For we have not an high priest which cannot be touched with the feeling of our infirmities; but was in all points tempted like as we are, yet without sin. Let us therefore come boldly unto the throne of grace, that we may obtain mercy, and find grace to help in time of need.

Hebrews xi. 4, 16—He being dead yet speaketh.—Now they desire a better country, that is, an heavenly: wherefore God is not ashamed to be called their God: for he hath prepared for them a city.

—— **xii. 1—3, 6, 11**—Wherefore seeing we also are compassed about with so great a cloud of witnesses, let us lay aside every weight, and the sin which doth so easily beset us, and let us run with patience the race that is set before us, looking unto Jesus, the author and finisher of our faith; who for the joy that was set before him endured the cross, despising the shame, and is set down at the right hand of the throne of God. For consider him that endured such contradiction of sinners against himself, lest ye be wearied and faint in your minds.—Whom the Lord loveth he chasteneth, and scourgeth every son whom he receiveth. Now no chastening for the present seemeth to be joyous, but grievous: nevertheless afterward it yieldeth the peaceable fruit of righteousness unto them which are exercised thereby.

James i. 12—Blessed is the man that endureth temptation: for when he is tried, he shall receive the crown of life, which the Lord hath promised to them that love him.

1 Peter v. 4—When the chief Shepherd shall appear, ye shall receive a crown of glory that fadeth not away.

—— **v. 7**—Casting all your care upon him; for he careth for you.

Revelation i. 17, 18—Fear not; I am the first and the last. I am he that liveth, and was dead; and, behold, I am alive for evermore, Amen; and have the keys of hell and of death.

—— **iii. 19**—As many as I love, I rebuke and chasten: be zealous therefore, and repent.

—— **vii. 13—17**—And one of the elders answered, saying unto me, What are these which are arrayed in white robes?

and whence came they? And I said unto him, Sir, thou knowest. And he said to me, These are they which came out of great tribulation, and have washed their robes, and made them white in the blood of the Lamb. Therefore are they before the throne of God, and serve him day and night in his temple: and he that sitteth on the throne shall dwell among them. They shall hunger no more, neither thirst any more; neither shall the sun light on them, nor any heat. For the Lamb which is in the midst of the throne shall feed them, and shall lead them unto living fountains of waters: and God shall wipe away all tears from their eyes.

Revelation xiv. 13—And I heard a voice from heaven saying unto me, Write, Blessed are the dead which die in the Lord from henceforth: Yea, saith the Spirit, that they may rest from their labours; and their works do follow them.

—— **xix. 5—9**—And a voice came out of the throne, saying, Praise our God, all ye his servants, and ye that fear him, both small and great. And I heard as it were the voice of a great multitude, and as the voice of many waters, and as the voice of mighty thunderings, saying, Alleluia: for the Lord God omnipotent reigneth. Let us be glad and rejoice, and give honour to him: for the marriage of the Lamb is come, and his wife hath made herself ready. And to her was granted that she should be arrayed in fine linen, clean and white: for the fine linen is the righteousness of saints. And he saith unto me, Write, Blessed *are* they which are called unto the marriage supper of the Lamb. And he saith unto me, These are the true sayings of God.

—— **xxi. 3, 4**—And I heard a great voice out of heaven saying, Behold, the tabernacle of God is with men, and he will dwell with them, and they shall be his people, and God himself shall be with them, and be their God. And God shall wipe away all tears from their eyes; and there shall be no more death, neither sorrow, nor crying, neither shall there be any more pain: for the former things are passed away.

—— **xxii.** 1—5—And he shewed me a pure river of water of life, clear as crystal, proceeding out of the throne of God and of the Lamb. In the midst of the street of it, and on either side of the river, was there the tree of life, which bare twelve manner of fruits, and yielded her fruit every month: and the leaves of the tree were for the healing of the nations. And there shall be no more curse: but the throne of God and of the Lamb shall be in it; and his servants shall serve him: and they shall see his face; and his name shall be in their foreheads. And there shall be no night there; and they need no candle, neither light of the sun; for the Lord God giveth them light: and they shall reign for ever and ever.

Introductory.

IN THE BEGINNING WAS THE WORD.—*John i., 1.*

THE COMMON GRIEF.

REV. DAVID RUSSELL.

MAN is born to troubles, and Christians are not exempted from them. Of all forms of trial to which they are liable, that of the loss of children by death may be regarded as one of the very greatest. In most cases it is not known what trial means till Death enters the dwelling, and carries off to his cold and dark dominions the child who has been the joy, the hope, the idol of its parents. Job bore with apparent composure the tidings of disaster upon disaster, till at last, the announcement was made of the sudden death of his children; then he "arose, and rent his mantle, and shaved his head, and fell down upon the ground, and worshipped, and said, 'Naked came I out of my mother's womb, and naked shall I return thither: the Lord gave, and the Lord hath taken away; blessed be the name of the Lord.'" How many mourners, royal and not royal, have experienced sorrow as great as David's when he mourned for Absalom, and have grieved as bitterly as Rachel when she "wept for her children, and refused to be comforted, because they were not." Christian parents, then, should remember that if their trial has been a great one, it is by no means a rare one; and the commonness of the affliction should in some degree temper their sorrow when bereaved of their children, they should regard the words of Peter as applying to them, "Beloved, think it not strange concerning the fiery trial which is to try you, as though some strange thing happened unto you." True, the commonness of the grief is but a poor consolation to the desolate heart of a parent; perhaps, as the poet represents, it may sometimes aggravate rather than assuage the bitterness of his sorrow:—

> "One writes, that 'Other friends remain,'
> That 'Loss is common to the race,'
> And common is the commonplace,
> And vacant chaff well meant for grain.
>
> That loss is common would not make
> My own less bitter, rather more:
> Too common! Never morning wore
> To evening, but some heart did break."

Yet the circumstance should not be altogether overlooked by mourners in Zion. Parents are too apt to suppose that no loss is so great as theirs; that no child was so dear, so clever, so good as theirs, and that, therefore, no sorrow can be like unto theirs, till they look abroad and try to weigh the distresses of others against their own. Then there is this result arising from the commonness of sorrow, that abundance of precious sympathy is at hand for the bereaved in the day of their calamity. One who has lost a child in infancy, for example, may learn how to bear his sorrow from considering the case of Jairus, the ruler of the synagogue. If it is a heavy trial to part with a child who is a mere infant, how much sorer the trial when, the dangers of infancy over, that child is at the interesting age of twelve years, and day by day is unfolding new beauties of mind, and heart, and body, and daily entwining itself more firmly around the parents' heart. If there were sons in the family of Jairus, it would have been a bitter trial to have had one of them taken from him; and had God asked him to choose which he would most readily surrender, we can imagine the perplexity of his heart, and how readily he would refer the matter back to God, to do as seemed good to him. But an only daughter! She would be the very last that he could think of giving up, and he would entreat most earnestly that God would, in mercy, spare *her*. She was, perhaps, not merely an only daughter, but an only child, in which case the anguish of his heart would be intensified in an inconceivable degree; for of all griefs that for an only child is, by universal consent, regarded as the most poignant—

> "But one, poor one, one poor and lovely child—
> But one thing to rejoice and solace in—
> And cruel death hath snatch'd it from my sight."

Bereaved parent! has your loss been as great as was that of Jairus? Even if it has, can you think of none who have been tried beyond what you have been? Then go where Jairus went for sympathy and succor. Be not afraid of "troubling the Master." What troubles Him is the want of faith and want of prayer. Hear his words, "Fear not; only believe," and "Thy daughter is not dead, but sleepeth." You may not expect your child to be restored to a life of sin and sorrow on earth. Would you wish it? But He who restored the daughter of Jairus after only a few hours' death, can restore yours, and will restore him though thousands of years should have to elapse ere the trump shall sound

which the dead shall hear, and, hearing, shall arise.
Then may Christian parents hope that they and their
children shall rise together, to mingle their voices
in the sound, ever old, ever new, "Unto him that
loved us, and washed us from our sins in His own
blood, and hath made us kings and priests unto God
and His Father; to Him be glory and dominion for
ever and ever. Amen!"

FRIEND AFTER FRIEND DEPARTS.

JAMES MONTGOMERY.

FRIEND after friend departs;
   Who hath not lost a friend?
There is no union here of hearts
   That finds not here an end!
Were this frail world our final rest,
Living or dying, none were blest.

Beyond the flight of time,—
   Beyond the reign of death,—
There surely is some blessed clime
   Where life is not a breath;
Nor life's affections transient fire
Whose sparks fly upwards and expire.

There is a world above,
   Where parting is unknown;
A long eternity of love,
   Formed for the good alone:
And faith beholds the dying here
Translated to that glorious sphere!

Thus star by star declines,
  Till all are past away;
As morning high and higher shines
  To pure and perfect day:
Nor sink those stars in empty night,
But hide themselves in heaven's own light.

"We miss them when the board is spread,
  We miss them when the prayer is said;
Upon our dreams their dying eyes
In still and mournful fondness lies."

NEWMAN.

COMPARE YOUR AFFLICTIONS WITH THOSE OF OTHERS.

JOHN FLAVEL.

SAY not, there is no sorrow like your sorrow. You have lost one child; but Aaron lost two, and Job all; and lost them by an immediate, instantaneous stroke of God. The children of some pious parents have died victims to public justice. Others have lived to sin so grievously, that their broken-hearted parents were ready to wish they had died from the womb. A third class have experienced such protracted and intolerable sufferings on a sick bed, that even a fond mother has wished and prayed for the closing moment. O think of these things, and acknowledge that your lot has been comparatively merciful.

HOW TO SYMPATHIZE WITH MOURNERS.

Rev. Charles J. Vaughan, D.D.

SORROW is a great test of truth. Nothing which has the slightest tinge of unreality, whether in the form of exaggeration or of affectation, has a chance of acceptance with persons in deep trouble. There must be, as a first condition, the recognition of the existence in the sufferer's case of that which is hard to bear; and there must be, as a second condition, the presentation of that which is perfectly supporting, because absolutely true, to meet it, if a man would minister with any effect to one on whom pain or loss, anxiety or desolation, has laid a heavy hand. Too often there is an attempt to ignore the sorrow; to treat it as if it were made too much of; almost to reprove it, as if it were fanciful or voluntary. It is difficult for health and sickness, ease and distress, a whole heart and a wounded heart, to meet and sympathize: grief is suspicious of gladness, and is slow to be persuaded that he who comes to the house of mourning from the dwelling of cheerfulness can bring with him a just appreciation of the calamity which he seeks to soothe. To be able to *weep with them that weep* is a necessary requisite in one who would be, in the divine sense, *a son of consolation*.

It is the first object of sorrow, if we recognize in it any object at all, that it be felt. If there is a remedial purpose in it, or if there is even a chastising and a humbling purpose in it, this can only be answered by the entrance of the pain itself into the very soul's soul. This is what an inexperienced comforter will not let it do. He acts, with his spiritual comfort, just as he thinks it wrong and shocking for another to act with his worldly comfort. He counts it a great sin to drown sorrow by letting in the din of the world upon it; but does he not himself seek to overbear sorrow in an opposite manner, by haste and precipitation in administering the remedies of the Gospel? Truths which will be valuable and efficacious a month hence, may themselves be inoperative and inaudible to-day. And the wise physician, like Him whose hand is working with him from above, will abide and watch his time. He will be satisfied, in the first instance, that the soul should lay itself low and let the wave pass over it. Its foot must touch the bottom of the deep waters before it can safely rise again to their surface. All that we can desire to hear from the rent heart, in the first hours of anguish, is the simple confession, *It is the Lord.*

FRIENDS NOT LOST.—Thou hast lost thy friend:—say, rather, thou hast parted with him. That is properly lost which is past all recovery, which we are out of hope to see any more. It is not so with this friend thou mournest for: he is but gone home a little before thee; thou art following him; you two shall meet in your Father's house, and enjoy each other more happily than you could have done here below.

REV. ROBERT HALL.

COMFORT IN AFFLICTION.

Thomas Moore.

O THOU who dry'st the mourner's tear,
    How dark this world would be,
  If, when deceived and wounded here
    We could not fly to thee;
The friends who in our sunshine live,
    When winter comes, are flown;
And he who has but tears to give,
    Must weep those tears alone;
But thou wilt heal that broken heart,
    Which, like the plants that throw
Their fragrance from the wounded part,
    Breathes sweetness out of woe.

When joy no longer soothes or cheers,
    And ev'n the hope, that threw
A moment's sparkle o'er our tears,
    Is dimmed and vanished too!
O! who would bear life's stormy doom,
    Did not thy wing of love
Come brightly wafting through the gloom,
    One peace-branch from above?
Then sorrow, touched by thee, grows bright
    With more than rapture's ray;
As darkness shows us worlds of light
    We never saw by day.

To live in hearts we leave behind is not to die.
Alexander Campbell.

USES OF CHASTISEMENT.

Rev. James W. Alexander, D.D.

IT is only in the Word of God that we learn to consider affliction as a blessing. The utmost which the most refined philosophy can effect, is to remove from our sorrows that which is imaginary, to divert the attention from the cause of distress, or to produce a sullen and stoical resignation, more like despair than hope. The religion of the gospel grapples with the evil itself, overcomes it, and transforms it into a blessing. It is by no means included in the promises made to true Christians that they shall be exempt from suffering. On the contrary, chastisement forms a necessary part of that paternal discipline by which our heavenly Father fits his children for their eternal rest and glory. The Psalmist asserts the blessedness of the man who is chastened by the Lord, with this qualification as necessary to constitute it a blessing, that he is also instructed in divine truth. Psalm xciv. 12. By this we understand that the influence of chastisement is not physical; that mere suffering has no inherent efficacy; but that the afflictions of this life are, in the hand of God, instrumental in impressing divine truth upon the heart, awakening the attention of the believer to the consideration of his own character and situation, the promise of the gospel, and the rewards of heaven. The child of God is assured that all things work together for his good; in this is plainly included the pledge, that chastisements and afflictions shall eventually prove a blessing; and this is verified by the experience of the whole church.

Times of affliction afford some natural facilities for cultivating repentance. Occasions of sin are then removed; the world is excluded. The man confined to the silence of the sick-room, or the house of mourning, cannot, by idle pursuits, divert his mind. He is forced to think; and to think of his sins. He considers his ways, bewails his transgressions, and renews his covenant. He learns to confess, "Surely it is meet to be said unto God, I have borne chastisement, I will not offend any more; that which I see not teach thou me, and if I have done iniquity, I will do so no more."—Job xxxiv. 31.

Now, in these experiences of the afflicted, there is a real consolation. Such tears are sweet, and it will probably be the unanimous testimony of all true penitents, that they have enjoyed a tender and refined delight in those moments of grief in which they came to God as a forgiving God, and heard Him say to their souls, in accents at once of gentle rebuke and comfort: "Behold I have refined thee but not with silver; I have chosen thee in the furnace of affliction," "For mine own sake will I defer mine anger." "For a small moment have I forsaken thee, but with great mercies will I gather thee: In a little wrath I hid my face from thee for a moment, but with everlasting kindness will I have mercy on thee, saith the Lord thy Redeemer."

The apostle Peter, in comforting the dispersed saints, explains to them this end of their chastisement, "If need be, ye are in heaviness through manifold temptations, that the trial of your faith being much more precious than of gold that perisheth, though it be tried with fire, might be found unto praise, and honor, and glory, at the appearing of Jesus Christ."

There is no expression in the Word of God better suited to reconcile the Christian to trials than that of the Apostle Paul: " He (that is God) chastens us for our profit, that we may be partakers of His holiness!" What words are these! This is the very summit of your desires. This you have been toiling for, and longing after. This you have earnestly implored, and are you now ready to shrink from the very means by which your Father in heaven is about to promote your sanctification? By no means will you be led to relinquish this appointment of God for your good. No, it is by these very trials that your graces are to be invigorated. The most valuable truths of the Christian are, " the exceeding great and precious promises." He does not feel the need of these promises while he is indulging in that self-pleasing which usually accompanies prosperity. In penning these lines, it is said advisedly, no man can fully value health who has not been sick, nor appreciate the services of the kind and skillful physician until he has been healed by him. And thus also, no man can fully prize or fully understand the promises of the Scriptures until they are made necessary to his support in adversity. Many of the most precious portions of revelation are altogether a dead letter to such as have never been exercised by the trials to which they relate. The believer who is in sufferings or straits of any kind, comes to God by prayer; and in attempting to pray, seeks some promise suitable to his precise wants. Blessed be God! he needs not to search long—so rich are the treasures of the Word. These promises he takes are the very truth of God. He pleads them at the throne of grace; he believes them, relies on them, rejoices in them. Taste of the sweetness of his promises, and each of you shall say with David: "It is good for me that I have been afflicted."

It is common to hear those who are ignorant of the Scriptures cavilling at the representation of Job as a man of eminent patience, but where, except in his biography, shall we look for the instance, suffering in one day the total loss of immense wealth, and of ten beloved children, and still saying, "The Lord gave, and the Lord hath taken away, blessed be the name of the Lord." It was, no doubt, a visitation sudden and alarming as a stroke of lightning, when Aaron beheld his sons consumed by fire from the Lord. It was an awful sanction to that rule, "I will be sanctified in them that come nigh me, and before all the people I will be glorified." Yet on seeing and hearing these things, the bereaved father, "held his peace," Lev. x. 3. It is a bitter medicine, but the soul which is convinced of God's justice and goodness lays down every thought of rebellion and discontent.

This is the temper which sanctified affliction always begets, so that the prostrate soul dares no longer to impose terms on Jehovah, but yields itself to his sovereign discretion. There is peace in such a surrender, a peace which is altogether independent of any expected mitigation of the stroke. Wave after wave often goes over the child of God, before he is brought to this state of self-renunciation. Murmuring may for a time prevail, yet the Great Physician, who applies the painful remedy, cannot be baffled, and triumphs to his own glory, and the unspeakable benefit of the believer's soul. Chastisement is useful, because it leads the believer to look for complete happiness in heaven only.

He is the happy man who dwells most on the thoughts of heaven. Like Enoch he walks with God. Like Job, he can say, "I know that my Redeemer liveth," etc. Like David, he glories, "Thou wilt show me thy salvation." Like Paul, he triumphs, "For I am now ready to be offered," etc. In every case of suffering it is the prime wisdom of the Christian to fix his eyes upon the heavenly crown. In every other hope you may be disappointed, in this you cannot. Try as you may all other fountains for your solace, there is a time coming when you must be driven to this. Become familiar with the meditation of heavenly glory! Daily contemplate that joyful deliverance from evil, that indissoluble and ecstatic union with the Lord Jesus Christ! Then, when death lays upon you his cold hand, you can say, "I am prepared for this hour. I have longed for this deliverance to meet my Lord in His temple. I have lived in communion with the blessed Lord of heaven." "Lo, this is my God, I have waited for Him, and He will save me; this is the Lord, I have waited for Him; I will rejoice and be glad in His salvation."

THE NECESSITY OF AFFLICTIONS.

Rev. John R. Macduff, D.D.

WHAT a blessed motto and superscription over the dark lintels of sorrow!—"IF NEED BE!" Every arrow from the quiver of God is feathered with it! Write it, child of affliction, over every trial thy God sees meet to send! If he calls thee down from the sunny mountain-heights to the darksome glades, hear Him saying, "*There is a need be.*" If he have dashed the cup of earthly prosperity from thy lips, curtailed thy creature comforts, diminished thy "basket and store," hear Him saying, "*There is a need be.*" If He has ploughed and furrowed thy soul with severe bereavement—extinguished light after light in thy dwelling—hear Him thus stilling the tumult of thy grief—"*There is a need be.*"

Yes! believe it, there is some profound *reason* for thy trial, which at present may be undiscernible. No furnace will be hotter than He sees to be needed. Sometimes, indeed, His teachings are mysterious. We can with difficulty spell out the letters, *God is love!*—we can see no "bright light"—no luminous Bow in "our Cloud." It is all mystery; not one break is there in the sky! Nay! "Hear what God the Lord doth speak"—"*If need be.*" He does not long leave His people alone, if He sees the chariot-wheels dragging heavily. He will take His own means to sever them from an absorbing love of the world—to pursue them out of self and dislodge usurping clay-idols that may have vaulted on the throne which He alone may occupy. Before thy present trial He may have seen thy love waxing cold—thy influence for good lessening. As the sun puts out the fire, the sun of earthly prosperity may have been extinguishing the fires of thy soul. Thou mayest have been shining less brightly for Christ, effecting some guilty compromise with an insinuating and seductive world. He has appointed the very discipline and dealing needful;—nothing *else*—nothing *less* could have done!

Be still, and know that He is God! That "*need be*," remember, is in the hands of Infinite *Love*, infinite *Wisdom*, infinite *Power*. Trust Him in *little* things as well as in *great* things—in trifles as well as in emergencies. Seek to have an unquestioning faith. Though other paths, doubtless, would have been selected by thee had the choice been in thy hands, be it thine to listen to His voice at every turn of the road, saying, "This *is the way, walk ye in it*."

We may not be able to understand it now—but one day we shall come to find that AFFLICTION is one of God's most blessed angels;—a ministering spirit, "sent forth to minister to them who are heirs of salvation." There would be no *Bow* in the material heaven but for the *Cloud!* Lovelier, indeed, to the eye is the azure blue—the fleecy summer vapor—or the gold and vermilion of western sunsets. But what would become of the earth if no dark clouds from time to time hung over it; distilling their treasures—reviving and refreshing its drooping vegetable tribes?

Is it otherwise with the soul? Nay. The cloud of sorrow is *needed*. Its every rain-drop has an inner meaning of LOVE! If, even now, afflicted one, these clouds are gathering, and the tempest sighing, lift up thine eye to the divine scroll gleaming in the darkened heavens, and remember that He who has put the Bow of promise there, saw also a "*need be*" for the cloud on which it rests!

There is therefore reason for this chastisement, for "Whom the Lord loveth he chasteneth." Heb. xii. 6.

What! God *loveth* me when He is discharging His quiver upon me!—emptying me from vessel to vessel!—causing the sun of my earthly joys to set in clouds? Yes! O afflicted, tossed with tempest —He *chastens* thee BECAUSE He *loves* thee! This trial comes from His own tender, loving hand—His own tender, unchanging heart!

Art thou laid on a *sick bed*—are sorrowful months and wearisome nights appointed unto thee? Let this be the pillow on which thine aching head reclines. *It is because he loves me!*

Is it *bereavement* that has swept thy heart and desolated thy dwelling? He appointed that chamber of death—He opened that tomb *because he loves thee!* As it is the suffering child of the family which claims a mother's deepest affections and most tender solicitude, so hast thou at this moment embarked on thy side the tenderest love and solicitude of a chastening Heavenly Father. He loved thee *into* this sorrow, and He will love thee *through* it. There is nothing capricious in His dealings. LOVE is the reason of all He does. There is no drop of wrath in that cup thou art called upon to drink.

"I do believe," says Lady Powerscourt, "He has purchased these afflictions for us as well as every thing else. Blessed be His name, it is a part of His covenant to visit us with the rod." What says our adorable Lord himself? The words were spoken, not when He was on earth, a sojourner in a sorrowing world, but when enthroned amid the glories of heaven, "*As many as I* LOVE, *I rebuke and chasten.*" Rev. iii. 19.

Believer! rejoice in the thought that the rod, the chastening rod, is in the hands of the living, loving Saviour who died for thee! *Tribulation* is the King's Highway, and yet that highway is paved with love. As some flowers before shedding their fragrance require to be pressed, so does thy God see meet to *bruise* thee. As some birds are said to sing their sweetest notes when the thorn pierces their bosom, so does He appoint affliction to lacerate, that thou mayest be driven to the wing, singing, in thy upward soaring, "*My heart is fixed, O God, my heart is fixed!*" "Those," says the heavenly Leighton, "He means to make the most resplendent, He hath oftenest His tools upon." "Our troubles," says another, "seem in His Word to be ever in His mind. Perhaps half the commands and half the promises He gives us there, are given us as *troubled* men."

Be it ours to say, "Lord, I will love Thee, not only despite of Thy rod, but *because* of Thy rod." I will rush into the very arms that are chastising me! When Thy voice calls, as to Abraham of old, to prepare for bitter trial, be it mine to respond with bounding heart, "*Here am I!*"—and to read in the Bow which spans my darkest cloud, "*He chastens* because *He loves!*" And He pities because He loves. A father bending over the sick bed of his weak or dying child, a mother pressing, in tender solicitude, an infant sufferer to her bosom,—these are the earthly pictures of God. "*Like as a father pitieth.*" "*As one whom his mother comforteth, so will I comfort you!*"

When tempted in our season of overwhelming sorrow to say, "Never has there been so dark a cloud, never a heart so stript and desolate as mine," let this thought hush every murmur, "It is *your* Father's good pleasure!" The love and pity of the tenderest earthly parent is but a dim shadow compared to the pitying love of God. If your heavenly Father's smile has for the moment been exchanged for the chastening rod; be assured there is some deep necessity for the altered discipline. If there be unutterable yearnings in the soul of the earthly parent as the lancet is applied to the body of his child—infinitely more is it so with your covenant God as He subjects you to these deep woundings of heart! Finite wisdom has no place in His ordinations. An earthly father *may* err—is ever erring; but, "*as for God His way is perfect.*" This is the explanation of His every dealing—"*Your heavenly Father knoweth ye have need of all these things!*"

Trust Him when you cannot trace Him. Do not try to penetrate the cloud which He "brings over the earth," and to look *through* it. Keep your eye steadily fixed on the Bow. The mystery is God's, the promise is yours. Seek that the end of all His dispensations may be to make you more confiding. Without one misgiving commit your way to Him. He says, regarding each child of His covenant family, what He said of Ephraim of old (and never more so than in a season of suffering), "*I do earnestly remember him still.*" Whilst now bending your head like a bulrush—your heart breaking with sorrow—remember His pitying eye is upon you. Be it yours, even through blinding tears, to say, "*Even so,* FATHER!" For he doth not afflict willingly.

In our seasons of trial, when under some inscrutable dispensation, how apt is the murmuring thought to rise in our hearts—"*All things are against me.*"

Might not this overwhelming blow have been spared? Might not this dark cloud, which has shadowed my heart and my home with sadness, have been averted? Might not the accompaniments of my trial have been less severe—"*Surely the Lord hath forgotten to be gracious?*"

Nay, these afflictions are errands of mercy in disguise!—"*He afflicteth not willingly.*"

There is nothing capricious or arbitrary about thy God's dealings. Unutterable *tenderness* is the character of all His allotments! The world may wound by unkindness;—trusted friends may become treacherous;—a brother may speak with unnecessary harshness and severity; but the Lord is "*abundant* in goodness and in truth." He appoints no needless pang. When he *appears*, like Joseph, to "speak *roughly*," there are gentle undertones of love. The stern accents are assumed, because He has precious lessons that could not otherwise have been taught!

Ah! be assured there is some deep *necessity* in all He does. In our calendars of sorrow we may put this luminous mark against every trying hour, "*It was needed!*" Some redundant branch in the tree required pruning. Some wheat required to be cast overboard to lighten the ship and avert further disaster. Mourning one!—He might have dealt far otherwise with thee! He might have cut thee down as a fruitless, worthless cumberer! He might have abandoned thee to drift, disowned and unpiloted on the rocks of destruction;—joined to thine idols, He might have left thee "alone" to settle on thy lees, and forfeit thine eternal bliss! But he loved thee better. It was kindness, infinite kindness, which blighted thy fairest blossoms, and hedged up thy way with thorns.

"Without this hedge of thorns," says Richard Baxter, "on the right hand and on the left, we should hardly be able to keep the way to heaven."

CALAMITY RESULTING IN VICTORY.—I honestly believe that many a sick bed has delivered the sufferer from a bed in perdition. Pain often drives to prayer. The door that shuts a man out from the world shuts him into reflection, and, finally, into the ark of safety. "There it is," said a young man, as he pointed to a diseased limb, which was eating away his life; "and a precious limb it has been to me. It took me away from a career of folly. It brought me to myself, and to this room of trial, where I have found Christ. I think it has brought me a great way on the road to heaven." It was the testimony of a Christian who had lost his eyesight, after a long confinement to a dark room, "I could never see Jesus until I became blind."

THEODORE L. CUYLER, D.D.

GOD'S POWER TO COMFORT.

Rev. T. De Witt Talmage, D.D.

WHEN a man has trouble, the world comes in and says: "Now get your mind off this; go out and breathe the fresh air; plunge deeper into business." What poor advice! Get your mind off of it! when everything is upturned with the bereavement, and everything reminds you of what you have lost. Get your mind off of it! They might as well advise you to stop thinking. And you cannot stop thinking in that direction. Take a walk in the fresh air! Why, along that very street, or that very road, she once accompanied you. Out of that grass-plot she plucked flowers or into that show-window she looked, fascinated, saying, "Come, see the pictures." Go deeper into business! Why, she was associated with all your business ambition, and since she has gone you have no ambition left.

Oh, this is a clumsy world when it tries to comfort a broken heart! I can build a Corliss engine, I can paint a Raphael's "Madonna," I can play a Beethoven's "Symphony" as easily as this world can comfort a broken heart. And yet you have been comforted. How was it done? Did Christ come to you and say, "Get your mind off this; go out and breathe the fresh air; plunge deeper into business?" No: There was a minute when He came to you— perhaps in the watches of the night, perhaps in your place of business, perhaps along the street—and He breathed something into your soul that gave peace, rest, infinite quiet, so that you could take out the photograph of the departed one, and look into the eyes and the face of the dear one, and say: "It is all right; she is better off; I would not call her back. Lord, I thank Thee that Thou hast comforted my poor heart."

There are Christian parents here who are willing to testify to the power of this Gospel to comfort. Your son had just graduated from school or college and was going into business, and the Lord took him. Or your daughter had just graduated from the young ladies' seminary, and you thought she was going to be a useful woman, and of long life; but the Lord took her, and you were tempted to say, All this culture of twenty years for nothing!" Or the little child came home from school with the hot fever that stopped not for the agonized prayer or for the skillful physician, and the little child was taken. Or the babe was lifted out of your arms by some quick epidemic, and you stood wondering why God ever gave you that child at all, if so soon He was to take it away. And yet you are not repining, you are not fretful, you are not fighting against God.

What enabled you to stand all the trial? "Oh," you say, "I took the medicine that God gave my sick soul. In my distress I threw myself at the feet of a sympathizing God; and when I was too weak to pray, or to look up, He breathed into me a peace that I think must be the foretaste of that heaven where there is neither a tear nor a farewell nor a grave." Come, all ye who have been out to the grave to weep there—come, all ye comforted souls, get up off your knees. Is there no power in this Gospel to soothe the heart? Is there no power in this religion to quiet the worst paroxysm of grief? There comes up an answer from comforted widowhood, and orphanage, and childlessness, saying, "Ay, ay, we are witnesses!"

CONSOLATION SOUGHT AND FOUND.

JOHN BOWRING.

WHEN the clouds of desolation
   Gather o'er my naked head,
   And my spirit's agitation
Knows not where to turn or tread;
When life's gathering storms compel me
   To submit to wants and woes,
Who shall teach me, who shall tell me
   Where my heart may find repose?

To the stars I fain would reach me;
   There the God of light must dwell;
Sacred teachers! will ye teach me?
   Blest instructors! will ye tell?
How my voice may reach that portal
   Where the seraphs crowd in throngs;
How the lispings of a mortal
   May be heard 'midst angel songs!

God and Father! Thou didst give me
   Sorrow for my portion here;
But thy mercy will not leave me
   Helpless, struggling with despair;
For to Thee, when sad and lonely,

Unto Thee, alone, I turn;
And to thee, my Father! only
Look for comfort when I mourn.

Nor in vain—for light is breaking
'Midst the sorrows, 'midst the storms;
And methinks I see awaking
Heavenly hopes and angel forms;
And my spirit waxes stronger,
And my trembling heart is still;
And my bosom doubts no longer
Thine inexplicable will.

PRAYER FOR SANCTIFICATION OF SORROW.

Archbishop Fenelon.

IT is but a poor consolation to tell you that I have a deep sense of your calamity. It is, nevertheless, all that human weakness can do, and to do any thing more we must have recourse to God. It is to Him, then, that I address myself; to that comforter of the afflicted and protector of the weak. I beg of Him not to deliver you from your trouble, but that He may make it profitable to you, that He would give you strength to bear it. The sovereign remedy against the great evils of our nature, is sharp affliction; it is in the midst of sorrows that we accomplish the great mystery of Christianity, that is to say, the inward crucifixion of the old man. It is here the virtue of grace unfolds itself, and operates most intimately, which is to teach us not to have a dependence on ourselves.

We must come out of ourselves to be able to resign ourselves to God. Thus, our heart wounded in the most tender part, troubled in its sweetest, most just, and innocent attachments, perceives it can no longer keep possession of itself, and is drawn from itself, that it may advance towards God. This is the great remedy against the evils sin has oppressed us with; the remedy is severe, but the evil also is very deep. God often inflicts upon two friends endeared to each other a stroke which proves an unspeakable good to each: He takes one to heaven, and renders this afflictive stroke salutary to the other, who remains on earth. This is what God has done for you. May He, by His Holy Spirit, awaken your faith, so that you may be penetrated with these truths!

WHEN we are under any affliction we are generally troubled with a malicious kind of melancholy; we only dwell and pore upon the sad and dark occurrences of Providence; but never take notice of the more benign and bright ones.

BISHOP HOPKINS.

AFFLICTIONS show us the darkness of the world and the brightness of heaven, and they stimulate to perseverance to death, in order to receive the radiant crown of everlasting life; they are designed to brighten the graces of God's people—to strengthen their faith and patience.

REV. W. NICHOLSON.

BENEFITS OF AFFLICTIONS.

RICHARD BAXTER.

AFFLICTIONS are God's most effectual means to keep us from losing our way to our heavenly rest. Without this hedge of thorns on the right hand and on the left, we should scarcely keep in the way to heaven. If there be but one gap open, how ready are we to find it, and turn out at it! When we grow wanton, or worldly, or proud, how doth sickness, or other affliction, reduce us! Every Christian, as well as Luther, may call affliction one of his best schoolmasters, and with David may say, "Before I was afflicted, I went astray; but now have I kept thy word." Many thousand recovered sinners may cry, "O healthful sickness! O comfortable sorrows! O gainful losses! O enriching poverty! O blessed day that ever I was afflicted!" Not only the green pastures and still waters, but the rod and staff, they comfort us. Though the Word and Spirit do the main work, yet suffering so unbolts the door of the heart that the Word hath easier entrance.

SANCTIFIED afflictions are an evidence of our adoption; we do not prune dead trees to make them fruitful, nor those which are planted in a desert; but such only as belong to the garden, and possess life.

REV. J. ARROWSMITH.

CALLING HIS CHILDREN HOME.

Rev. T. L. Cuyler, D.D.

GOD often calls these children home. This is the bitter cup he gives us to drink. He knows our soul's disease. He is the wisest and best of physicians, never selects the "wrong bottle," and never gives one drop too much of the correct medicine. He does all things well. His children must trust their Father. He chastens for our profit that we may be partakers of his holiness.

God sees that some one in the family has need of his spiritual skill—from indulged sin, from weakening of the graces, and he gives a cup of bitter disappointment—the gourd that was so grateful and refreshing withers. Patient submission, humble acquiescence, and unfaltering trust and hope are the lessons God would teach and what the soul's disease requires. If the cup had not been drunk the blessings would have been lost; if the child had not died, the idol would have been enthroned.

God's cups may be bitter, and you may be long in draining them; at the bottom lies a precious blessing. Rich graces lie there. For this reason the "trial" of faith is precious. So Abraham and Job and all God's children have found it.

Be not surprised when God mixes such a bitter cup for you as the death of a child. You need that medicine. The best tonic medicines are bitter. They have a merciful purpose. It is your Father's cup. Drink it, unhesitatingly, uncomplainingly, and with the spirit of that Beloved Son, who said, "Not my will but thine be done."

WE ARE GOING ONE BY ONE.

Mrs. M. E. Carmichael.

ONE by one we all are going,
  Where the stream of death is flowing;
  One by one we ford that river,
That once crossed is crossed forever.

One by one our friends are falling,
As the voice of God is calling;
One by one is illness wasting
Those who to the grave are hasting.

One by one earth's joys are waning,
And decay o'er all is reigning;
One by one is death still slaying
In each land with no delaying.

One by one the hours are flying,
Filled with anguish and with sighing;
One by one they leave us weeping,
While God's Spirit watch is keeping.

One by one we feel deep sorrow,
And for grief there's no to-morrow;
One by one afflictions chasten,
As through life's dark shades we hasten.

One by one are angels bringing
Christians to the land of singing;
One by one their burdens fall,
And Christ their Lord is all in all.

THE MINISTRY OF TROUBLE.

REV. T. DE WITT TALMAGE, D.D.

IT is easy enough to explain a smile, or a success, or a congratulation; but, come now, and bring all your dictionaries and all your philosophies and all your religions, and help me to explain a tear. A chemist will tell you that it is made up of salt and lime, and other component parts, but he misses the chief ingredients—the acid of a soured life, the viperan sting of a bitter memory, the fragments of a broken heart. I will tell you what a tear is; it is agony in solution.

If it were not for trouble, this world would be a good enough heaven for me. You and I would be willing to take a lease of this life for a hundred million years, if there were no trouble.

The earth cushioned and upholstered and pillared and chandeliered with such expense, no story of other worlds could enchant us. We would say: "Let well enough alone. If you want to die and have your body disintegrated in the dust, and your soul go out on a celestial adventure, then you can go; but this world is good enough for me." You might as well go to a man who has just entered the Louvre at Paris, and tell him to hasten off to the picture galleries of Venice or Florence. "Why," he would say, "what is the use of my going there? There are Rembrandts and Rubens and Raphaels here that I haven't looked at yet." No man wants to go out of this world, or out of any house until he has a better house.

After a man has had a good deal of trouble, he says, "Well, I am ready to go. If there is a house somewhere whose roof doesn't leak, I would like to live there. If there is an atmosphere somewhere that does not distress the lungs, I would like to breathe it. If there is a society somewhere where there is no tittle-tattle, I would like to live there. If there is a home circle somewhere where I can find my lost friends, I would like to go there." He used to read the first part of the Bible chiefly, now he reads the last part of the Bible chiefly. Why has he changed Genesis for Revelation? Ah! he used to be anxious chiefly to know how this world was made, and all about its geological construction. Now he is chiefly anxious to know how the next world was made, and how it looks, and who live there, and how they dress. He reads Revelation ten times now where he reads Genesis once. The old story, "In the beginning God created the heavens and the earth," does not thrill him half as much as the other story, "I saw a new heaven and a new earth." The old man's hand trembles as he turns over this apocalyptic leaf, and he has to take out his handkerchief to wipe his spectacles. That book of Revelation is a prospectus now of the country into which he is to soon immigrate; the country in which he has lots already laid out, and avenues opened, and trees planted, and mansions built. The thought of that blessed place comes over me mightily, and I declare that if this house were a great ship, and you all were passengers on board it, and one hand could launch that ship into the glories of heaven, I should be tempted to take the responsibility, and launch you all into glory with one stroke, holding on to the side of the boat until I could get in myself! And yet there are people to whom this world is brighter than heaven. Well, dear souls, I do not blame you. It is natural. But, after a while, you will be ready to go. It was not until Job had been worn out with bereavements and carbuncles and a pest of a wife that he wanted to see God. It was not until the prodigal got tired of living among the hogs that he wanted to go to his father's house. It is the ministry of trouble to make this world worth less, and heaven worth more.

••••••••••••••••••••••••••••••••

USE OF AFFLICTIONS.—"Extraordinary afflictions are not always the punishment of extraordinary sins, but sometimes the trial of extraordinary graces." Job's friends, such as they were, insisted that his extraordinary afflictions were a just punishment of sins. But God vindicated Job against this charge, and demonstrated to all the world, that the "trial of our faith worketh patience," and all the other Christian graces. Some one has said, "Afflictions are God's polishing brushes," which brighten us for this world and the world to come.

Let us ever remember, that when the founder has cast his bell, he does not at once place it in the steeple, but, before doing so, he tries it with his hammer, beating it on every side, to see if there is any flaw in it. Afflictions drive us more closely under the wing of our Divine protector.

R. MACDUFF, D.D.

"JESUS WEPT."

Rev. John Eadie, D.D.

MARVELLOUS spectacle! Jesus wept, as the mourners about him wept! The sight of such sorrow overpowered Him, and He could not refrain. That was a true manhood, which felt this touch of nature, and burst into tears. There was no Stoicism in His constitution. There was no attempt to train down His sympathies, and educate Himself to a hard and inhuman indifference. Neither was He ashamed of His possession of our ordinary sensibilities. He felt it no weakness to weep in public with them that wept. So sinful did sin appear in its penalty of death—so saddening was the desolation which death had brought into that happy home—so humbling was the picture of Lazarus, alive and active but a few days before, but now laid in the narrow vault, and carefully concealed from view, that the Saviour bowed to the stroke, and, under the impulse of genuine sympathy, "Jesus wept." Perhaps the prospect of His own death and entombment rose up suddenly before Him,—the thought that He should soon be as Lazarus now was, a cold and inanimate corpse, with weeping mourners making a similar procession to His tomb. And though He had but to take a few steps more, and the greatest of His miracles should be achieved, and he that was dead should be raised—so powerful and tender were His mingled sensations that "Jesus wept."

Shall we use the common term, and say that He

was "unmanned?" No. Such an epithet originates in a grievous misinterpretation of our nature. Is man to be denied the relief of tears, and woman only to be so privileged? Is it beneath his masculine robustness to show a moistened eye? Is he to be a traitor to deepest and purest emotion, and to attempt to cauterize the fountain of tears? No. Christ, the model of manhood, the mirror of all that was noble and dignified, did not deny Himself the relief; and shall men be looked upon as effeminate, as falling from the dignity of their sex, if, with emotions like Christ's, they shed tears like Him? No. Perish that dignity which would aspire to a transcendental apathy that man was not made for, and which Jesus despised! The tear is as genuine as the smile. He who would do such violence to his nature insults its Creator, and would foolishly set himself above the example of the Redeemer. Instead of raising himself above humanity, he sinks beneath its level. The brow that never wore a smile is not more unnatural than the eye that never glistened with a tear.

Therefore do we vindicate for the afflicted mourner the privilege of tears. You are not giving way to sin when you are giving way to tears. Man is not disgracing his manhood, nor woman showing herself to be but a woman, when they weep under bereavement. Try not to be above the Saviour. It is not sin to mourn, but the sin is to murmur,—to fall into querulous repining as if God had wronged you, and it needed an effort on your part to forgive Him. We are sure that Jesus harbored no grudge of this nature against His Father in heaven; and yet He wept. To forbid tears is to impose a cruel penance,

—is to deny a luxury to the mourner in which his Lord indulged. O thou of the bruised heart! when thou goest to the sepulchre where the beloved dust is garnered, weep, but not in dejection,—weep, but repine not; disturb not the unbidden tear, as thou art in the place of burials. The dust thou sorrowest over cannot indeed respond; but the time is coming when thy tears shall be wiped away by the very hand that inflicted the stroke. . . .

Whichever form of bereavement oppresses you, oh, be comforted by the thought that "Jesus wept;" that He who so wept is still unchanged in nature; that the heart which was so troubled is as susceptible now as then, and beats in unison and sympathy with you under such trials and sorrows. What a comforter is the Elder Brother, who knows what it is to be bereaved, and will, out of such experience, soothe and solace His people! Nay, more: for eighteen years the Man Jesus has been employed in binding up the bleeding in heart and healing all their wounds. Every variety of grief He has dealt with, and with every element and form of it He is perfectly familiar. If there be power in human sympathy to lighten the load of woe, O how much more in the sympathy of Him who "bore our griefs and carried our sorrows"—whose words of comfort reach the heart—who gives Himself to be loved in room of the object taken away—and gathers the departed into a blessed company before the throne, with the prospect of a happy and unclouded reunion! Let the mourner never forget the image of the weeping Saviour. O how it will re-assure him, and fill him with unspeakable consolation! Thou weepest—but "JESUS WEPT!"

THE SEXTON AND HIS LITTLE GRAVES.

DAVID RAE, EDINBURGH.

IN the churchyard, and in matters connected with it, John Brown seemed quite a different man from what he was anywhere else. Genial, free, and hearty in his own house and the village, he was grave and taciturn in the discharge of his funereal duties, and watched over the place of tombs with a jealous care. This part of his character no one could read but the parish minister; he alone had the key to it. The secret, however, was this. The deepest affections of his soul centred on the enclosed two acres, which he had tended for twenty years. He regarded it with a pride and even a love as great as, and very similar to, that with which an enthusiastic gardener looks upon his domain, and cherishes its floral treasures. Every new-made grave was to John like a flower which he had planted, and it was added in his memory to the many hundreds which covered the surface of the enclosure; to be thought of and cherished according to the degree of respect and reverence which the sexton had for its inmate. As a gardener has his favorite flowers, so John had his favorite graves, and spent additional time on their adornment. Hence one grave might be seen with a smooth velvet turf, and a flower or two blooming upon it, while those surrounding it were covered with rank masses of grass; thus, by looking at any one grave, it could be known what was the state of John's feelings toward the mouldering dust beneath. His professional love was particularly lavished on the little ones. For the children's graves he had a peculiar affection and reverence. Not one of them was suffered to go to waste; and long after the little mound had disappeared, the small level spot was easily found by patches of white clover,—for John invariably sowed this on the little graves, and on none other. Mr. Gray had not been long minister of the parish till he noticed the odd practice of his gravedigger; and one day when he came upon John smoothing and trimming the lowly bed of a child which had been buried a few days before, he asked him why he was so particular in dressing and keeping the graves of the children. John paused for a moment at his work, and looking up, not at the minister, but at the sky, said, "Of such is the kingdom of heaven."

"And on this account you tend and adorn them with so much care," remarked the minister, who was greatly struck with the reply.

"Surely, sir," answered John; "I canna make ower braw and fine the bed-coverin' o' a little innocent sleeper that is waitin' there till it is God's time to wauken it and cover it with the white robe, and waft it away to glory. When sic grandeur is awaitin' it yonder, it's fit it should be decked oot here. I think the Saviour that counts its dust sae precious will like to see the *white clover sheet spread abune't;* dae ye no think sae tae, sir?"

"But why not thus cover larger graves?" asked the minister, hardly able to suppress his emotion.

"The dust of all His saints is precious in the Saviour's sight."

"Very true, sir," responded John, with great solemnity, "but I canna be sure wha are His saints and wha are no. I hope there are mony o' them lyin' in this kirkyard; but it wad be great presumption in me to mark them oot. There are some that I'm gey sure aboot, and I keep their graves as nate and snod as I can, and plant a bit floure here and there as a sign o' my hope; but I daurna gie them the white sheet. It's clean different, tho,' wi' the bairns. We hae His ain word for their up-going, and sae I canna mak' an error there. Some folks, I believe, are bauld enough to say that it's only the infants of the guid that will be saved."

"And do you adhere to that doctrine?" inquired Mr. Gray.

John answered by pointing to a little patch a few paces off, which was thickly covered with clover.

"That ane," he said, "is the bairn o' Tam Lutton, the collier. Ye ken Tam, sir?"

Mr. Gray did, indeed, know Tam, for he was the most notorious swearer, liar, and drunkard in the parish; and John did not require to say any more to show that he disbelieved the doctrine of the condemnation of infants.

"It's no only cruel and blasphemous," he continued, in a dry, sarcastic way, "but it's quite absurd. Jist tak' that bairn o' Tam's as an example. According to their belief it's lost; because we may, without ony breach o' charity, say that Tam is at present a reprobate. But he is still in the place of hope, sir; and it is quite possible that he may be converted. What comes o' the bairn then? Na, na," he added, looking reverently upward, "God is merciful, and Jesus died; and it was He that said, 'Of such is the kingdom of heaven.'"

Mr. Gray was much struck by the deep feeling and fervent piety manifested by the grave-digger, and thought he would extract more of his ideas regarding the subject on which they had been speaking. For this purpose he pointed to the little grave which John was trimming so neatly, and, knowing it to be that of a still-born child, he observed,

"Is it not mysterious, John, that the little human form lying there should not have been permitted to cross the porch of existence? I saw it as it lay so still and beautiful in its snowy robe, and as I noticed its perfect form, with every organ and every limb complete, I was almost tempted to ask why God had made such a beautiful temple in vain."

"'In vain!' say ye," returned John. "Na, no in vain. God mak's naething in vain, far less a form like that in His ain image. Omnipotent as He is, and infinite in His perfections, He canna *afford* tae fashun sic a glorious object only that worms might prey on it. The little marble image lying below this sod is as great a thing as ever God made on this earth. Adam, when he rose up frae the green sward o' Eden, wasna mair physically perfect. He was bigger, nae doot, but nae better formed; and was the ane made in vain any mair than the ither? Na, na, na! The bairnie, puir lammie, 'll ken naething o' the joys and sorrows, the sunshine and shadow o' this life; but he'll be a pure, unsullied sharer o' the life that is ayont this, and higher than this; for I aye cast anchor on the blessed words spoken by the Redeemer o' men and infants, 'Of such is the kingdom of heaven;' and when I think o' a still born wean, I think o' a human being, made, no' for time *but for immortality.*"

The minister took John's hand, and silently pressed it. He had got the key to his deeper nature, and was thrilled by its unexpected richness.

....

OUR COMING LIFE.

JOHN G. WHITTIER.

WE shape ourselves the joy or fear
   Of which the coming life is made,
And fill our future's atmosphere
   With sunshine or with shade.

The tissue of the life to be
   We weave with colors all our own,
And in the field of destiny
   We reap as we have sown.

Still shall the soul around it call
   The shadows which it gathered here,
And, painted on the eternal wall,
   The past shall reappear.

Think ye the notes of holy song
   On Milton's tuneful ear have died?
Think ye that Raphael's angel throng
   Has vanished from his side?

Oh, no! we live our life again;
   Or warmly touched, or coldly dim,
The pictures of the past remain—
   Man's works shall follow him.

WOULD YOU CALL THEM BACK TO EARTH AGAIN?

Rev. G. Whyte.

COULD you be so selfish, and so cruel? Could you wish them back—back from the presence of the Lamb,—back from the sweets of glory to the bitterness of time,—back from those rivers of pure pleasure which flow full and large at God's right hand, to the streams of mingled enjoyment in this vale of sorrow? After they have reached the haven of rest, would you recall them to struggle again with the storm? Is there anything in the state or employments of those who surround the throne which you are called upon to contemplate with sadness, or to deplore in the language of despair? Is it any subject of regret to them that their sun went down while it was yet day?

Resurrection Thought.—"Whether buried in the earth, or floating in the sea, or consumed by the flames, or enriching the battle-field, or evaporated in the atmosphere,—all, from Adam to the latest-born, shall wend their way to the great arena of the judgment. Every perished bone and every secret particle of dust shall obey the summons and come forth. If one could then look upon the earth, he would see it as one mighty excavated globe, and wonder how such countless generations could have found a dwelling beneath its surface."

Rev. Gardiner Spring, D.D.

WHAT MAKES HEAVEN FOR US?

D. L. MOODY.

IT won't be the pearly gates; it won't be the jasper walls, and the streets paved with transparent gold, that shall make it heaven for us. These would not satisfy us. If these were all, we would not want to stay there forever. I heard the other day of a child whose mother was very sick; and while she lay very low, one of the neighbors took the child away to stay with her until the mother should be well again. But instead of getting better, the mother died; and they thought they would not take the child home until the funeral was all over; and would never tell her about her mother being dead. So a while afterward they brought the little girl home. First she went into the sitting-room to find her mother; then she went into the parlor, to find her mother there; and she went from one end of the house to the other, and could not find her. At last she said, "Where is my mamma?" And when they told her her mamma was gone, the little thing wanted to go back to the neighbor's house again. Home had lost its attractions to her, since her mother was not there any longer. No; it is not the jasper walls and the pearly gates that are going to make heaven attractive. It is the being with God. We shall be in the presence of the Redeemer; we shall be forever with the Lord.

WHAT TAKES PLACE AT DEATH.

Rev. Fergus Ferguson, D.D.

ONE reason why our grief at the loss of dear friends is often so excessive as to verge upon the borders of sinfulness, is, that we do not realize sufficiently the joy and the blessedness of the heavenly world. If Christian people would only take the full advantage, in a time of bereavement, of what they profess to believe, "we would have far more white than black at the funeral—far more of the bridal blended with the burial." Let us try to picture out *what takes place at death*, that the dying who read these lines may be cheered, and that mourners may be comforted. The Lord will not be offended at some little play of the imagination, when the intimations of Scripture, and the inferences of analogy, are made the basis of our somewhat conjectural representation.

In the first place, it is highly probable that, in many instances, our dying friends do not suffer so much as they may seem to do. The moorings are being loosed—the immortal spirit is being freed from its confining cage of clay. It is being deadened to pain, as well as to the world. A dear young lady, over whom her mother bent, about a year ago, in sympathizing sorrow, as she lay on what appeared to be her difficult death-bed, expressed the feelings of multitudes who depart, when she said in broken whispers, "Mamma, don't grieve so much for me—I don't suffer much—I'm only weary, weary in my body—but my soul is happy, happy, happy!"

We will not enter on that debated point, "How does the soul leave the body?" On such points we cannot decide, speculate as we may. But let us contemplate "the better part," when just being released from the crumbling prison-house. It is probable that some little time may elapse before it is completely detached from its old companion. Immediately after all seems over, and even when we have reverently closed the lips and eyes, a life-like expression still lingers upon the countenance—which, however, in a short time, disappears, and is followed by the unmistakable impress of dissolution. But see now how beauteous a being has risen from that abandoned, prostrate form, fair as an Aphrodite emerging from the wave! It is probable that heavenly glory forthwith invests and gilds the newly liberated spirits of all little children and of all the righteous. This is the first instalment of "the building of God, the house not made with hands, eternal in the heavens." And, O! what an expression of holy happiness will now sit upon the countenance of the spirit thus set free! That look, if interpreted, would speak in some such words as these: "If we had but known to what liberty, and peace, and blessedness we were being led through that dark valley from which we have just escaped, we would never have murmured once, or sought to prolong our stay on the earth at all. And if the friends whom we have left only knew how happy we are, they would not be lamenting over our clay, as we fear they may be doing. Surely they could not be so selfish as to wish us back from this superior state to our former confinement and many imperfections."

Disembodied spirits cannot see this material world which they have just left, even as we, still shut up within walls of flesh, cannot see them. But if we could see them, we would be able to recognize them. The old look will be there, in the midst of all the glory and bliss. For when we gaze into the face of a friend on earth, that which pleases and thrills us is not a mere material picture, but the glowing outcome of a loving, valuable soul behind. Now, the spirit will wear, when set free from flesh, its own characteristic look of kindness and purity. And the kinder and holier we have been in heart before we die, the kinder and holier shall be the expression of our several countenances whenever we have been disembodied. Without doubt, we shall know one another in the world to come. Whenever our dear ones leave us, they are made conscious of the presence and companionship of guardian angels. When human nurses can do no more, the seraphic and celestial conductors strike in and gladly perform their part. If they are "all ministering spirits, sent forth to minister for them who shall be heirs of salvation" (Hebrews i. 14), we would expect them to be at hand, when urgently needed, at Jordan's swollen flood. If all Christ's "little ones" have angels (Matthew xviii. 10), who "behold the face of His Father in heaven," in all likelihood these bright messengers will be commissioned to conduct both infants and believers to that glorious presence, when their own countenances have been changed and darkened. If the beggar Lazarus was carried up by "angels" to Abraham's bosom, will they not wait on all humble mendicant-like suppliants who "enter heaven by prayer?" Some dying people seem to get a glimpse of these expectant attendants through the chinks of the prison walls before dissolution has taken place; but assuredly they will be made manifest to all the heirs of heaven when completely emancipated. It is possible, too, that the spirits of dear friends, "not lost but gone before," may hover near. A mother or a father may be there ready to meet a departed child. O, how joyous a meeting that shall be! Just as there are affectionate salutations here when friends see one another again who have been long separated, marked demonstrations of joy and welcome shall be made shortly after the weary pilgrim has breathed his last, both on his part and on that of the heavenly convoy that have come to guide him home.

Our departed friends pass quickly from earth to heaven. "Absent from the body," they are immediately made "present with the Lord." Angels "fly swiftly." Spirits move "quick as thought." The bright squadrons we have pictured out shall "climb the ether" with the rapidity of the lightning. The soul of the penitent thief went "that day" with Christ to Paradise. The good old man in Ayr, long ago, was quite right who asked that his fingers might be put on Rom. viii. 38, 39, as he felt the blindness of death coming over him, and exclaimed, "Children, I have breakfasted with you this morning: I shall sup to-night with my Lord Jesus."

What comfort there is to the bereaved in these simple considerations! When the evening shades darken down for the first time on the cold clay, so strangely silent and so sadly shrouded, let them only remember that already the departed has passed the pearly gate; has trodden the golden streets; sees "face to face;" and "knows as he is known." Instead of seeming to chide the Lord by the vehemence of their grief, and to wish to draw back the departed from "an exceeding weight of glory," let them seek from the ever-present Paraclete the spiritual benefit which the chastisement is intended to impart, and go through the world with their hearts more than ever in heaven, because their precious treasures have gone there before them.

Infant Salvation.

OF SUCH IS THE KINGDOM OF HEAVEN.—*Matt. xix: 14.*

INFANT SALVATION.

WILLIAM ANDERSON, D.D.

THOSE who die in infancy form by far the greatest proportion of Redeemed Spirits. And when the heart of the Christian is ready to fail within him for grief, when among adult men and women he can discover so little which will reward the Redeemer for the travail of His soul, how reviving it is to look upward, and contemplate the innumerable multitude of those who were rescued in infancy from the corrupting power of the world, and safely secured for Himself in His heavenly pavilion! It is astonishing, on the one hand, that there should be found so many who have dark misgivings of heart on the subject of the salvation of these infants; and, on the other, that among those who do not question it, so little account should be taken of them in estimating the glory of the kingdom — despising these little ones, and scarcely reckoning them in the number of the Saved: whereas it would be a less improper way of calculation to say, that the kingdom belongs to children, and that the adults who are saved are a few who are admitted to a share of their inheritance.

Therefore, with regard to the deceased infant children of believers, *their* salvation, at least, is as sure as the salvation of the parents themselves. What was the promise worth, yea, what did it mean, if it contained nothing for the spirits of his infant offspring, when the Lord said to Abraham, the type of all believing parents, "I will establish my covenant between me and thee, to be a God unto thee, and to thy seed after thee," and commanded that they should be circumcised, as well as himself, as a token of their interest in the promised salvation? Are not the blessings of God especially blessings for eternity? "Wherefore God is not ashamed to be called their God, for He hath prepared for them a city." And can infants renounce the God of their parents, as those may do who have grown up to years of personal responsibility? Oh, happy children, ye who were laid hold of by the Redeemer and appropriated to Himself, before ye could apostatize like your wretched brothers and unhappy sisters, who have broken the household covenant and abjured the family's Saviour! Then, said I to the father and mother, as they wept, Your children who have died are a better portion to you than those who live: weep for the living and not for the dead: it is the living you have lost; the dead are safely reserved for you. Again: when believing parents made their way so earnestly through the obstructing disciples, to place their children before the Redeemer that He might bless them, what otherwise was His reception of them worth, yea, what did it mean, when "He was much displeased" with his disciples, "and said unto them, Suffer the little children to come unto Me, and forbid them not: for of such is the kingdom of God," and then, "took them up in His arms, put His hands upon them, and blessed them?" If any of these children had presently died—and there can be little doubt that some of them did die in childhood—how vain it had been for them to be blessed by the Redeemer, if there be no heavenly inheritance for those who die in early years?

It is most injurious, however, to the cause of infants, to plead it on ground so low as this. Instead of merely vindicating their admission, and some consideration for them, I regard them as being generally the best welcomed spirits which pass into the eternal world. The whole of our Lord's treatment of them is calculated to produce this impression. Besides, contemplating the subject in the light of reason—Is not the intellectual and moral structure, I ask, of an infant's spirit the same as that of a full-grown man? And who shall dispute, that some of the brightest geniuses and most amiable hearts of our race may have been withdrawn—in the love and valuation of them withdrawn—after a short time's breathing of the pestilential air of this earth, yea, before a breath of it was inhaled, to be secured and nursed in the Paradise of God? As I think of it, I become the more persuaded, that this securing of many of the *best* by early death may be a principle of the divine administration. It is true, they passed away without having acquired any of this world's learning; but irrespectively of God's standard of measurement being a moral one, how insignificant, I appeal, will not even Newton's science appear in yonder Temple of Light! Will the infant spirit have any sense of inferiority from the want of it? Will it appear disrespectable for the want of it in the estimation of the Eternal One? It is true, again, that they passed away without any prayers in which their infant knees had bowed; and without any psalms of praise which their infant lips had sung; but what, brethren, I, a second time, appeal, is the chief characteristic of a religious life in this world? Is it not to have our hearts brought back to their infant state? To have them cleansed of those pollutions, and divested of those perverse habits which we have contracted since we were like these children, who were early withdrawn from the corrupting influences to which we have been exposed? Accordingly, Christ's great lesson for us is, Learn to be like a child. And, a third time, if there are a few deeds of charity, of the performance of which we can speak for ourselves, oh, is it not all more than counterbalanced when these infants can plead in reply, that they were guilty of no envious thoughts, no bitter or slanderous speeches, no impure imaginations or devices, no fretfulness against the Providence of God,—of nothing at all which can be charged against them as either a dereliction or transgression of duty! Who of us shall presume to compare himself with an infant, or forbid that its spirit go to the Saviour of its pious father, or the Saviour of its pious mother?

And further, in regard to those children dying in infancy who are the offspring of ungodly parents— equally of such do I believe that they shall all be saved; though not with a salvation so glorious as that of the offspring of the saints. It is not by any means for the relief of the anxiety of those wicked parents that I express myself thus confidently about the salvation of their children; but for magnifying the grace of God, and rejoicing the hearts of the saints on the subject of the magnificence of the

Redeemer's kingdom, and the splendor of His reward. . . . . We claim them for the kingdom. When the Son of God was incarnated, He became these infants' Brother; and when *they* have not rejected Him, will *He* disown them?

INFINITE wisdom has determined that trouble, of one description or another, shall constitute part of the discipline to which every human being must be subjected.

In the present provisional state of things, afflictive dispensations "must needs be."

We do not at present inquire why it is that this element of suffering interpenetrates to so large an extent the fabric of human society. We take our position upon the undisputed and indisputable fact that trouble, in one form or another, is universal; and withdrawing our attention from all other developments of this ubiquitous ingredient in human life, we fix it upon one of the most painful forms in which it is found, and over the bier of the departed infant we would ask, "Is it well with the child?"

Tender as are the ties that bind the parental heart to those little undeveloped but ever-developing Living Objects which enable parents to realize that they are parents, these very ties are destined to be often agonizingly ruptured. Comparatively few are the households in which there have not been "mourning and bitterness" for some child that was, and is not. Many are the Rachels who have been bowed down under bereaving affliction, and have wept, and "refused to be comforted," because their sons or their daughters "are not." The "places that once knew" multitudes of dear little Miniatures of fathers and mothers, now "know them no more." And fathers and mothers go about the streets mourning; or, refusing consolation, they languish in retirement.

But is there no balm for the wounds of bereaved parents? Is there no physician to heal their broken spirit? There is a physician, all-skillful to cure. He has a balm which is the very essence and elixir of consolation: "It is well with the child." The child is not lost, but gone before. Its "death is gain." Though it is "absent from the body," it is "present with the Lord," which is "far better." It is in "Abraham's bosom." And what is grander still, it is in the bosom of Infinite Love. Its voice to its parents, if that voice could be heard by earthly ears, would be, "Weep not for me." Such is our deliberate opinion concerning departed little ones.

There is a positive foundation on which the doctrine of the everlasting bliss of all who die in infancy may be securely built up.

(1) It may be proved from the fact *that, in consequence of the interposition of the work of Christ, there is to be a universal resurrection of the bodies of men.* It will be admitted that there was no provision made for the resurrection of the bodies of men except in the restorative dispensation of mercy through Christ. As it is "in Adam" that all die, so is it "in Christ" alone that all shall be made alive again. It is the "second Adam" who is the Cause, or Occasion, of the universal resurrection.

But in the resurrection of the body and its reunion to the soul, there will be to the glorified a vast addition to their means of bliss; and there will be to the lost a vast addition to their woe. The bodily organism must, according to the condition in which it is placed, minister largely to the happiness or to the misery of the soul. Can we suppose, then, that any of those who die in infancy, and who have never had the opportunity of rejecting the propitiation of Christ, will be subjected, on account of that gracious work, to greater woes than they would have been called to endure had there been no Saviour at all? Can we suppose that Christ will be an unmitigated and inevitable curse to any of mankind? Surely we cannot cherish such a supposition, when we remember that He came into the world not to condemn it, but to save and to bless it. But if we cannot cherish such a supposition, we cannot suppose that any infants dying in infancy will be lost.

(2) This reasoning is fortified *by the express teaching of our Lord himself*. We learn from the Gospels, as for example from Matt. xix. 13, that on a certain occasion there were brought to Him "little children," that He might put his hands on them and bless them. His disciples rebuked the parents. But Jesus said, "Suffer little children to come unto me, and forbid them not, *for of such is the kingdom of heaven*." This does not seem to mean, "for of persons resembling little children is the kingdom of heaven." The term rendered "of such" has naturally a demonstrative import. Our Saviour elsewhere employs it when He says, "The hour cometh, and now is, when the true worshipper shall worship the Father in spirit and in truth; for the Father seeketh such to worship Him;" that is, "seeketh these to worship Him." It occurs in many other portions of the New Testament with the same demonstrative im-

port, as for example in Acts xxii. 22, in which passage we learn that the Jews in Jerusalem cried out on a certain occasion, in reference to Paul, "away with *such* a fellow from the earth;" that is "away with *this* fellow from the earth." Jesus then means "for of *these* is the kingdom of heaven." The kingdom of heaven belongs to "little children." This interpretation is confirmed by the consideration that we should otherwise be at a loss to discover any peculiar propriety in our Saviour's action, when He took up the little ones in His arms and blessed them. If the reason of His procedure resolved itself simply into the fact that *the adult subjects of the kingdom of heaven are childlike*,—the same reason might have led Him to take up lambs in His arms and bless them, inasmuch as the adult subjects of His kingdom are lamb-like as well as child-like.

It is true that it is added, in Mark x. 15, that our Saviour said, after blessing the little children, "Verily I say unto you, whosoever shall not receive the kingdom of God *as a little child*, he shall not enter therein." But still even here, it is supposed that the kingdom of heaven belongs to little children; for when it is said "whosoever shall not receive the Kingdom of God *as a little child*," the meaning surely must be, "as a little child receives it." *Whosoever shall not receive the kingdom of God without seeking to present anything of the nature of personal meritoriousness, shall in no wise enter therein.*

If it should be said that "the kingdom of heaven" spoken of by our Lord is the kingdom of heaven upon earth, we would reply, that the kingdom of heaven is not entirely upon earth. It is partly and principally in heaven. And moreover, if there be no obstacles to the infant's admission into the earthly province of the heavenly empire, there can be none to its admission into that larger and more glorious province above, which, from its vastitude and vast pre-eminence, gives the denomination to the whole domain.

(3) We might add to these considerations the fact that *throughout the Scriptures God is frequently represented as cherishing a special regard for little children.* We see this in the rebuke administered to Jonah,—" And should I not spare Nineveh, that great city, wherein are more than six score thousand persons that cannot discern between their right hand and their left hand." We see it in the words of Jeremiah xix. 4, "They have filled this place with the blood of innocents." And again, in the words of Joel ii. 16, "Gather the people, sanctify the congregation, assemble the elders, *gather the children and those that suck the breast,* etc., then will the Lord be jealous for the land, and pity his people." And in Ezekiel xvi. 21, God calls the little children of the Israelite *His children,* and pours terrible denunciations upon the people for causing them to pass through the fire to Moloch:—"Thou hast slain *my children,* and delivered them to cause them to pass through the fire."

On the whole, then, every line of Scripture-truth, when we follow it out undeviatingly, leads us up to the conclusion, that "it *is* well" with all the "little children" who have been carried away from the unfolding arms, though not from the infolding hearts and memories, of bereaved parents. They have been taken up "higher." They have been committed to wiser and more tender keeping. "Their angels" have got them; and in the immediate vicinity of the throne, they are undergoing a training, which is absolutely free from all those elements of imperfection which might have resulted in moral deviation, defilement, and death, had they remained on the earth. "It *is* well."

JAMES MORISON, D.D.

We arrive at the conclusion, so delightful in itself and so consolatory to parents in the hour of bereavement, that their precious children whom, in the sweetness of their infantile innocence, the cold hand of death has rifled from their bosoms, are translated to the regions of the blest. Those delicate flowers, which the rude storms of our inclement atmosphere have blighted, unfold in eternal fragrancy beneath the pleasant beams of the sun's celestial glory. Those bright, but little stars, which to us seem prematurely quenched, do but sink beneath the horizon till, with new lustre and augmented magnitude, they repair their drooping radiance, and "Flame in the forehead of the morning sky." Those gems, more precious than pearls or rubies, of which the anguished mother has been despoiled, are set in deeper brilliance in that glorious mediatorial diadem which encircles the Redeemer's brow. Those infantile voices, which had scarce learnt to lisp His name, now sing in lofty descants, "Salvation to him that sitteth upon the throne, and to the Lamb." Then let the stricken hearts of parents, whom death has made childless, no longer indulge an immoderate grief. Your beloved and lamented offspring, looking down from their heavenly spheres, would chide your sorrow. Among the ransomed they have taken their immortal stations.

EDWARD STEANE, D.D.

ONE of the most beautiful incidents of the Redeemer's life affords to the question of infant salvation a most decisive and satisfactory solution. There stands the Incarnate God! Truth beams from His lips, and healing power radiates from His omnipotent touch. Mothers in Israel gather around Him, and anxiously present their children for His benediction. The disciples, ignorant of the depth and tenderness of His sympathies, and knowing as yet but little of the benign purpose of His coming, rebuke the tender women for their intrusion, and thrust them and their children away from His presence. But He, the messenger of truth, and the procurer of life and salvation for all, bids the trembling women draw near to Him, and welcomes their children to His loving arms, uttering those memorable words — "Suffer the little children to come unto me, and forbid them not: for of such is the kingdom of God." (Mark x. 14.) Nor can the word "such" be frittered down to mere likeness; and, if it were, the likeness itself would indicate a fitness for the kingdom; and if a fitness, a title thereto through grace. But another text gives the meaning of the word a direct personal application to children themselves as such:—"Take heed that ye despise not one of these little ones [little children being then in His presence]: for I say unto you that in heaven their angels do always behold the face of my Father which is in heaven." (Matt. xviii. 10.) These plain and striking words settle for ever the question of infant salvation. In heaven the little ones are angels, blessed spirits, dwelling in God's immediate presence, beholding His face, and rejoicing in the light of His countenance.

Parents, wipe away your tears: your little ones are safe. Though severed from your embrace, they are received into the embraces of Him who died for them and rose again. Lift up your eyes then from the gloomy sepulchre to the radiant throne, and there behold them resplendent in robes of purity, and exultant in the bliss of the Divine presence. Prepare to meet them in that bright world, where the parting tear shall never be shed, and the sad farewell shall never be heard. Meanwhile, be unceasingly careful to train your surviving offspring to a meetness for that blessed inheritance, that at the last day, when standing in His glorious presence, you may say respecting both them and yourselves, "Here, Lord, are we, and the children Thou hast given us."

WILLIAM COOKE, D.D.

IF infants are raised from the dead through the mediation of Christ, and if, as we have seen, they cannot be raised to misery, they are, of course, delivered from the penal sentence pronounced on them on the ground of Adam's transgression; and if so, they are also delivered from that spiritual death into which they fell through the loss of those holy principles which were enjoyed by Him as their head and representative: for, were it otherwise, the blessing of the resurrection would be rendered worse than nugatory. As they have not been accountable agents, their deliverance from the one result of the sin of Adam, must be connected with deliverance from the other, and this again with eternal life in the heavenly paradise. It was in consequence of the sin of Adam, that special holy influence was withdrawn; and it is in consequence of the perfect righteousness of Jesus as the second Adam, that this hallowed gift is restored. And if it was as the descendants of Adam, our public head, that we were involved in this loss, so it is as connected with Christ as our Head that we came to partake of the sacred influence of His Spirit. If, then, this gift be bestowed on deceased infants, it must be given them as members of His spiritual body, and, of course, must be given to make them meet for the special privileges and blessings of His kingdom. The resurrection of infants, then, including, of course, the recall of their spirits from the separate state, is connected with their previous deliverance, at least at the time of their death, from the power of original sin, and, consequently, with their final enjoyment of the celestial inheritance. . . . .

These reflections appear decidedly to show that the question respecting the salvation of infants ought not to be shunned as an intrusion into those "secret things" which belong only to God. It seems to be an evident conclusion, from every view which the Scriptures exhibit of the will of the Almighty, that all of them dying in infancy are saved.

DAVID RUSSELL, D.D.

"While the child was yet alive, I fasted and wept; for I said, Who can tell whether God will be gracious to me, that the child may live? But now he is dead, wherefore should I fast? can I bring him back again? I shall go to him, but he shall not return to me." II. Samuel, xii., 22, 23.

LET not this be interpreted as the language of *insensibility*. The general character of David, and his previous behavior on the same occasion, ought to save him from every imputation of this kind. No. His heart was full of paternal and conjugal tenderness. Fain would he have brought back his babe to his own fond embrace, and to the breast of its disconsolate mother. But the thought was vain. All was now over. The last sigh with which the infant spirit escaped to wing its way to the world of light, had settled the case with regard to the child. David had found his consolation in God, and he had the richest and sweetest of all comforts respecting his infant. The language, "*I shall go to him,*" is evidently the language of comfort, by which he was supported under the anguish that would otherwise have been intolerable in the thought of what follows: "*but he shall not return to me.*" It does not, then, it *cannot* refer to *the grave.*" The child was not in the grave when the words were uttered; nor do I believe there was any thought of the grave in the bereaved parent's mind. What consolation could there have been in *that*, that *he*, too, should lie down a cold, inanimate corpse? This was not *going to him* in any sense that could impart the slightest satisfaction to the afflicted spirit. The words clearly imply firm conviction of his child's existence and happiness. "I shall go to him," means, I shall go whither he has now gone. And if his afterwards joining him there was an object of hope, there is necessarily implied the persuasion of his having gone to a place of happiness. How sweetly soothing, how inestimably precious is the same thought still to the agonized bosom of parental love! How delightfully tranquillizing, when the first burst of nature's agony has a little subsided, the reflection that your child has been taken away from the evil to come—taken, to spend those years in heaven, which he must otherwise have spent amidst sin, and temptation, and sorrow, in the valley of tears: that he has been spared all the perils, and fatigues, and fightings of the wilderness, and has been received at the better country, even the heavenly; that the tender and lovely plant which you had begun to cherish with so much care has been happily removed from all the chilling frosts and withering blasts of this inferior clime, and has found its place in the garden of God above, there to drink the dews of paradise, and to flourish in unfading beauty! It is a settled, undoubting, delightful serenity which the soul enjoys in contemplating the departure of *little children*. Think of what the kind and gracious Redeemer said of them when, with a frown on those who would have forbidden their being brought to him, and a smile of ineffable benignity on the little immortals themselves, He said: "Suffer the little children to come unto me, and forbid them not: for of such is the kingdom of God;" and, taking them up in His arms, He blessed them. Think, then, of their blessedness, and that will soothe your grief.

RALPH WARDLAW, D.D.

"Your little ones, which ye said would be a prey, and your children, which in that day had no knowledge between good and evil, *they shall go in thither.*"—Deut. i. 39.

You are in circumstances to welcome light from whatever quarter on the destiny of children dying in infancy.

I have lying before me the analysis of an argument from analogy on this subject, which made a great impression on me at the time I first saw it, and may be of use to you at present. The argument is based upon the admission of children into the mised land.

I need not remind you that there is an analogy between the land which was once the land of promise to the Jews and our heavenly home. From that land, for their sins, the fathers were excluded —Caleb and Joshua alone excepted. But of the children it is said—"*They* shall go in thither." If this was so in the case of the earthly Canaan; if the children of parents, who themselves were excluded, were favored in this way; if they were the subjects of mercy, while their fathers were the objects of punitive justice, how much more may we expect it to take place in respect to the heavenly Canaan? The point here is, that the exclusion of children does not follow the exclusion of parents. If it did, all would have been excluded except the children of Caleb and Joshua.

The *reason assigned by God* for this procedure is one which will be applicable at the day of judgment.

"Your children, which *in that day had no knowledge between good and evil*, they shall go in" It is true they were living when their fathers rebelled against God; but they were not partakers in the rebellion. In the day of provocation they were gambolling about the green fields in innocent ignorance of what was taking place: they were not yet capable of distinguishing between good and evil, and, therefore, they were not excluded. But since we are speaking of the dealings of the unchangeable God, we may safely conclude that He will acknowledge the force of the same reasons in the final judgment. The infants who die, carry with them towards the judgment throne no knowledge of good or evil, no experience of the bitterness of offending God. And they will not be involved in the condemnation of the wicked.

If you next consider the purposes for which children were admitted into Canaan, you will see that similar purposes require fulfillment in their admission into heaven. One of these purposes is referred to in the verse quoted at the top: "Your little ones, which *ye said should be a prey*." If you read carefully the fourteenth chapter of Numbers, verses 1–3, you will understand the force of the rebuke. Sin had blotted out their faith in God. "Their children were sure to perish!" They themselves, too, would perish. So they thought. And *they* were indeed to perish. But the helpless ones, the innocent, the unpartaking, were to go free. Now the admission of the children into Canaan, after the expression of unbelief on the part of the parents, was a vindication of God's ways, an answer to the unbelief of the parents, and a perpetual token that God deals with infants on the ground of saving mercy. It is glorious to think that God is preparing a reply to the doubts and disbeliefs of all who are far from

Him, by a similar exercise of grace. Sceptics, infidels, heathens, expect nothing for *their* children but death, temporal and eternal. How will they be amazed when they discover, in another state, that God has been better than their thoughts; and although they (because of their sins) are excluded, their children have been admitted into His presence. Still further, God had this purpose in bringing the children into Canaan, that they should advance His standard into new territory, build up His kingdom, and be the organ of His praise. Has He not the same purpose in respect of heaven? He chooses not to be alone throughout eternity. And (blessed prospect!) from the mouth of babes and sucklings He ordains the strength of His eternal hallelujahs. He who could raise up children to Abraham from the stones, will not want the power to fill heaven with their loving and delightful songs.

ALEX. MACLEOD, D.D.

I MUST embrace this renewed opportunity of expressing my firm conviction, founded, I think, on the testimony of the divine record, that all infants, *without exception*, will, when they die, be introduced by the compassionate and Almighty Redeemer into that place where, "out of the mouth of babes and sucklings," He will then and to all eternity perfect His own praise; showing in them and by them the infinite value and efficacy of His own atoning blood. He who shed that blood for them on Calvary, and who, while yet in deep humiliation, said, "Suffer little children to come unto me," has now brought them near the exalted throne which

He occupies and adorns. There they are transformed into His likeness, because they now "see Him as he is." Their powers will thus be perfected, and their capacity for enjoyment accordingly enlarged. They were not permitted to serve, so as to enjoy fellowship with God here. But there they shall serve Him day and night in His temple. And what a source of consolation is this! Oh! can we grieve when we have reason to believe that our children are in heaven, freed for ever from all evil, and from the possibility of suffering or sorrow of any kind; but on the contrary rejoicing, as they shall to eternity rejoice, in the presence of God and of the Lamb! Who can doubt that their songs will be among the sweetest, and even the loftiest, to be heard in the celestial temple?

ADAM THOMSON, D.D.

I HAVE often been struck with the following passage in connection with the subject of infant salvation—"Out of the mouth of babes and sucklings hast thou ordained strength because of thine enemies, that thou mightest still the enemy and the avenger." (Ps. viii. 2.) The enemy and the avenger referred to here is, I think, Satan, who would avenge himself, if he could, by destroying the whole human race. But his revengeful desires have been thwarted, inasmuch as many helpless babes have been made the subjects of renewing grace. More than this; I suppose the majority of our race die in infancy; these, I believe, are all lambs of the "Good Shepherd," and are taken to Himself—"for of such is the kingdom of God." In this way the Father of mercy "ordains strength, stills the enemy and the avenger;" because, in the salvation of infants, the number of the saved is greater than the lost. Our Saviour quoted this ancient oracle, when the children sung His praises in the temple, and He silenced those who were instigated by the "enemy and the avenger" to find fault with the children and their songs. Many children now sing the praises of the "Good Shepherd" in the temple above, and your dear child is there too, and of her and many more are the ancient words true, "Out of the mouth of babes and sucklings hast thou ordained strength."

ALEX. WALLACE, D.D.

As partakers of a fallen nature, children are subject to disease and death. Much and tenderly as we love them, it is not unfrequently that we are called to follow them to the silence and the solitude of the tomb. More than one-third of the race die in infancy and childhood. What is their final condition? This is a question which often forces itself upon the thought of Christian parents, and which more or less disturbs their inward peace and quiet. But how tranquillizing and how assuring are the words of the Saviour—"of such is the kingdom of heaven!"—as if to intimate that heaven is their true and proper home—their Father's house in which only they can be for ever safe and happy. Of the salvation of infants there can be no possible doubt; for, "as in Adam all die, so in Christ shall all be made alive." Whatever may be the effects involved in man's transgression, these are all provided for and removed by the substitution and the work of

Christ; so that if there were no personal sin or actual guilt, the Saviour's mediation would result in the salvation of the whole race. From all such individual, actual guilt, infants are free; and the atonement insures their introduction into the family of God, with a full participation in the glory of the world to come. But myriads of children, no longer within the years of infancy, are permitted to light up our homes with their smiling, beaming faces for a longer or shorter period, and in many ways to add to the sum of our earthly joys, and yet are taken from us while the dew of youth is upon them, and sometimes amid the first and earliest buddings of their intellectual development and intelligence. What is *their* final condition? It is impossible to fix on any one uniform age in a child as the point at which responsibility begins; but let the age be what it may, we are firm in the belief that the Spirit whom the Saviour sent to glorify Him, and whose office it is to take of the things which are Christ's and show them to us, not only enlightens the minds of these little ones prior to their removal, but so reveals a Saviour's love to them and in them as to draw their young and susceptible hearts into union and fellowship with Himself here, and thus prepare and meet them for the life and the bliss of a higher state. If in all things Christ is to have the pre-eminence, then He will have the pre-eminence in numbers. The saved will far outnumber the lost; and among these redeemed and glorified ones, those whose hearts have been least defiled by actual sin, and who are most susceptible of receiving the impression of the Saviour's image, will occupy a conspicuous place. Just as a single dew-drop can reflect all the rays of the sun, so the mind of a child can take on and reflect the likeness of God—" of such is the kingdom of God." They are there in myriad throngs—pure, perfect, and forever blessed. They perfect the family of God. Their presence makes that home of the redeemed the brighter, and sunnier and more attractive.

There is no circle into which they do not enter, no scene in which they do not mingle, and no service in which they do not perform their part.

ROBERT FERGUSON, D.D.

THE argument for infant salvation rests, not on isolated passages, but on the genius of the Bible and its economy of grace. We muse upon the mission of Christ to find one of its principal glories in glorified infancy. The inhabitants of Christian and Pagan lands shall be judged respectively by the Gospel and by conscience, but to neither law can infants be subject. The death of children is traceable to the sin of Adam, and their glory to the righteousness of Christ. The only view which harmonizes universal scripture is, that the redemption by Christ completely covers the sin of Adam, that adults in Bible lands are judged according to their faith or unbelief in the Son of God, and that Christ's covenant with His Father carries the salvation of all infants.

There is an intuitive conviction that infants, who have not *personally* rejected the law and love of God, cannot be excluded from the kingdom, and that they are as fully identified with the second as with the first Adam. There may be a higher degree of glory given to some translated infants because of their godly parentage. But the soul of man clings to the thought of no infant being lost in the universe of that God, whose "tender mercies are over all His works."

J. LOGAN AIKMAN, D.D.

THE salvation of children seems thus clearly to be the doctrine of the Word of God. The opposite doctrine may become the worshippers of Moloch, but should be driven for ever from the creed of those who call upon Him whose name is "Love," who follow that "Good Shepherd" who "gathereth the lambs in His arms, and carrieth them in His bosom," and who put all their trust in Him whose latest instructions on earth were given to an apostle, in words ever memorable, as evidencing His own remarkable love for the young, and as affording a test by which others are to evidence their love for Himself—FEED MY LAMBS.

JOHN MACFARLANE, D.D.

I CANNOT believe that the Saviour, who evinced such attachment to children upon earth, who took them in His arms and blessed them, who rebuked the apostles for forbidding their approach to His person, who declared that "of such is the kingdom of heaven,"—I cannot believe that the infant flower, which so soon lies withered upon its stalk, is not transplanted into those unfading bowers where it will flourish in all the bloom and vigor of immortality.

THOMAS CHALMERS, D.D.

INFANTS, whose undeveloped minds cannot apprehend and appreciate the blessings of salvation, are saved. We doubt not their entrance into the kingdom of heaven. We doubt it not of all, whatever their descent, who die at that early age—the age which precludes moral discernment, and, therefore, responsibility.

R. WINTER HAMILTON, D.D.

I HAVE had six children, and I bless God for His free grace that they are all *with* Christ, or *in* Christ, and my mind is now at rest concerning them. My desire was that they should have served Christ on earth, but if God will choose to have them rather serve Him in heaven, I have nothing to object to it; His will be done!

CHARLES ELLIOT, D.D.

ONLY SLEEPING.—They have only gone an hour or two sooner to bed, as children are used to do, and we are undressing to follow. And the more we put off the love of the present world, and all things superfluous beforehand, we shall have the less to do when we lie down.

ARCHBISHOP LEIGHTON.

Consolation for Parents Bereft of Children.

Her Child was Caught up to God and to His Throne.—*Rev. xii.*, 5.

THE LIGHT THAT RADIATES AROUND THE INFANT'S TOMB.

REV. DR. THOMAS CHALMERS.

THIS text—Romans iv. 9-15—affords, we think, something more than a dubious glimpse into the question that is often put by a distracted mother when her babe is taken away from her—when all the converse it ever had with the world amounted to the gaze upon it of a few months, or a few opening smiles which marked the dawn of felt enjoyment—and ere it had reached perhaps the lisp of infancy, it—all unconscious of death—had to wrestle through a period of sickness with his power, and at length to be overcome by him. Oh, it little knew what an interest it had created in that home where it was so passing a visitant—nor, when carried to its early grave, what a tide of emotion it would raise among the few acquaintance it left behind! On it, too, baptism was impressed as a seal, while as a sign it was never falsified. There was no positive unbelief in its little bosom—no resistance yet put forth to the truth—no love at all for the darkness rather than the light—nor had it yet fallen into that great condemnation which will attach to all who perish because of unbelief, that their deeds are evil. It is interesting to know that God instituted circumcision for the infant children of Jews, and at least suffered baptism for the infant children of those who profess Christianity. Should the child die in infancy, the use of baptism as a sign has never been thwarted by it; and may we not be permitted to indulge a hope so pleasing as that the use of baptism as a seal remains in all its entireness,—that He who sanctioned the affixing of it to a babe will fulfill upon it the whole expression of this ordinance? And when we couple with this the known disposition of our great Forerunner—the love that He manifested to children on earth—how He suffered them to approach His person—and lavishing endearment and kindness upon them in the streets of Jerusalem, told His disciples that the presence and company of such as these in heaven formed one ingredient of the joy that was set before Him—tell us if Christianity do not throw a pleasing radiance around an infant's tomb? And should any parent feel softened by the touching remembrance of a light that twinkled a few short months under his roof, and at the end of its little period expired, we cannot think that we venture too far when we say that he has only to persevere in the faith, and in the following of the gospel, and that very light will again shine upon him in heaven. The blossom which withered here upon its stalk has been transplanted there to a place of endurance, and it will then gladden that eye which now weeps out the agony of an affection that has been sorely wounded; and in the name of Him, who, if on earth, would have wept along with them, do we bid all believers to sorrow not even as others which have no hope, but to take comfort in the thought of that country where there is no sorrow and no separation.

Oh, when a mother meets on high
The babe she lost in infancy,
Hath she not then, for pains and fears—
The day of woe, the watchful night—
For all her sorrow, all her tears—
An over-payment of delight?

A MOTHER'S FIRST GRIEF.

ROBERT SMYTH CHILTON.

SHE sits beside the cradle,
   And her tears are streaming fast,
   For she sees the present only,
While she thinks of all the past:
Of the days so full of gladness,
When her first born's answering kiss
Thrilled her soul with such a rapture
That it knew no other bliss.
O those happy, happy moments!
They but deepen her despair;
For she bends above the cradle,
And her baby is not there!

There are words of comfort spoken,
And the leaden clouds of grief
Wear the smiling bow of promise,
And she feels a sad relief;
But her wavering thoughts will wander,
Till they settle on the scene
Of the dark and silent chamber,
And of all that might have been.
For a little vacant garment,
Or a shining tress of hair,

Tells her heart, in tones of anguish,
That her baby is not there!

She sits beside the cradle,
But her tears no longer flow,
For she sees a blessed vision,
And forgets all earthly woe;
Saintly eyes look down upon her,
And the voice that hushed the sea
Stills her spirit with the whisper,
"Suffer them to come to Me."
And, while her soul is lifted
On the soaring wings of prayer,
Heaven's crystal gates swing inward,
And she sees her baby there!

BEREAVED PARENTS COMFORTED.

Rev. W. M. Taylor, D.D.

BEREAVED parents, do not sorrow murmuringly and without hope when your children are taken from you in death, for in such a dispensation Jesus is only saying to you in another form what He said to His disciples long ago, "Suffer the little children to come unto me, and forbid them not: for of such is the kingdom of God." Their death is but their going to Him, for I have no doubt whatever of the salvation of infants. It is not indeed a doctrine distinctly revealed; but it may, I think, be inferred from many passages of Scripture, and from the whole character of the gospel itself. The very words which I have quoted, even if there were no others, warrant the conclusion that infants are received into that kingdom of God which stretches into eternity; and if this be so, wherefore should you be like Rachel, "refusing to be comforted?"

Consider to whom they have gone. They have been taken to the arms of Jesus, and to the bright glory of the heavenly state. Nothing now can mar their felicity, or dim the lustre of their joy, or damp the ardor of their song; and could they speak to you from their abode of bliss, they would say to you, Weep not for us, but weep for yourselves, that you are not here to share our happiness.

Consider from what they have been taken. They have been removed from earth, with its pains and privations, its sufferings and sorrows. Look back upon your own chequered histories, and tell me if you can contemplate without a feeling of grief, the idea of your children passing through such trials as those which have met you in the world? Would you wish that their hearts should be wrung as yours have been, by the harshness of an unfeeling world, or by the ingratitude of those whom you have served? Nay, in view of the agony of this very bereavement, would you wish that a similar sorrow should be theirs? And yet does not their continuance in the world involve in it the endurance of all these things; and ought it not, therefore, to be a matter of thankfulness that they have reached heaven without having passed through the full bitterness of earth? Above all, can you contemplate the spiritual dangers with which the world is environed, and not feel grateful that your little ones are now eternally safe from them? Think of the temptations that have beset you, and of the dreadful battles which you fought with them, and how near you were to being conquered by them, and let me ask if in this view you can feel otherwise than glad that they have gained the victory without the perils and hardships of the fight? Perhaps, had they been exposed to these dangers they would have fallen before them; perhaps, had they lived they would have grown up only to fill your hearts with sadness, and "to bring your gray hairs with sorrow to the grave;" but all this is now impossible, for they are safe with Jesus. It *is* hard to part with your children; indeed there can be no severer bereavement, unless it be the death of a husband or a wife. But, oh! remember the death of your child is not the heaviest calamity that could befall you, for "a living cross is heavier than a dead one."

Consider again for what they are taken. Perhaps you have been wandering away from Christ, and He has taken this way to bring you back. Perhaps you have been centring your heart too much on the earthly object, and He has taken it to Himself, that your treasure may be still in Him. Perhaps you have never known Him, and He has taken this means of introducing Himself to you, coming to you as He did to His followers of old, over the very waves with which you are struggling, and saying, "It is I, be not afraid." Perhaps some other member of your family was to be led through this affliction to the Lord, and thus one little one was taken from you for a season, that another might abide with you forever. And if this should be so, can you repine?

Consider, finally, how this bereavement will appear when you come to lie upon your death-bed. I have seen mothers and fathers not a few at that solemn hour, but never one have I heard expressing anxiety for the little children who had gone before. The great concern, then, after their own eternal safety, has always been for those they were leaving behind. The Lord, thus, is afflicting thee now, that thy sorrow may be mitigated at the last. Think of all these things, mourning parents, and then your bereavement will seem to be, as it in reality is, a token of love and not of anger.

> "Oh, not in cruelty, not in wrath,
>   The Reaper came that day;
> 'Twas an angel visited the green earth,
>   And took the flowers away."

PARENTAL ANXIETY REMOVED BY THE EARLY DEATH OF CHILDREN.

REV. DR. JOHN MACFARLANE.

THE ardent love you have for your children is not altogether pleasurable. It necessarily carries you into many anxious thoughts about their welfare. In this sense they are a burden to you, and this burden becomes all the heavier the more you love them. Your own experience of this world has not exalted it, as a place of residence, in your estimation. You have tested its promises, and found them false and vain. You have tasted its pleasures, and found that they "bite like a serpent, and sting like an adder." You have groaned under its pains and penalties, and you have found out that help from man is in vain, and that miserable comforters are all that crowd around you in the night seasons of your soul, and sore disquietudes.

You, therefore, tremble when you think of your darling infants living to be cast upon such revolutionary periods in the troubled life of man, wherein, though they may preserve their integrity, they must endure hardships, but in which, also, they may lose their precious souls for ever. Their futurity, then, is at once your main difficulty, and your most fertile source of anxious foreboding. Now, has not their early death solved this difficulty for you, and ought it not, therefore, also to be your consolation? You will never have any more anxiety on their account. The various hiding-places in your hearts, from which these anxieties spring upon you, have been searched, and by death have been completely emptied.

Their Education is Completed.—They "know as they are known." Your utmost wish in this respect was to give them, if not a learned, at least a useful education. But God has been better than your wish. They are now in knowledge far beyond the most splendid scholars and most profound philosophers of this and of every age. Their intellectual stature is only to be accounted small when compared with the wisdom of God Himself. Neither before angels, nor the spirits of the just made perfect, have they to veil their faces.

Their Holiness is Perfected.—Not one of the infirmities they inherited from you now appertains to them; they are "holy as God is holy." Did you tremble at the thought of their exposure to the temptations of Satan and the flesh? Be assured now that they are "more than conquerors through Him that loved them." Exquisitely beautiful now are those dear creatures in all the graces of the family of God. Their thoughts, their desires, their actions are at this moment in perfect harmony with the mind of the Holy One of Israel. The same mind that is in Christ is in them; they do the will of their heavenly Father, and *He* is pleased with them every moment, and every moment delights their happy souls with His approving smile.

THEIR HAPPINESS IS CONSUMMATED.—You were not at ease as to measures for their future provision, and even with respect to the most likely ones, you feared that they might fail. To make them comfortable for life you were ready to sacrifice much, and you never wearied in efforts to secure for them an honorable independence. Their futurity was upon your minds all the day, and oft took from you the sleep of all the night. Surely, then, you may cease from lamentation, when you are certified that, as they shall sin no more, so neither shall they suffer any more. They are as happy now as they can be. God has provided for them in heaven. They are now inheriting the promises. They are now in actual possession and enjoyment of "that inheritance which is incorruptible and undefiled, and that fadeth not away." Within them is a "well of water springing up into everlasting life;" without them is the perennial flow of the river of life; above them is the unclouded sun of God's favor; and around them are gathered the inexhaustible fountains of celestial bliss. They are so happy now that they are for ever singing. And if ever there should be a "Selah" to their song, it is only to draw in a larger inspiration for a more melodious burst of praise. They would not return to you now, much though they loved you and you them. They do not miss you now, much though you miss them. Your sorrows do not diminish their joys, and their joys ought to diminish your sorrows. Oh, who would bring them back again *here*, to toil, and sweat, and suffer, and, perhaps, to sin without penitence, and to die without faith? You, O weeping parent, ought to be the very last to think of it, and yours should ever be the song of gratitude.

••••••••••••••••••••••••••••••

RESTORATION OF CHILDREN IN HEAVEN.

REV. DR. JOHN BROWN.

WITH what delight will parents, themselves released from the captivity of the grave, behold their early-lost, long-mourned children coming forth, not the pale, emaciated, lifeless, ghastly forms they reluctantly committed to the grave, but strong in incorruptibility, glorious in beauty, "fashioned like unto Christ's glorious body." Then shall it appear to the assembled universe that among the redeemed of the Lord, fathers have not hoped in vain, nor mothers brought forth for trouble. "They are the seed of the blessed of the Lord, and their offspring with them."

But it will be long, long ere they return. The captivity of death is measured, not by years, but by ages. What then? It is but the few, it may be the very few, remaining days of the years of our pilgrimage, which prevent our spirits from embracing theirs; and in the resting-places prepared for us, though we shall not cease to desire, we shall never weary for "the adoption, the redemption of the body." "Be patient, brethren, unto the coming of the Lord, Behold, the husbandman waiteth for the precious fruit of the earth, and hath long patience for it, until he receive the early and latter rain. Be ye also patient; and stablish your hearts." Then "those young and tender plants, which are now cut down, and withering around us, shall spring up in fairer and more durable forms." "The children of the resurrection cannot die any more, but are equal to the angels."

Having been raised from the dead, they shall "mount up together in the clouds," along with those who have been miraculously changed, "to meet the Lord in the air: and so shall they ever be with the Lord." Among that glorious company shall be found those infants and little children whose untimely departure to "the land of the enemy" drew forth such tender regrets and bitter tears. They shall not only "return," but "come to Zion, with songs and everlasting joy upon their heads: they shall obtain joy and gladness, and sorrow and sighing shall flee away." They shall not only leave for ever the dark and lonesome abodes of death, but they shall for ever dwell in the cheerful regions of perfect life, and light, and joy. They shall not only be brought from the land of the enemy, but they shall be "brought in and be planted in the mountain of Jehovah's inheritance, in the place which He has made for Himself to dwell in, in the sanctuary which His hand has established." There "Jehovah-Jesus shall reign for ever and ever," and there "they shall reign with Him." The long silence of the grave shall be exchanged for the ceaseless ever-new song of Moses and the Lamb. "Sing unto the Lord, for He hath triumphed gloriously."

Who is like unto Jehovah among the gods? Who is like unto Him, glorious in holiness, fearful in praises, doing wonders? He has ransomed us from the power of the grave. He has redeemed us from death. He has swallowed up death in life. O death, where is thy sting? O grave, where is thy victory? Thanks be to Him who has given us the victory. Salvation to our God and to the Lamb, for ever and ever. To Him who loved us, and washed us from our sins in His own blood; to Him be glory and honor for ever and ever. Worthy is the Lamb that was slain, slain for us. "Hallelujah!" And again and again the great multitude, with a voice as of many waters and mighty thunderings, shall shout "Hallelujah!" And none in all the happy company will sing more sweetly than the little children.

Then, indeed, shall be brought to pass the saying that is written, "Out of the mouth of babes and sucklings thou hast perfected praise."

THE LAMBS ALL SAFELY FOLDED.

UNKNOWN.

I LOVED them so,
That when the Elder Shepherd of the fold,
Came, covered with the storm, and pale and cold,
And begged for one of my sweet lambs to hold,
I bade Him go.

He claimed the pet;
A little fondling thing, that to my breast
Clung always, either in quiet or unrest;
I thought of all my lambs I loved him best,
  And yet—and yet—

  I laid him down,
In those white shrouded arms, with bitter tears;
For some voice told me that, in after years,
He should know nought of passion, grief, or fears,
  As I had known.

  And yet again
That Elder Shepherd came; my heart grew faint—
He claim'd another lamb, with sadder plaint.
Another! She, who, gentle as a saint,
  Ne'er gave me pain.

  Aghast I turned away;
There sat she, lovely as an angel's dream,
Her golden locks with sunlight all agleam,
Her holy eyes with heaven in their beam;
  I knelt to pray:

  "Is it Thy will?
My Father! say, must this pet lamb be given?
O, thou hast many such, dear Lord, in heaven!"
And a soft voice said, "Nobly hast thou striven;
  But—peace, be still!"

  Oh, how I wept
And clasped her to my bosom, with a wild
And yearning love—my lamb, my pleasant child:
Her, too, I gave—the little angel smiled,
  And *slept!*

"Go! go!" I cried:
For, once again, that Shepherd laid His hand
Upon the noblest of our household band;
Like a pale spectre, there He took His stand,
    Close to his side.

    And yet how wondrous sweet
The look with which He heard my passionate cry
"Touch not my lamb—for him O let me die!"
"A little while," he said, with smile and sigh,
    "Again to meet."

    Hopeless I fell;
And when I rose, the light had burned so low,
So faint, I could not see my darling go.
He had not bidden me farewell; but, ah!
    I *felt* farewell—

    More deeply far
Than if my arms had compass'd that slight frame;
Though could I but have heard him breathe my
  name—
"Dear mother!"—but in heaven 'twill be the same;
    There burns my star!

    He will not take
Another lamb, I thought; for only one
Of the dear fold is spared to be my sun,
My guide, my mourner when this life is done;
    My heart would break.

    O, with what thrill
I heard Him enter; but I did not know
(For it was dark) that He had robbed me so;
The idol of my soul—*he* could not go—
    O, heart, be still!

CONSOLATION FOR PARENTS.

   Came morning: can I tell
How this poor frame its sorrowful tenant kept?
For waking tears were mine; I, sleeping, wept,
And days, months, years, that weary vigil kept.
   Alas, "Farewell,"

   How often it is said!
I sit and think, and wonder, too, sometime,
How it will seem, when, in that happier clime,
It never will ring out like funeral chime
   Over the dead.

   No tears! no tears!
Will there a day come that I shall not weep?
For I bedew my pillow in my sleep.
Yes, yes, thank God, no grief that clime shall keep—
   No weary years.

   Ay, "It is well!"
Well with my lambs, and with their earthly guide:
There, pleasant rivers wander they beside,
Or strike sweet harps upon its silver tide—
   Ay, "It is well!"

   Through the dreary day
They often come from glorious light to me:
I cannot feel their touch, their faces see,
Yet, my soul whispers, they do come to me;
   Heaven is not far away!
  —The *Christian Witness*, DR. JOHN CAMPBELL, Editor.

....

AFFLICTIONS are the medicine of the mind; if they are not toothsome, it is not required in physic that it should please, but heal.

        BISHOP HEASHAW.

DIVINE BENEFICENCE IN THE DEATH OF CHILDREN.

Rev. Thomas Binney, D.D.

I AM fond of children. I think them the poetry of the world,—the fresh flowers of our hearths and homes, little conjurers, with their "natural magic," evoking by their spells the delight that enriches all ranks and equalizes the different classes of society. Often as they bring with them anxieties and cares, and live to occasion sorrow and grief, we should get on very badly without them. Only think —if there was never anything anywhere to be seen, but great, grown-up men and women! How we should long for the sight of a little child! Every infant comes into the world like a delegated prophet, the harbinger and herald of good tidings, whose office it is, "to turn the hearts of the fathers to the children," and to draw the "disobedient to the wisdom of the just." A child softens and purifies the heart, warming and melting it by its gentle presence; it enriches the soul by new feelings, and awakens within it what is favorable to virtue. It is a beam of light, a fountain of love, a teacher whose lessons few can resist. Infants recall us from much that engenders and encourages selfishness, that freezes the affections, roughens the manners, indurates the heart;—they brighten the home, deepen love, invigorate exertion, infuse courage, and vivify and sustain the charities of life. It would be a terrible world, I do think, if it was not embellished by little children; *but* it would be a far more terrible one *if little children did not die!* Many, I dare say, would be shocked by this assertion. It may be true, however, nevertheless.

I am quite aware that death is in itself a very fearful thing; and that *premature* death is thought to be "mysterious,"—something to be submitted to, as incapable of being reconciled with the idea of presiding wisdom and love,—to be mourned over as an unmixed evil, expressive only of the wrath of God and the misery of man! Now, I quite hold that death is *punitive*. I believe it to be the consequence and the proof of the apostasy. I take it to be the mode of departure from earth *which was introduced by sin*,—painful, appalling, dark,—instead of that bright and glorious translation which would probably have awaited successful virtue. You will please to observe, that, as no world of limited extent could have continued the fixed dwelling-place of immortals, whose numbers were perpetually receiving augmentation,—and as the primary law of all intelligence would seem to be that of progress and advancement,—the probability is, that man was never meant for this world only; departure from it would be the law of his creation; but, on the alternative of his retaining his loyalty to God, that departure would have occurred after the full development of his nature *here* had fitted him for a rise in the scale of being, and it would have come in the form of reward and honor, perhaps with visible and public splendor,—the joyous congratulations of those left on earth mingling with the welcome, the symphonies and the songs of those superior spirits, to whose higher sphere the individual ascended. Sin, however, reversed all this. Instead of it, Humanity had to "depart hence" by returning to the dust; to go down into the dark valley, and to pass thus towards the awful future,—the vast unknown!

Death, then, simply considered, having become the law by which man's residence here was to terminate; and Humanity having become what entirely changed its character and circumstances,—giving a new importance to the relationships of life, and impressing uncertainty, to say the least, on the future beyond it; this being the case, *to render life itself tolerable to man*, it was necessary that the fixed general law should be softened and modified by two others. That is to say, it was necessary that death should so occur as not to be of the nature of a distinct, positive, and public *revelation* of the precise *future* into which each individual passed; and, that men should live *utterly uncertain* as to when they were to die. The punitive character of the original law being admitted, anything that would modify it in these two respects, would be of the nature of *benevolent relief*. This relief is accorded to us. The first is provided for by death happening *alike to all;*—and the second by its occurring *at all ages*. Whatever the character of individuals may be, however possible it is for any to acquire a fitness for a higher sphere, (and that, as we believe, is pre-eminently possible now through Christ)—still, *all* die, and, as a general rule, under the like circumstances of pain and suffering, and very generally, too, with similar feelings to themselves and to survivors. There is not such a difference between the death-beds of the religious and the worldly, except in particular cases, as some may suppose; and there is always that ignorance in relation to the dead, which makes it possible to the living to hope. So far, therefore, as all the *circumstantials* of death are concerned,—the precursors and attendants and immediate results, disease, pain, dissolution, corruption,—which in all ages have constituted topics of pathetic discourse, or subjects for odes and songs of lamentation,—so far as these are concerned, they are the benevolent products of a modifying law, with which God in His goodness has softened the rigor of the original infliction.

The same principle applies to premature death. All of you can see that a general law, terminating life in all cases on a precise day, would be painful and intolerable; it would poison life from first to last, and it might provoke and exasperate license and lust. It is important, both for happiness and virtue, that no one should know when he is to die. This object, however, can only be secured by death happening at every moment throughout the entire period allotted to man—extreme cases, even, such as death before leaving the spring-head and fountain of life, and death being delayed beyond all known or ordinary instances,—these are alike the working out of the same law. To secure, then, the proposed object,—to place humanity under the most gracious and benevolent constitution of things at all *possible* now,—in order that men might so live as to *enjoy* life, because happily ignorant respecting its termination,—on this account it is, that infants and children die; that youths and maidens die; that the young man splendidly endowed, the young woman beautiful and accomplished, die; the bride in her day of tremulous delight, the mother in the hour of her new joy, the strong man in the glory of his strength, — on *this* account they die. They die, — *that all who live* may live on under the blessed consciousness that they know not when *they* are to die. The whole race reaps the benefit of premature mortality. The glow and brightness of all life is connected with the graves and sepulchres of the young. Those who die early, or in the midst of their days, enjoy the advantage while they live. But the law would be infringed, and would be contradictory and unnatural if *parents* were to be *sure* that no child could possibly die till it was a day old, or a month, or a year, or two years, or ten;—to be thoroughly kind, the law must be carried out to its farthest extent, and come into play from the very first moment of possible vitality. Hence it is that infants die;—they die through the working of a most benevolent secondary law, brought in to break the rigor of the first. And they die *for the benefit of the race*. Their lives are taken for the sake of securing the happiness of the world. I had almost said,—and I *may* say it as speaking *in a figure*,—that a babe in its coffin may be supposed to look, to its weeping parents, like a little "dead Christ!" It has died vicariously—to secure a temporal advantage for the world, even as Christ died vicariously to secure for it a spiritual redemption. The one dies, that we may not know *when* we shall die; the other died that we *might* know "that our Redeemer liveth." By the one fact we are enabled to endure life; by the other we are taught to die in hope, and to look forward to the resurrection of the dead. Let a halo of glory, then, seem to encircle that fair brow, the brow of that little babe, lying cold and dead there, on the lap of its mother! Poor mother! thy sorrow is great! Weep away;—let the hot tears gush out;—it is not the time to speak to thee now. But very soon thou wilt come to understand how, all thy life, thou hast been reaping advantages *that came to thee by the death of the infants of others;* and thou wilt learn to acquiesce in what is really the result of one of the most benevolent of God's arrangements. The death of thy child, *as a human being,* is from sin; but his death *as a child* is, because he is one of the chosen of the race, whose lot and mission are not to live to *do* and to *enjoy,* but simply to *die,*—but to die for the benefit of the whole species, the world over!"

She died in beauty, like a rose blown from its parent stem;
She died in beauty, like a pearl dropped from some diadem;
She died in beauty, like a lay along a moon-lit lake;
She died in beauty, like the song of birds amid the brake;
She died in beauty, like the snow on flowers, dissolved away;
She died in beauty, like a star lost on the brow of day.
She lives in glory, like night's gems set round the silver moon.
She lives in glory, like the sun amid the blue of June.

Unknown.

"IS IT WELL WITH THE CHILD?"

REV. C. H. SPURGEON.

"Is it well with the child? And she answered, It is well."

NOW let every mother and father know assuredly that it is well with the child, if God hath taken it away from you in its infant days. You never heard its declaration of faith—it was not capable of such a thing—it was not baptized into the Lord Jesus Christ, not buried with him in baptism; it was not capable of giving that "answer of a good conscience toward God;" nevertheless, you may rest assured that it is well with the child, well in a higher and better sense than it is well with yourselves; well without limitation, well without exception, well infinitely, "well" eternally.

. . . .

I now come to make a PRACTICAL USE OF THE DOCTRINE.—First, let it be a *comfort to bereaved parents*. You say it is a heavy cross that you have to carry. Remember, *it is easier to carry a dead cross than a living one.* To have a living cross is indeed a tribulation,—to have a child who is rebellious in his childhood, vicious in his youth, debauched in his manhood! Ah, would God that he had died from the birth; would God that he had never seen the light! Many a father's hairs have been brought with sorrow to the grave through his living children, but I think never through his dead babes; certainly not if he were a Christian, and were able to take the comfort of the apostle's words—"We sorrow not as they that are without hope." So you would have your child live? Ah, if you could have drawn aside the veil of destiny, and have seen to what he might have lived! Would you have had him live to ripen for the gallows? Would you have him live to curse his father's God? Would you have him live to make your home wretched, to make you wet your pillow with tears, and send you to your daily work with your hands upon your loins because of sorrow? Such might have been the case; it is not so now, for your little one sings before the throne of God. Do you know from what sorrows your little one has escaped? You have had enough yourself. It was born of woman, it would have been of few days and full of trouble as you are. It has escaped those sorrows; do you lament that? Remember, too, your own sins, and the deep sorrow of repentance. Had that child lived, it would have been a sinner, and it must have known the bitterness of conviction of sin. It has escaped that; it rejoices now in the glory of God. Then would you have it back again?

Bereaved parents, could you for a moment see your own offspring above, I think you would very speedily wipe away your tears. There among the sweet voices which sing the perpetual carol may be heard the voice of your own child—an angel now, and you the mother of a songster before the throne of God. You might not have murmured had you received the promise that your child should have been elevated to the peerage; it has been elevated higher than that—to the peerage of heaven. It has received the dignity of the immortals; it is robed in better than royal garments; it is more rich and more blessed than it could have been if all the crowns of earth could have been put upon its head. Wherefore, then, could you complain? An old poet has penned a verse well-fitted for an infant's epitaph:—

> Short was my life, the longer is my rest;
> God takes those soonest whom he loveth best;
> Who's born to-day, and dies to-morrow,
> Loses some hours of joy, but months of sorrow;
> Other diseases often come to grieve us,
> Death strikes but once, and that stroke doth relieve us."

Your child has had that one stroke and has been relieved from all these pains, and you may say of it, This much we know, he is supremely blessed, has escaped from sin, and care, and woe, and with the Saviour rests. "Happy the babe," says Hervey, "who,

> Privileged by faith, a shorter labor and a lighter weight,
> Received but yesterday the gift of breath,
> Ordered to-morrow to return to death."

While another says, looking upward to the skies,—

> "O blest exchange, O envied lot,
> Without a conflict crowned,
> Stranger to pain, in pleasure bless'd,
> And, without fame, renowned."

So is it. It is well to fight and win, but to win as fairly without the fight! It is well to sing the song of triumph after we have passed the Red Sea with all its terrors; but to sing the song without the sea is more glorious still! I do not know that I would prefer the lot of a child in heaven myself. I think it is nobler to have borne the storm, and to have struggled against the wind and the rain. I think it will be a subject of congratulation through eternity, for you and me, that we did not come so easy a way to heaven, for it is only a pin's prick after all, this mortal life; then there is exceeding great glory hereafter. But yet I think we may still thank God for those little ones, that they have been spared our sins, and spared our infirmities, and spared our pains, and are entered into the rest above. Thus saith the Lord unto thee, O Rachel, if thou weepest for thy children, and refusest to be comforted because they are not: "Refrain thy voice from weeping, and thine eyes from tears: for thy work shall be rewarded, saith the Lord; and they shall come again from the land of the enemy."

The next and perhaps more useful and profitable inference to be drawn from the text is this: many of you are parents who have children in heaven. Is it not a desirable thing that you should go there too? And yet have I not in these galleries and in this area, some, perhaps many, who have no hope for hereafter? In fact, you have left that which is beyond the grave to be thought of another day, you have given all your time and thoughts to the short, brief, and unsatisfactory pursuits of mortal life. Mother, unconverted mother, from the battlements of heaven your child beckons you to Paradise. Father, ungodly, impenitent father, the little eyes that once looked joyously on you look down upon you now, and the lips which had scarcely learned to call you father, ere they were sealed by the silence of death, may be heard as with a still small voice, saying to you this morning, "Father, must we be for ever divided by the great gulf which no man can pass?" Doth not nature itself put a kind of longing in your soul that you may be bound in the bundle of life with your own children? Then stop and think. As you are at present, you cannot hope for that; for your way is sinful, you have forgotten Christ, you have not repented of sin, you have loved the wages of iniquity. I pray thee go to thy chamber this morning, and think of thyself as being driven from thy little ones, banished for ever from the presence of God, "cast" where "their worm dieth not, and the fire is not quenched." If thou wilt think of these matters, perhaps the heart will begin to move, and the eyes may begin to flow, and then may the Holy Spirit put before thine eyes the cross of the Saviour, the holy child Jesus! And remember, if thou wilt turn thine eye to Him thou shalt live; if thou believest on Him with all thy heart thou shalt be with him where He is,—with all those whom the Father gave Him who have gone before. Thou needest not to be shut out. Wilt thou sign thine own doom, and write thine own death warrant? Neglect not this great salvation, but may the grace of God work with thee to make thee seek, for thou shalt find—to make thee knock, for the door shall be opened—to make thee ask, for he that asketh shall receive! Oh, might I take you by the hand,—perhaps you have come from a newly-made grave, or left the child at home dead, and God has made me a messenger to you this morning,—oh, might I take you by the hand and say, "We cannot bring him back again, the spirit is gone beyond recall, but you may follow!" Behold the ladder of light before you! The first step upon it is repentance, out of thyself; the next step is faith, into Christ, and when thou art there, thou art fairly and safely on thy way, and ere long thou shalt be received at heaven's gates by those very little ones who have gone before, that they may come to welcome thee when thou shouldst land upon the eternal shores.

HAPPY EVA.

JOHN G. WHITTIER.

DRY thy tears for holy Eva!
With the blessed angels leave her;
Of the form so soft and fair
Give to earth the tender care.

In the better home of Eva
Let the shining ones receive her,
With the welcome voiced psalm,
Harp of gold and waving palm!

All is light and peace with Eva;
There the darkness cometh never;
Tears are wiped and fetters fall,
And the Lord is all in all.

Weep no more for happy Eva,
Wrong and sin no more shall grieve her;
Care, and pain, and weariness
Lost in love so measureless.

Gentle Eva, loving Eva,
Child confessor, true believer,
Listen at the Master's knee,
"Suffer such to come to me!"

O for faith like thee, sweet Eva,
Lighting all the solemn river,
And the blessings of the poor
Wafting to the heavenly shore!

THE FADED FLOWER.

REV. JOHN JAMESON.

SO quickly, so lightly, and so placidly passed she, that ere we had the courage to think she was going, already she was not. With all the simplicity of an infant, she had said to her mother, the day before she fell ill, that she was going to die. Just as she was departing, she revived for a moment, gathered strength, and throwing one full look of kindness on her trembling parent, breathed her last. "That look," said her mother to me, "I can never forget; that look was all the portion she had to bequeath; and that look now lifts me up." There was something very fine in the scene. Little Johnnie, heedless of his own grief,—and he, too, had been crying bitterly,—when he beheld his mother weeping, sprung to her, clasped her in his arms, *clapped* her with all his gentleness, and kissed the tears from her cheeks.

This world of ours, my dear Mary, is just a greenhouse, where there are flowers of every standing. Those, generally, of a commoner and lowlier sort hang long, and from month to month, unfading still, deal out, with unchanging hue, their daily meed of fragrance,—it may be, little felt and little noticed, but still they are there. Those, again, of grander flowering, with their bright and delicate and sparkling beauty, which rivets our gaze, soon, right soon, alas! fade away. There is a flower, they tell us, the most exquisite of all that blossoms, which blooms during night, as if day were too strong for the delicacy of its sweetness. In such haste is it to be gone, that in the self-same hour in which it opens and spreads its loveliness, it sheds it, and its leaf falls off. The gardener alone, curious and deeply interested, who has sat up and watched to see, has catched and felt the pleasure of the passing sight. Your little Maggie was such a flower. Why should we think it strange when the flower is faded?— "the Spirit of the Lord bloweth upon it." The flower has lived its own, its appointed time; and could tarry no longer, by no means. A child may cry when its lovely flower is gone; far otherwise the gardener himself,—he is satisfied, nay, is quite delighted, that ever such a flower was his.

THE MOTHER'S BLIGHTED HOPES.

REV. JOHN KITTO, D.D.

WHEN [referring to the death of the widow of Zarephath's only son] we behold that a child so dear—

. . "Like a flower crusht with a blast is dead,
And ere full time hangs down his smiling head,"

how many sweet interests in life, how many hopes for the time to come, go down to the dust with him! The purest and most heart-felt enjoyment which life offers to a mother in the society of her little child, is cut off for ever. The hope—the mother's hope, of great and good things to come from this her son, is lost for her. "The live coal that was left," and which she had reckoned that time would raise to a cheerful flame, to warm her home, and to preserve and illustrate the name and memory of his dead father, is gone out—is quenched in darkness. The arms which so often clung caressingly around her, and whose future strength promised to be as a staff to her old age, are stiff in death. The eyes which glistened so lovingly when she came near, now know her not. The little tongue, whose guileless prattle had made the long days of her bereavement short, is now silent as that of the "mute dove." Alas! alas! that it should ever be a mother's lot to close in death the eyes of one whose pious duty, if spared, should be in future years to press down her own eyelids. This is one of the great mysteries of life, to be solved only thoroughly, only fully to our satisfaction, in that day, when passing ourselves the gates of light, we behold all our lost ones gathered around our feet.

""""""""""""""""""""""""""""

"A LITTLE CHILD SHALL LEAD THEM.

Rev. William Blair, M.A.

THE house is dark, the house is sad,
    The house is hushed to rest;
In every heart sits grief, the guest
    Unbidden and unblest.

One leaf is lost, one bud is shed,
    One flower less sees the sun;
A pulse has paused, a soul has fled,
    A little life has run.

We miss the music of a voice
    That warbled once so sweet;
The sparkle of two laughing eyes,
    The patter of two feet.

The trifles of the passing hour,
    The toys that pleased the while,
The lingering words at parting said,
    The dimpling, welcome smile.

Such garnered things of memory
    We keep a sacred trust;
The relics of our vanished joy,
    The rose-leaves turned to dust.

We grieve not for thy early bliss,
    Thy sudden glory given;
The chill of earth escaped, to wear
    The shining robe in heaven.

No more the stress of pain or grief
    Shall press thee—happy now;
The strife is waged, the victory won,
    The laurel on thy brow.

The flower that faded here below
    Now blooms a flower above;
The star that set at early dawn
    Now shines in realms of love.

An Eastern star to Bethlehem's babe
    Did wondering sages bring;
The star that leads our steps beams o'er
    The place where Christ is King.

THE child is dead; it lived a little while in a world of which it knew nothing; and is gone to another in which it is already become wiser than the wisest it has left behind.

WILLIAM COWPER.

THE CHARM OF CHILDHOOD.

REV. GEO. GILFILLAN.

THE charm of childhood,—who has not felt it?—although it may not always be easy to analyze its elements. Some of them, however, are obvious enough, and are found in the young of all animals, and in all youthful things. The full-grown tree has much beauty, but more still belongs to the tender sapling, which the snow almost breaks as it descends upon it, and which seems so helpless, yet interesting, in its infancy. The full-blown rose is a gorgeous object, but sweeter still the rosebud, peering out timidly through its half-opened eye into the strange atmosphere of earth, and making you cry with the poet,

> "Sweet flower, thou'rt opening on a world
>   Of sin and misery;
> But this at least consoles my mind,
>   They cannot injure thee."

The river, mature in age, swelled by a hundred tributaries, arisen in flood, and raging in wrath from bank to brae, may be a sublime sight; but surely it is more attractive in its youth, when a narrow strip of green, amidst barren moors, is its only boundary, and one star reflected on it from the proud heavens, is its sole companion. You tremble at the eagle, swooping and screaming through the upper ether, with the lightning in his eye, and the lamb in his talons; but you love to look at the young eaglet, lying secure in its lofty eyrie, and expecting the arrival of its food-bearing father. The old sparrow is a thief—and, as such, detested—but the young sparrow is the favorite and pet of the child—herself a pet and a favorite. The sheep seems silly enough, while bleating in her pastures, and running away when no one pursueth; but how lovely and dear the lamb, suddenly appearing by her mother's side, as if dropped from one of the white spring clouds, or meekly following in her train, even though it be to slaughter and death! And so with the children of the human family. Coming out of the awful cloud of darkness which enshrouds birth, they come out as stars. Taken out of earth's lowest parts, they shine forth as gems of the purest water, and the brightest colors. Bursting up, as it were, from the bowels of the world, they burst up as flowers of the sweetest fragrance and the most variegated hues. Purity, simplicity, instinct, and unconsciousness, compose at first the elements of a child's existence. There it lies—like a thing of heaven and eternity, amidst the bustle, and care, and evil, of the world—nourished on smiles, turning, sweet satellite! round the orb of its mother's face—sending up aimless, but beautiful smiles of its own—both when awake and when asleep—and dreaming that "strangest of all things, an infant's dream." In what innocence it is wrapped—as if in swaddling-bands of snow! No envy wrinkles that smooth brow—no lust and no hatred lurk in that heart—no fury burns in that clear, mild eye—its only food is milk, and its only sin is tears. In what blessed ignorance it dwells? It knows not of God—but neither does it know of His many foes and rebellious creatures. It knows not of good—but neither does it know of evil. The alarm of war it never heard—the blood-spotted and tear-stained records of the sad history of humanity it never read—of the folly, falsehood, cruelty, impiety, and madness which dwell in the heart and blacken the life of man, it is altogether unaware; and yonder spring rosebud, first meeting the smile of the light, is not more unconscious of the rude realities of the world than that newly-budded babe. Beautiful all this; but there is a period a little farther on when the child becomes more interesting far; that is, when the soul awakes within it—and the coming forth of the evening star from a mass of clouds is not so beautiful as the first awaking of immortal mind in a child's eye; and when the heart awakes within it, and its smiles are no longer undistinguishing and no longer aimless, but become deeper in their significance, while equally sincere; and the understanding awakes within it, and proceeds to ask questions which no philosophy and no theology have yet been able to resolve; and the power of speech awakes within it, and its tongue overflows with that artless but piercing prattle which is more delightful than the murmur of streams, than the bleat of lambs, or than the stir of wind-swept flowers; because, while equally unconscious and equally musical, it is full of articulation, of meaning, and of love.

"Be worthy of death; and so learn to live
   That every incarnation of thy soul
     In other realms, and worlds, and firmaments
   Shall be more pure and high."

ADDRESS ON THE DEATH OF A CHILD.

Rev. Joseph P. Chown.

WE must all sympathize with the grief of bereaved parents. I do not know that I have ever felt more of it than during the past week, over the sights I have witnessed in the cemetery on the hill-side. I have seen the coffins of two little ones placed side by side in the chapel, and another coffin by *their* side, containing the remains of a mother, and the motherless children and the childless mother were sorrowing together. And I have seen another dear one lowered into its last resting-place, and the parents almost dragged from the spot, as though they could not leave it there. And I have seen another laid side by side with its grandsire, as old age and infancy slept together in their cold chamber. And yet another laid in its narrow resting-place, and then the little ones that were left dropping their white roses,—the parents' tears, precious dew-drops, falling with them,—upon the dear babe whose spirit had gone to glory, and whose body was left to moulder to its native dust. There is generally, however, in such a case, much to console us in our sorrow, if it may never be entirely taken away.

Sometimes the child is taken, when God sees if it were spared it would engross too much of the parents' affections, it would be *idolized* instead of *loved*—would be in the place of the Saviour and heaven to the parents, and that would not be well either for them or the child. Sometimes the child is taken instead of the parent. Justice does not say, "Thou fool, this night thy soul shall be required of thee," but Mercy says, instead, "I will call the child, and that may arrest him in his course, and the shock may break the ties that bind him to sin." And so the child, who is ready for heaven, is taken—the parent, who must have been cast down to hell, is spared. Sometimes God sees that our affections are becoming too closely entwined around earthly objects, and He takes the child, that those affections may be drawn up to heaven with it; it needs a painful wrench to tear them away, and it is thus He snatches from us a present treasure, to lead us to seek after future and everlasting joys. And then we know they are not lost—these dear departed children. The flower was given, and had just begun to bloom in its beauty and breathe its fragrance through your dwelling, and now it is gone; but it is not withered, it is not stolen, it is not destroyed; the Lord of the garden has sent His messenger, and he has plucked it, and borne it up from the desert world, whose rude blasts chilled it, to the Paradise where it shall bud and bloom in the sunlight of heaven for ever. Remember, too, how many parents would have rejoiced if their flowers had been taken to Paradise, instead of being spared to be the poor wretched, withered, down-trodden things they are now,—rather weeds, indeed, than flowers,—or crushed, it may be, almost out of existence altogether. And think, also, that if our little ones were taken from heaven to earth, or even if it were from earth to an unknown place, or to a worse place, then we might grieve over it; but it is not so; if we have them not here we have them in heaven. About whomsoever we may have doubts over their departure, there is no room for doubt here; the Saviour who gathered them around Him upon earth, and blessed them, is gathering them around Him in heaven, and blessing them in a manner of which we can form no conception; and so they are there, dwelling in His presence, blessed in His smile, rich in His glory, and waiting to welcome those who shall follow them, to their portion of everlasting peace and joy.

GOD'S RELATIONSHIP TO CHILDREN.

REV. JOHN GUTHRIE, D.D.

OUR Father in Heaven, the infinite Parent of us all, and the Saviour, who did what no parent has done,—shed His blood to redeem them,—have a closer relation to our children, and a better right to them, than we. Be it the endeavor, then, of mourning parents to exclaim with the bereft patriarch, and as much as possible in that patriarch's spirit and power, "The Lord gave, and the Lord hath taken away; blessed be the name of the Lord!" Yea, let them overflow with hallelujahs, that, in the Atonement of Jesus, they have such an impregnable ground of hope in respect to their deceased children. The fact that these children are in heaven, among the shining throng, white-robed, and vocal with the praises of redeeming love, should endear Jesus to them the more, through the ransom of whose precious blood their darlings are now in an infinitely happier than the parental home. This will help you, desolate parent, better to appreciate and realize the claims of that bright world to which they have been summoned. You know not what use God may have for them there. Who knows to what glorious account Jesus, even now while you weep, may there be turning their little radiant spirits? He has the ripened spirits there of "just men made perfect;" and with these He gems and jewels His crown of many stars. But He has also use there for the infant spirit in its loveliness. If the ripened saints are the stars that grace His crown, He whose delight is to take the lambs into His arms may well cull also the buds and flowerets of childhood to cluster as a garland round His bosom of love. Your children's precious dust is at present in the hands of the enemy; but that enemy,—"the last enemy," —shall be destroyed, and you and the tender objects of your regret, if you are only faithful to that Saviour whose blood has saved them, and persevere in the faith and love of Him to the end, will meet again ere long, triumphant over death, the grim foe that has despoiled you, and spend a long and happy Forever in the presence of your Lord.

We would say, in conclusion, to the bereft parent, through whose heart grief has driven its rude ploughshare, and whose wounds, it may be, are yet green. "Mourn not as those who have no hope," for, as respects your children, "there is hope in their end." In their material part only, they are, like Rachel's of old, "in the land of the enemy:" their nobler part is in the land, and in the embrace, of the Infinite Friend. Nor is that Friend forgetful of their sleeping dust. It is precious in his sight.

"The redemption of the body" is as sure as the redemption of the soul." That enemy, "the last enemy," shall one day be destroyed; and on that eventful day, "your children shall come again." Only see to it, *now*, like David, that you will, by faith, "go to them," and Jesus will see to it *then* that they shall "come to you." "Thus saith the Lord; refrain thy voice from weeping and thine eyes from tears; for thy work shall be rewarded, saith the Lord; and they shall come again from the land of the enemy." What a rapturous prospect for the Christian parent?

....

THE CHILDREN SAFELY FOLDED.

REV. JOSEPH BROWN, D.D.

I HAVE a full persuasion in my own mind that "it is well with the child" that dies in infancy; and I have often felt thankful that I had satisfied myself on that head before I was led to secure the possession of a burying place for my own infant children; but my faith rests less on any particular passage than on the genius of the gospel scheme. Just as I find that the divinity of our Lord is the key to the interpretation of the current representation of Scripture, so I think that the salvation of infant children is in best accordance with many portions of the holy oracles.

I had occasion to glance at the subject of infant salvation recently, when speaking of Christ's being "glorified in" the *number* of "His saints in that day," and in endeavoring to establish the position that the redeemed will greatly outnumber those that perish. I believe that even in past times the number of the saints may have been greater than a contracted charity has supposed, than the spirit of bigotry has allowed. I believe that, in the long ages of rest and triumph in store for the Church, "the nations of the saved" will soon counterbalance the deficiencies of many generations. And even in reference to those periods in which sin and Satan have most prevailed, I comfort myself with the thought that death has been employed by Him who has the power of the keys, in securing a great ingathering into the kingdom of heaven from those who have died in fancy.

I remember conversing, many years ago, on this subject, with the late Ebenezer Brown, of Inverkeithing, and of marking the delight he seemed to gather from the thought that the multitudes of children who die in heathen countries, and in the heathen parts of our own country, ay, and even those that are violently taken away by the cruel hands of superstition and idolatry, are "caught up to God and to His throne," to swell the numbers of the ransomed, and to enlarge the honors of the Redeemer.

SAFE WITH CHRIST.

REV. CHARLES GARRETT.

OH weeping, trembling mother, the Good Shepherd who carries the lambs in His bosom, looks pityingly upon you, and says in loving tones, "Can you not trust your child with *Me?*" Surely your heart, in the midst of its agony, will reply,

"Yes, Lord, I can." You have often said to an earthly friend, "I have no fear nor anxiety about my child when it is with *you*." And if this be true, for it to be with *Christ* must be far better. Think of His unerring wisdom, His almighty power, His boundless resources, His unutterable tenderness, and, above all, His infinite love, and your faith will be strengthened and steadied. Remember that He loves your sainted child as tenderly as if there were not another child in the universe, and, oh, how safe, how happy it must be with *Him!* Bear in mind also that the separation is only for a "little while," as little as is consistent with your eternal welfare. Your heavenly Father is far more anxious to have you in heaven than you are to get there. All the events of your life are working together for this end. You may not be able to see how this can be, but His eyes are clearer than yours. He sees the end from the beginning. If, therefore you cannot *praise* Him for this "fiery trial," don't *murmur*—be dumb, and open not your mouth, because He has done it. He will understand your silence. "He knoweth our frame; He remembereth that we are dust." His purposes will soon be accomplished, and then amidst the glories of heaven you will meet again; so shall you "obtain joy and gladness, and sorrow and sighing shall flee away."

"A PATH that must be trod,
If man would ever pass to God."

THOMAS PARNELL.

AN APPEAL TO PARENTS.

Rev. William Bathgate.

CHRISTIAN parent, bereaved of an infant-child, one word of appeal to you. Sore was your heart in the sad hour which struck the departure, to another home and bosom, of your darling child. Though seasons may have come and gone, though years of vicissitude may have fled since you kissed for the last time the infant-clay in its snow-white dress, or heard the first clod fall relentlessly on the coffin which contained the pride of your heart, the tear still starts, and the lip still quivers, over the name and image of your beloved infant. Sorrow not for him. He stands on the other bank of the Jordan, ready to hail you as you rise from the troubled river. He tunes his infantine harp to give you a gladsome welcome to the mansions above. Wish him not "back again," for the wish is unkind as well as vain. Comfort yourself with the assurance that you "shall go to him." Your child is not among strangers. The angels wait on him. The Saviour carries him in His bosom. Never was he so much at home. He has the blessed fortune to advance beneath the care and education of heaven. He is in the train of the blessed Saviour, for whose glorious appearing you daily look. O let your affections be *fixed* on the heavenly world. The Great Spirit will not charge you with idolatry should you quicken your pace to glory because your departed child wearies for your coming. God smilingly looks on the reunion of sire and son.

CHRISTLESS PARENT, bereaved of an infant-child, what shall we say to you? It is well even with the spirit of your little one. This is a gratifying, gladdening truth, even to a parent bound for a dread futurity. But, then, though you are welcome to all the consolation which such a truth is fitted to impart, does not the truth flash across your benighted soul a terrible suggestion? O, see you not that if you die Christless as you are living Christless, your little one and you shall never meet. Should it often watch for its mother's spirit emerging with a song of victory from the billows of the Jordan, it shall watch in vain. Should it on the morning of judgment recognize its mother's face and hold aloft its tiny hands, it shall hold them up in vain. Ah! bereaved mother, you have drunk the bitterest of earth's cups. Death tore from you the idol of your heart. But, continue Christless, remain unsaved, and you will see your child rising in glory, while you yourself are sinking into hell. Can you stand *that prospect?* Take your infant's Saviour as your Saviour. Rend not the heart of the soul-loving and soul-saving Jesus by continuing unsaved, and constraining Him to bid you depart far from your child, and far from Himself.

MOURN for those who are left; mourn not for the one taken by God from earth; he has entered into eternal rest; while we are bowed with sorrow.

TALMUD.

A TRANSPLANTED FLOWER.

WM. A. BRADBURY, MUSICAL COMPOSER, NEW YORK.

KATIE is gone. Where? To heaven. An angel came and took her away. She was a lovely child—gentle as a lamb; the pet of the whole family; the youngest of them all. But she could not stay with us any longer; she had an angel sister in heaven, who was waiting for her. The angel sister was with us only a few months, but she has been in heaven many years, and she must have loved Katie, for everybody loved her. The loveliest flowers are often soonest plucked. If a little voice sweeter and more musical than others was heard, I knew Katie was near. If my study-door opened so gently and slyly that no sound could be heard, I knew that Katie was coming. If, after an hour's quiet play, a little shadow passed me, and the door opened and shut as no one else could open and shut it, "so as not to disturb papa," I knew Katie was going. When, in the midst of my composing, I heard a gentle voice saying. "Papa, may I stay with you a little while? I will be *very* still," I did not need to look off my work, to assure me that it was my little lamb. You stayed with me too long, Katie, dear, to leave me so suddenly; and you are *too still* now. You became my little assistant—*my home angel*—my youngest and sweetest singing-bird, and I miss the little voice that I have heard in the adjoining room, catching up and echoing little snatches of melody as they were being composed. I miss those soft and sweet kisses. I miss the little hand that was always first to be placed upon my forehead, to "drive away the pain." I miss the sound of those little feet upon the stairs. I miss the little knock at my bedroom door in the morning, and the triple good-night kiss in the evening. I miss the sweet smiles from the sunniest of faces. I miss— oh! how I miss the foremost in the little group who came out to meet me at the gate for the first kiss. I do not stoop so low now, Katie, to give that first kiss. I miss you at the table and at family worship. I miss your voice in "*I want to be an angel,*" for nobody could sing it like you. I miss you in my rides and walks. I miss you in the garden. I miss you everywhere; but I will try not to miss you in heaven. "Papa, if we are good, will an angel truly come and take us to heaven when we die?" When the question was asked, how little did I think the angel was so near! But he did "truly" come, and the sweet flower is translated to a more genial clime. "I do wish papa would come." Wait a little while, Katie, and papa will come. The journey is not long. He will soon be "Home."

A FLOWER TRANSPLANTED.

HERE lies a rose, a budding rose,
   Blasted before its bloom;
Whose innocence did sweets disclose
   Beyond that flower's perfume.

To those who for her loss are griev'd
   This consolation's given—
She's from a world of woe receiv'd
   And blooms a rose in Heaven.

ROBERT BURNS.

PURPOSES OF DIVINE MERCY IN EARLY DEATH.

Rev. John Ker, D.D.

THE death of the child Abijah, recorded in the 14th chapter of the first book of Kings, occurred in a time and place in which hopeless degeneracy reigned among the more mature. God wished to show how He could still make up the jewels for His crown—gathering them out of the darkest pits of this earth and showing us their glitter, before He gave them their heavenly setting. It is a ground of great comfort and hope, when our eye and heart are wearied with sights and histories of full-developed wickedness among heathen at home and abroad. Where the death of the young is most sadly abundant, may we not reverently trust, that behind the physical causes which are working there, a purpose of mercy lies hidden?—as if the gleaming form of the angel of life could be discerned hastening to bind up the sheaves which the death-reaper is cutting down. There are other methods of delivering from the Sodoms and Gomorrahs of the world than flight by the way of the plain; and God has higher mountains to carry His elect to than that which was a refuge for righteous Lot.

The notice of this life is very brief. Little could be said of it on this world's side; it was so colorless and unsensational. How far it had passed from infancy into childhood we cannot say—probably only a few short steps. But the great end of life had been gained, even in regard to character; not its maturity indeed, but its direction. This is the main thing in our present life. "Even a child is known by his doings, whether his work be pure and whether it be right." The first step has been taken in the path which leads to everlasting life, and if death comes, it is God's acceptance of the traveller's aim—the seal of perpetuity set upon that Zionward look. The Hosanna passes at once into a Hallelujah. The way in which this tendency of character is described, is very tender and very comforting to those who have lost little children. "In him there is found some good thing toward the Lord God of Israel in the house of Jeroboam." The very vagueness and indefiniteness of it are full of kindness and charity; for though the "*some*" is not expressed in the original, it is really implied. An indescribable *somewhat*, different in different natures, and discernible oftentimes only by a parent's eye, will show how a very young child's heart turns to the thought of God and Christ, and the heavenly world. It is perhaps realized only when the child has been taken away; and he must be cold and hard who can listen with indifference to a parent, while the smallest of these tokens are fondly rehearsed—the slightest motions of the tender blade as it quivered beneath the Spirit's breath. He does not despise these tokens who quenches not the smoking flax, and who, when there was no loving paternal eye here to make search, came and sought them out Himself. There must be some such force in the words "*there is found*," as if God were seeking something which His eye could rest on with complacency in this monarch's house, and found it in the heart of this young child feebly feeling after Him. It was the one great treasure of the palace in the sight of Him who knows to discriminate the gold from the dross.

There is a testimony to the power of the grace of God in the words—"*in the house of Jeroboam.*" It was certainly He who found the good thing in the child's heart who had first hidden it there. There is none good but one, that is God; and there is nothing good toward Him but what comes from Him. To find the treasure in such a palace was as rare a thing as marvellously beautiful—the equivalent in the Old Testament of "saints in Cæsar's household," and more of a miracle in its way than that of him who was kept from the lion's mouth, or those who passed through the fiery furnace without the smell of fire on their garments. What means God's providence employed to carry the seed of that good thing into the heart, we cannot tell. Whether the mother did not wholly share the father's godless life, or whether there was some nurse or attendant who became a foster-parent to the soul, we know not. The power of God's Spirit to teach was in any case the same. In nothing, perhaps, is the divinity of the Scripture revelation more apparent, than in the way in which the mind of the youngest child can not only touch but comprehend its grandest truths —grasp with its infant hand the infinite. The breath that inspired the Bible comes evidently from Him who breathes into us the breath of life; they are so fitted to each other. This is a never-failing encouragement to parents to begin early the religious training of their children; and it is a sure ground of hope, that the soul which, in its first essay, can take such a hold of the highest truth, is made for an immortal life. There are deaths of babes and sucklings from which God can perfect praise, so as to still the enemy and the avenger. He can kindle a little lamp in our earthly homes, so bright, that we can see Him carrying it up to make of it a star in the highest firmament. When, as in this instance, it is kindled we know not how—when it shines solitary but steadfast through some cloud-rift in a troubled sky, it lets us see a peculiar power in His grace; but in every instance in which we see Him writing His new name upon a young heart before He takes it to Himself, we are bound to look upon His work with a very loving and hopeful admiration. Never is it more manifest that it is not for time but for eternity He is doing it; that He is taking up the lamp of our home to shine in the sky above all cloud and tempest. "It shall never perish, neither shall any pluck it out of my hand."

The death of the child of Jeroboam, no less than the good thing found in his life, has lessons of encouragement and comfort. As it regarded the family from which he was taken, his death is spoken of as a judgment; but it is only because they refused to understand its true meaning. The history looks at it in the light of the result; but in the Divine intention it was sent in kindly warning. Jeroboam had been a sinner and a seducer to sin, and he had been repeatedly admonished in vain. His right arm had been withered and healed again, and still he resisted. A child was sent to him, in whose young heart there was some good thing toward God, and he despised the attraction; and now that child is removed, "if" his heart may be melted by the tenderness of sorrow, and led to hear a voice from its grave. Happy for him if the death of his child had proved the life of his soul. Then though the child had not been restored, he would have been enabled to say, "I shall go to him." But he went on frowardly in the way of his heart, and the death which was sent in mercy is written down in judgment. It is our own use of these events which makes them gentle or stern: as we bear ourselves to them, they turn to us their side of light, or frown upon us from the cloud, till the chariot-wheels of the heart drive heavily. Never does God woo more tenderly, or seek to win for heaven more attractively, than in the love of a child taken to the skies in its opening months or years. If we have been lying fettered in worldly sloth and sin, He is sending His angel to deliver us out of the prison.

But if there was mercy offered to the parents in the death of the child, there was the full accomplishment of it to the child himself. Could we but see the future in this world from which a premature departure saves, and the future in another to which it conveys, it would help to reconcile us to the frost which withers many an opening blossom. There were trials lying in wait for his spiritual life which could be in no other way escaped. The good thing which was in him as a child would be for a while reckoned by the father a childish caprice; but as it grew with his years and strengthened with his growth, it would have encountered stern opposition, and the allurements of his position would have laid many a snare for his feet. He was yet in the peaceful harbor, but soon he must venture out on the open sea, with its fierce storms, its adverse currents, and its deceitful eddies. God's power could, and doubtless would, have kept him safe amid all; but He deemed it more merciful to spare him the struggle, and to hasten the course of the frail bark, like that of the ship into which the Saviour entered, immediately to the land whither it was going. "The Lord knoweth how to deliver the godly out of temptations,"—some by grace in this world, others by an early call from it.

He was saved from witnessing and sharing the suffering and ruin which soon afterwards overtook his father's house. The catastrophe had been delayed, perhaps by the unconscious intercession of this young life; but it could not be averted. The axe is lying at the root of the barren and withered tree which has cumbered the ground so long; but first the tender vine which has clasped its arms so lovingly around it must be gently untwined and transplanted to a place of safety, where it may flourish in a better soil and under a more peaceful sky. A flood of desolating waters is about to sweep over the wide land of Israel, but God must prepare an ark for His young servant, ere the storm can break. What though that ark be his grave? It is full of happiness and hope to those who are shut in by the hand of God. "Thou wilt hide me in the grave; thou wilt keep me secret, until thy wrath be past; thou wilt appoint me a set time, and remember me." "The righteous is taken away from the evil to come."

The mercy of the early death is still more clear, when we think of what the child was taken to. When faith lets us look within the veil, we see Him who long afterwards assumed bodily form and speech, beginning his gracious invitation, "Suffer the little children to come unto me, and forbid them not: for of such is the kingdom of heaven." Surely He was in this place though they knew it not. Neither was it far from this in time or place that a prophet was about to speak of Him—" He shall feed his flock like a shepherd: He shall gather the lambs with his arm, and carry them in His bosom;" and here already He is bringing home the firstlings of His flock. There were many bright hopes before the child to human eyes; but such a word of invitation might well outweigh them all. He was taken from the expectation of an earthly crown to the possession of a heavenly one; from the troubled and precarious dominion of Israel to a kingdom that cannot be moved; from the protection of a father who, however well he loved him, knew not his true interests, to the care and nurture of the Father of spirits; from an earthly mother's tenderness to Him who created it, and who says, "As one whom a mother comforteth, so will I comfort you;"—from the loud wail of a sorrowing nation to the joyful acclaim of the nations of the saved; from the tears of kindred to the bosom of the family where they weep no more. Is it well with the child? and shall we not answer? It is well.

It is a blessed thing when bereaved parents can so reply, when faith can lean on God, and hope can look up to heaven, and love can tenderly smooth the short green grave where God has hidden their heart's desire—His precious seed—and they, mourning but not murmuring, can patiently bide the time till He shall give it back to them, in the day when flower and fruit, freshness and ripeness, are found united, and a joy with them like unto the joy of harvest. Let us not ask why the child entered this world only to quit it, and made its brief home in our hearts to leave them more lonely and desolate. It is one token that there is another world, when there are so short sojournings in this. The entrance of the child into the life of earth, however narrow its space, is as true a beginning of the life that never ends, as the threescore years and ten—and its share in the great atonement as real and full as that of him who has borne, through all the appointed hours, the burden and heat of the day! Its release and his labor are alike of grace, and have their place and purpose in the innumerable family of the redeemed. There must be many varied voices in the harmonies of heaven, as well as in the choirs of earth. There, too, "both young men and maidens, old men and children, must praise the name of the Lord." Nor has its short life been in vain, even on earth, if it has drawn the affections of any to a heavenly world —if the sweet bird of passage which nestled beneath our eaves has attracted the heart to the sun and summer of a better land.—Then, "the child dies an hundred years old." Only let it be the earnest wish and effort of parents who have lost their children, to make sure of this—to see to it that the separation is not perpetual, and that the bond be made as eternal as it is deep and dear. There is no judgment in such deaths, no sting in such sorrows; but goodness and mercy—pure, unmingled, and everlasting—to parent and to child.

AFFLICTION is a winged chariot that mounts up the soul toward heaven.

T. ADAMS.

PARENTAL CONSOLATION.

Rev. John Guthrie, D.D.

WHEN troubles like a tempest sweep,
    And tides of fierce temptation roll,
As deep, remorseless, calls to deep,
    Around my whelmed and sinking soul;
Lo! He is near, my Saviour dear,
    Who trode affliction's path;
Who walked the wave, despoiled the grave,
    And plucked the sting from death.
If in bereavement's bitter cup
    Some dregs continue to the end,
As memory wakes the image up
    Of parent, brother, sister, friend;
My Lord who wept o'er him that slept,
    And soothed the sisters twain,
From heaven on high, with tender eye,
    Still marks the mourner's pain.
When weeping o'er my children's grave,
    As if to rescue from its gloom
The golden hopes that childhood gave,
    Now quenched and buried in their tomb;
Thou fondling arm, thou bosom warm,
    Where babes of old were pressed,
I joy to see my lambs with Thee,
    Safe folded on Thy breast!
If infants none in heaven were found,
    To glad its golden street,
But only star-bright victors crowned,
    Then heaven were incomplete.

Such stars may gem Christ's diadem,
　　Yet infants too have place;
These flowerets young are garlands strung,
　　Sweet trophies of His grace.

GONE TO PARADISE.

Charles Wesley.

WHEREFORE should I make my moan,
　　Now the darling child is dead?
　　He to rest is early gone,
　　He to Paradise is fled
I shall go to him, but he
Never shall return to me.
God forbids his longer stay,
　　God recalls the precious loan!
He hath taken him away,
　　From my bosom to His own.
Surely what He wills is best;
Happy in His will I rest.
Faith cries out, "It is the Lord!
　　Let Him do what seems Him good:
Be Thy holy name adored,
　　Take the gift awhile bestowed;
Take the child, no longer mine;
Thine he is, for ever Thine!"

Death is the privilege of human nature,
And life without it were not worth our taking.
Thither the poor, the prisoner and the mourner
Fly for relief, and lay their burdens down.

Rowe.

"A SWEET SORROW."

PHILIP SCHAFF, D.D.

WHAT can parents ask more than that their infants should be in heaven? The feelings which become them, when they for the last time draw near the coffin of the infant sleeper, and lay their warm hands once more, as an affectionate farewell, upon its brow, are beautifully expressed by Dr. Schaff who himself experienced the "sweet sorrow."

"NOW, farewell, my precious boy! Till I see thee again, farewell! With a saddened heart have I performed the last act of earthly love; and now I resign thee into the hands of higher and better parental care. Short was thy visit in this rough and tempestuous world! The heavenly gardener has early transplanted the fragrant lily of thy life into a milder and purer clime. Thy life was not yet darkened and embittered by the fearful curse of sin and death. As a tender lamb of Christ, thou didst bear thy cross in friendly innocence, like the infants of Bethlehem, who were slain by the tyrant sword of Herod. as the first martyr-fruits offered to the new-born Saviour, to whom the ancient church has devoted the third day after Christmas as an anniversary-day of special remembrance. Thou art now happy with them, and with the pleasant angels, far away from the sultry and sickly atmosphere of earth and sin. in serene celestial heights, in the green peaceful bowers of Paradise, led, and fed, and refreshed by the Great Shepherd of the sheep and of the lambs, who was Himself once a child, that He might sanctify the tender age of infancy, and who, in the days of His flesh, pressed infants to His bosom, speaking those words of comfort: "Suffer little children to come unto me, and forbid them not: for of such is the kingdom of God." His thou wert by birth; and, as He formed thy beautiful body, so did He also, by His Holy Spirit, silently, and unconsciously to thee, early prepare thy spirit for that holy world where now thou art at home. It was He that taught thee to lisp, as thou didst in the midst of thy suffering, with infant joy: "Heaven is a beautiful place: God is there, Christ is there, the angels are there, all good people are there!" Yes, my hopeful, pious boy! they are all there, old and young, great and small,—all who have overcome in the blood of the Lamb! There also dost thou bloom for ever, in the unfading beauty of the loveliest age! Thither also do thy parents, by God's grace, hope to arrive, when their hour shall strike, to embrace thee, the beloved of their hearts, in glorified youth, and to lose thee no more for ever! Oh, the joy of such a meeting!

DEATH loves a shining mark, a signal blow.
YOUNG.

WHEN musing on companions gone,
We doubly feel ourselves alone.
WALTER SCOTT.

BEREAVED PARENTS COMFORTED.

Rev. Dr. Russell.

WHEN a bereaved parent feels all the force and tenderness of parental love, and while his heart bleeds for the loss of his children, let him ponder this precious record, "Like as a father pitieth his children, so the Lord pitieth them that fear Him;" and let the disconsolate mother dwell on these words, "As one whom his mother comforteth, so will I comfort you;" and surely while they are charmed with their beauty, the soul will draw from these declarations the richest, the most endearing, and the most effectual consolations. Their own feelings will help them to understand the warmth and the tenderness of the love of heaven.

It is delightful to repose on Him who can enter into our every feeling, can effectually succor us in the day of trial, and with power can say, "Weep not, the child is not dead but sleepeth." "I am the resurrection and the life." "O thou afflicted, tossed with tempest; when thou passest through the waters, I will be with thee." Let the thought, then, of the blessedness of their departed infants, quicken the progress of Christians to the land of immortality, holiness, and joy. Let them rest on that word, which is able to fill with confidence and hope, even when descending the vale of the shadow of death, when, like a ship unmooring from its anchor they are about to launch into a world of spirits, when eternity is bursting on their view, and when called to that solemn meeting, which every individual must one day have with "Him whose eyes are as a flame of fire." Let them wait for that "happy, happy hour, when on bursting the veil of mortality," and entering into the celestial paradise, they shall find their infants in the bosom of Him who hath graciously said, "Of such is the kingdom of heaven."

> "A few short years of evil past,
> We reach the happy shore,
> Where death-divided friends at last
> Shall meet to part no more."

GERMS OF IMMORTALITY.

Rev. John Cumming, D.D.

CHRISTIANITY alone looks with sympathy on infants, loves them more than angels, provides for their future state, and plants in the sorrowing hearts of those who have lost them bright hopes of restored union and communion in glory. Christianity takes the infant close to her mother-bosom, spreads over it the warm wing of love, sprinkles on its bright brow waters from that river whose streams make glad the city of our God, and gives utterance to the deep sympathies of her heart in these words,—"Suffer little children to come unto me, and forbid them not: for of such is the kingdom of heaven." Babes are not too insignificant in her thoughts. Her Incarnate One controls the exalted hierarch beside the throne, and also stoops to teach and bless an orphan child. Never did He who spake as never man spake breathe a more beautiful or touching thought, or bequeath to mourning mothers bereaved of their infants a more precious legacy, than when He rebuked the stern frowns which His disciples cast on the mothers that crowded round Him with their babes, and took up the unconscious infants in His arms, and blessed them and said, "Suffer little children to come unto me, and forbid them not; for of such is the kingdom of heaven." Whosoever may undervalue these germs of immortality, these folded buds of promise, these tenants of earth in training for heaven,—the Son of God does not. He spreads over them the shield of His power, and covers them with the feathers of His wing. He saw immortality beam from their countenances, in their bosoms His ear heard the beatings of a life that can never die; and capacities which all the treasures of time and earth cannot fill disclosed themselves to the eye of Him to whom the most secret structure of mind and body is thoroughly unveiled. It is relation to eternity that makes the feeblest strong, and the smallest great.

THE FLOWERS OF PARADISE.

Rev. Thomas Guthrie, D.D.

HEAVEN is greatly made up of little children,—sweet buds that have never blown, or which Death has plucked from a mother's bosom to lay on his own cold breast, just when they were expanding, flower-like, from the sheath, and opening their engaging beauties in the budding time and spring of life. "Of such is the kingdom of heaven."

How soothing these words by the cradle of a dying infant! They fall like balm drops on our bleeding heart when we watch the ebbing of that young life, as wave after wave breaks feebler, and the sinking breath gets lower and lower, till with a gentle sigh, and a passing quiver of the lip, our sweet child leaves its body lying like an angel asleep, and ascends to the beatitudes of heaven and the bosom of its God. Perhaps, God does with His heavenly garden as we do with our own. He may chiefly stock it from the nurseries, and select for transplanting what is yet in its young and tender age,—flowers before they have bloomed, and trees ere they begin to bear.

....

THE GRAVE A WARDROBE.

MATTHEW HENRY.

BLESSED be God for the covenant of grace with me and mine, it is well ordered in all things and sure. O that I could learn to comfort others with the same comforts with which, I trust, I am comforted of my God! This comes near, but O Lord I submit! I am much refreshed with 2 Kings iv. 26. "Is it well with thee? is it well with thy husband? is it well with the child? and she answered, It is well." Although I part with so dear a child, yet I have no reason to say otherwise but that it is well with us, and well with the child, for all is well that God doeth; He performeth the thing that He appointed for me, and His appointment of this providence is in pursuance of His appointment of me to glory, to make me meet for it.

After the funeral he thus writes: "I have been

this day doing a work that I never did, burying a child. A sad day's work; but my good friend Mr. Lawrence preached very seasonably and excellently in the afternoon, from Psalm xxxix. 9. 'I was dumb, I opened not my mouth; because Thou didst it.' My friends testified their kindness by their presence. *Here is now a pretty little garment laid up in the wardrobe of the grave, to be worn again at the resurrection:* Blessed be God for this hope!"

....

CHRIST BLESSING LITTLE CHILDREN.

REV. JOHN BROWN, D.D.

LET us consider that most delightful incident recorded by three of the evangelists. "They brought young children to Jesus that he should touch them, and his disciples rebuked those who brought them. But when Jesus saw it, He was much displeased, and said unto them, 'Suffer little children to come unto me, and forbid them not, for of such is the kingdom of God: and He took them in His arms, put His hands on them and blessed them.'" I will not dogmatize as to the precise meaning of a passage, which admits of more than one interpretation, but I will say, in the cautious language of John Newton, "I think it at least highly probable that in these words our Lord does not only, if at all, here intimate the necessity of our becoming as little children in simplicity, as a qualification without which (as He expressly declares in other places) we cannot enter into His kingdom, but informs us of a fact, that the number of infants who are effectually redeemed to God by His blood, so greatly exceeds the aggregate of adult believers, that comparatively, His kingdom may be said to consist of little children."

A MOTHER COMFORTED.

Rev. John Morrison, D.D.

NOW good and merciful are God's concealments! He will not disclose to us the painful future, because we could not bear it, and because He means, in all our hidden trials, with a Father's love to sustain and cheer us. And so it will be, my dear Madam, with you. He bestowed on you that precious gift, which you so much valued; and now that He has seen fit, in inscrutable wisdom, to resume His own gift, He will prove to you that, in His own unchangeable and everlasting love, He will make up the sad loss by filling your heart with the sweet sense of His loving-kindness and tender mercy. It is all well—supremely well—with the dear child. Your sympathizing Redeemer has taken him into His own bosom, and he is safe for ever from the ills to which he would have been exposed in this sinful and sorrowing world. Hereafter he will welcome his loving, though now afflicted parents, into everlasting habitations; and though he hath a father on earth, and a Father in Heaven, *you* will be his only recognized mother to all eternity. May God be with you, to pour His own balm into your wounded heart! and enable you to say "It is well."

Submit to bereavements; from them we often may date God's richest mercies to us.

T. Goodwin.

MY DARLING'S SHOES.

Unknown.

GOD bless the little feet that can never go astray,
For the little shoes are empty, in the closet laid away!
Sometimes I take one in my hand, forgetting, till I see
It is a little half-worn shoe, not large enough for me;
And all at once I feel a sense of bitter loss and pain,
As sharp as when, two years ago, it cut my heart in twain.
O little feet that wearied not! I wait for them no more,
For I am drifting on the tide, but *they* have reached the shore;
And while the blinding tear-drops wet these little shoes so old,
She stands unsandled in the streets that pearly gates enfold;
And so I lay them down again, but always turn to say:
God bless the little feet that *now so surely* cannot stray.
And while I thus am standing, I almost seem to see
Two little forms beside me, just as they used to be;
Two little faces lifted, with their sweet and tender eyes.
Ah me! I might have known that look was born of Paradise.
I reach my arms out fondly, but they clasp the empty air,

There's nothing of my darlings but the shoes they
    used to wear.
Oh! the bitterness of parting cannot be done away,
Till I see my darlings walking where their feet can
    never stray;
When I no more am drifted upon the surging tide,
But *with them safely* landed upon the river-side;
Be patient, heart! while waiting to see *their* shin-
    ing way,
For the little feet in the golden street can never go
    astray.

GONE TO SLEEP.

Archbishop Leighton.

INDEED, it was a sharp stroke of a pen that told me your pretty Johnny was dead. Sweet thing! and is he so quickly laid asleep? Happy he! Though we shall have no more the pleasure of his lisping and laughing, he shall have no more the pain of crying, nor being sick, nor of dying; and hath wholly escaped the troubles of schooling, and all other sufferings of boys, and the riper and deeper griefs of riper years; this poor life being all along nothing but a linked chain of many sorrows and many deaths. Tell my dear sister she is now much more akin to the other world; and this will be quickly passed by us all. John has but gone an hour or two sooner to bed, as children used to do, and we are undressing to follow. And the more we put off the love of this present world, and all things super-fluous beforehand, we shall have the less to do when we lie down.

THE LOSS OF CHILDREN.

John Flavel.

MOURNER, whatever may be your grief for the death of your children, it might have been still greater for their life. Bitter experience once led a good man to say, "It is better to weep for ten children dead, than for one living." Remember the heart-piercing affliction of David, whose son sought his life. Your love for your children will hardly admit of the thought of such a thing as possible in your own case. They appeared innocent and amiable; and you fondly believed that, through your care and prayers, they would have become the joy of your hearts. But may not Esau, when a child, have promised as much comfort to his parents as Jacob? Probably he had as many of their prayers and counsels. But as years advanced, he despised their admonitions, and filled their hearts with grief. As a promoter of family religion, who ever received such an encomium from the God of heaven as Abraham? How tenderly did the good man pray for Ishmael! "O that Ishmael might live before thee!" Yet how little comfort did Ishmael afford.

Alas! in these days of degeneracy, parents much more frequently witness the vices of their children than their virtues. And even should your children prove amiable and promising, you might live to be the wretched witness of their sufferings. Some parents have felt unutterable agonies of this kind.

God may have taken the lamented objects of your affection from the evil to come. When extraordinary calamities are coming on the world He frequently hides some of His feebler children in the grave. Surely, at such a portentous period, it is happier for such as are prepared to be lodged in that peaceful mansion than to be exposed to calamities and distresses here. Thus intimates the prophet Jeremiah, "Weep not for the dead, neither bemoan him; but weep sore for him that goeth away; for he shall return no more, nor see his native country." It was in a day when the faith and patience of the saints were peculiarly tried, that the voice from heaven said, "Write, blessed are the dead, which die in the Lord, from henceforth."

A BUD OF BEAUTY.

Rev. Robert Hall.

THIS eloquent divine, in speaking of the death of his little boy, says, "God dries up the channels, that you may be haply compelled to plunge into an infinite ocean of happiness." Blissful thought! Father, mother, you who mourn over the grave of your little one, look up! know that the chastening rod is in your heavenly Father's hand, and that if He hath taken away, He first did give, and He doeth all things well. He gave you the bud of beauty, and you centred your happiness in its being. He saw that this was not for your good, so He took away the child, whose presence had been as a leaping, sparkling streamlet to your heart's love, that that heart, which had before tasted of earthly, might be lost in the immensity of heavenly love.

It is a very solemn consideration that a part of myself is in eternity, in the presence, I trust, of the Saviour. How awful will it be, should the branch be saved and the stock perish!

****

BETTER TO BE WITH CHRIST.

Rev. Philip Doddridge, D.D.

COULD I wish that this young inhabitant of heaven should be degraded to earth again? Or would it thank me for that wish? Would it say that it was the part of a wise parent to call it down from a sphere of such exalted services and pleasures to our low life here upon earth? Let me rather be thankful for the pleasing hope, that though God loves my child too well to permit it to return to me, He will ere long bring me to it. And then, that endeared parental affection, which would have been a cord to tie me to earth, and have added new pangs to my removal from it, will be as a golden chain to draw me upwards, and add one farther charm and joy even to Paradise itself. And oh, how great a joy to view the change, and to compare that dear idea, so fondly laid up, so often reviewed, with the now glorious original, in the improvement of the upper world! Was this my desolation, this my sorrow, to part with thee for a few days, that I might receive thee for ever, and find thee what thou art? It is for no language but that of heaven to describe the sacred joy which such a meeting must occasion!

"Lord!" should each of us say in such a case,

"I would take what Thou art doing to my child as done to myself; and as a specimen and earnest of what shall shortly be done." *It is* therefore *well.*

VICTORY WITHOUT CONFLICT.

REV. JAMES HERVEY, A.M.

YONDER white stone, emblem of the innocence it covers, informs the beholder of one who breathed out its tender soul almost in the instant of receiving it. There the peaceful infant, without so much as knowing what labor and vexation mean, "lies still and is quiet; it sleeps and is at rest." Staying only to wash away its native impurity in the laver of regeneration, it bade a speedy adieu to time and terrestrial things. Happy voyager! no sooner launched than arrived at the haven!

> "Happy the babe, who, privileg'd by fate
> To shorter labor, and a lighter weight,
> Receiv'd but yesterday the gift of breath,
> Order'd to-morrow to return to death."

Consider this, ye mourning parents, and dry up your tears. Why should you lament that your little ones are crowned with victory before the sword is drawn, or the conflict begun. Perhaps the Supreme Disposer of events foresaw some inevitable snare of temptation forming, or some dreadful storm of adversity impending. And why should you be so dissatisfied with that kind precaution which housed your pleasant plant, and removed into shelter a tender flower before the thunders roared, before the lightnings flew, before the tempest poured its rage? O remember! they are not lost, but "taken away from the evil to come."

THE FLOWER PLUCKED BY THE MASTER.

A GENTLEMAN'S gardener had a darling child, in whom his affections seemed to be centred. The Lord laid His hand upon the babe: it sickened and died. The father was disconsolate, and murmured at the dealings of Providence.

The gardener had in one of his flower-beds a favorite rose. It was the fairest flower he had ever seen on the tree, and he daily marked its growing beauty, intending, when it was full blown, to send it to his master's mansion. One morning it was gone: some one had plucked it. Mortified at what he thought was the improper conduct of one of the servants, he endeavored to find the culprit. He was, however, much surprised to find that it was his master who, on walking through the garden, had been attracted by the beauty of the rose, and, plucking it, had carried it to one of the beautiful rooms in the Hall. The gardener's anger was changed into pleasure.

He felt reconciled when he heard that his master had thought the flower worthy of such special notice. "Ah! Richard!" said the gentleman, "you can gladly give up the rose, because I thought it worthy of a place in my house. And will you repine because your heavenly Father has thought wise to remove your child from a world of sin, to be with Himself in heaven."

THERE is no grief like the grief which does not speak. LONGFELLOW.

THE CROWN OF LIFE.

Rev. Richard Cecil.

I PERCEIVE I did not know how much my life was bound up in the life of a creature. When she went, nothing seemed left me; one is not, and the rest seem a few thin and scattered remains. And yet how much better for my lamb to be suddenly housed, to slip unexpectedly into the fold to which I was conducting her, than remain exposed here; perhaps become a victim. I cried, "O Lord, spare my child!" He did; but not as I meant; He snatched it from danger, and took it to His own home.—Part of myself is already gone to Thee: help what remains to follow!

He who removed our infant has seemed to say, "What I do thou knowest not now, but thou shalt know hereafter; patiently suffer this little one to come unto me, for of such is my kingdom composed. Verily, I say unto you, their angels do always behold the face of my Father. If I take away your child, I take it away to Myself." Is not this infinitely beyond any thing you could do for it? Could you say to it if it had lived, thou shalt "weep no more, the days of thy mourning are ended?" Could you show it any thing in this world like "the glory of God and of the Lamb?" Could you raise it to any honor here like "receiving a crown of life?"

────────────────

Every one can master a grief but he that has it.
Shakspeare.

THE CHILD IN HEAVEN.

MARY HOWITT.

WE meet around the board, thou art not there;
    Over our household joys hath passed a gloom;
  Beside the fire we see thy empty chair,
    And miss thy sweet voice in the silent room.
What hopeless longings after thee arise!
Even for the touch of thy small hand I pine;
  And for the sound of thy dear little feet.
    Alas! tears dim mine eyes,
Meeting in every place some joy of thine,
  Or when fair children pass me on the street.
Beauty was on thy cheek; and thou didst seem
  A privileged being, chartered from decay;
And thy free spirit, like a mountain stream
  That hath no ebb, kept on its cheerful way.
    Thy laugh was like the inspiring breath of spring,
That thrills the heart, and cannot be unfelt,
  The sun, the moon, the green leaves and the flowers,
    And every living thing,
Were a strong joy to thee; thy spirit dwelt
  Gladly in life, rejoicing in its powers.
Oh! what had death to do with one like thee,
  Thou young and loving one; whose soul did cling,
Even as the ivy clings unto the tree,

To those that loved thee! Thou, whose tears would spring
　Dreading a short day's absence— didst thou go
Alone into the future world unseen,
　Solving each awful untried mystery,
　　The dread unknown to know;
To be where mortal traveller hath not been
　Whence welcome tidings cannot come from thee?
My happy boy! and murmur I that death
　Over thy young and buoyant frame hath power?
In yon bright land love never perisheth,
　Hope may not mock, nor grief the heart devour.
　　The beautiful are round thee; thou dost keep
Within the Eternal presence; and no more
　May'st death or pain, or separation dread:
　　Thy bright eyes cannot weep,
Nor they with whom thou art thy loss deplore;
　For ye are of the living, not the dead.
Thou Dweller with the unseen, who hast explored
　The immense unknown; thou to whom death and heaven
Are mysteries no more; whose soul is stored
　With knowledge for which man hath vainly striven;
　　Beloved Child, oh! when shall I lie down
With thee beneath fair trees that cannot fade?
　When from the immortal rivers quench my thirst?
　　Life's journey speedeth on;
Yet for a little while we walk in shade;
　Anon by death the cloud is all dispersed,
Then o'er the hills of heaven the eternal day doth burst.

LITTLE ONES IN HEAVEN.

Rev. Robert Ferguson, D.D.

WE are not forbidden to mourn over the loss of those who have been taken from us; but our sorrow should be moderated by the reflection that our loss is their gain. The joy which was felt, and whose expression could not be repressed at the birth of the child, is surely not to become extinct in the event of his departure and introduction to a nobler state of being. Are all those delightful emotions which took possession of our breasts when he began to develop his intellectual power, or his spiritual life, to die out when that very same child is taken up into the society of perfected spirits, in whose midst his mental powers and his inner life will be revealed as they never could have been in this inferior state? Is it nothing that we have given birth to one who is now numbered with the sons of glory, and whose presence in heaven has widened the circle of the redeemed around the throne of God? If death be a condition of life, then those whom we may have lost by death are not lost, but gone before. They are not dead, but live; and with the living only do they hold communion.

Christian parent! dry up thy tears; or if you must weep, make a rainbow of your tears. Let joy rise above grief as heaven rises above earth. If the birth of your child filled your breast with emotions which no human words can express, and if on his being born again you became the subjects of feelings yet more tender and peculiar, then think of him now amid the beatitudes and the blessedness of the heavenly world, sinless in character, deathless in life, exhaustless in energy, ceaseless in activity, and through the ages on ages, ever moving in the light of the throne, expatiating amid its unquenchable glories, and in communion with the Eternal.

How delightful the idea that some of our little ones are there, ever beholding the face of their Father, reposing in His immutable love, and being filled with the fulness of joy! How cheering the thought that they have been admitted to the society and the fellowship of perfected spirits, are now the companions and associates of patriarchs, and prophets, and apostles, of martyrs and confessors, of the mightiest and the noblest dead, and hold the most intimate intercourse with them on all that is holy and true, unchangeably good and sublimely grand! How inspiring the belief, that they are now waiting our arrival, and are beckoning us onward and upward to join their wider circle, to enter with them on brighter scenes, and to enjoy life with them in its fulness and its fruitions! If we have ties on earth, we have ties also in heaven. Nor let us forget that heaven is our home, as it is the home of those little ones now in glory. It is there that we are to meet them again, to be reunited in indissoluble bonds, and to dwell in endless life. Their very existence there is meant to charm our spirits up to their bright abode. Let us, then, set our affections on that higher world; let us yield to its attractive influence; and let us rejoice in this prospect of mingling for ever with our little ones and our loved ones in scenes of ineffable light and life, of glorious love and boundless joy.

THE INFANT CHOIR IN HEAVEN.

JAMES MONTGOMERY.

HAPPY, thrice happy were they thus to die,
　　Rather than grow into such men and women—
　　Such fiends incarnate as that felon sire
Who dug its grave before his child was born;
Such miserable wretches as that mother
Whose tender mercies were so deadly cruel!
I saw their infant's spirit rise to heaven,
Caught from its birth up to the throne of God;
There, thousands and ten thousands I beheld
Of innocents like this, that died untimely,
By violence of their unnatural kin,
Or by the mercy of that gracious Power,
Who gave them being, taking what He gave
Ere they could sin or suffer like their parents.
I saw them in white raiment, crowned with flowers,
On the fair banks of that resplendent river
Whose streams make glad the city of our God—
Water of Life as clear as crystal, welling
Forth from the throne itself, and visiting
Fields of a Paradise that ne'er was lost;
Where yet the Tree of life immortal grows,
And bears its monthly fruits, twelve kinds of fruit,
Each in its season, food of saints and angels;
Whose leaves are for the healing of the nations.
Beneath the shadow of its blessed boughs
I mark'd those rescued infants, in their schools,
By spirits of just men made perfect, taught

The glorious lessons of Almighty Love,
Which brought them thither in the readiest path
From the world's wilderness of dire temptations,
Securing thus their everlasting weal.
Yea, in the rapture of that hour, though songs
Of cherubim to golden lyres and trumpets,
And the redeemed upon the sea of glass,
With voices like the sound of many waters,
Came on mine ear, whose secret cells were open'd
To entertain celestial harmonies—
The small, sweet accents of those little children,
Pouring out all the gladness of their souls
In love, joy, gratitude, and praise to Him—
Him who had lov'd and wash'd them in his blood;
These were to me the most transporting strains;
Amidst the hallelujahs of all Heaven.
Though lost awhile in that amazing chorus
Around the throne, at happy intervals
The shrill hosannas of the infant choir,
Singing in that eternal temple, brought
Tears to mine eye, whilst seraphs had been glad
To weep, could they have felt the sympathy
That melted all my soul, when I beheld
How condescending Deity thus deign'd,
Out of the mouths of babes and sucklings here,
To perfect His high praise;—the harp of heaven
Had lack'd its least but not its meanest string,
Had children not been taught to play upon it,
And sing, from feelings all their own, what men
Nor angels can conceive of creatures, born
Under the curse, yet from the curse redeem'd,
And placed at once beyond the power to fall—
Safety which men nor angels ever knew,
Till ranks of these and all of those had fallen

GOOD BYE.

Unknown.

GOOD bye, good bye, it is the sweetest blessing,
   That falls from mortal lips on mortal ear,
  The weakness of our human love confessing,
   The promise that a love more strong is near.
      "May God be with you."

Why do we say it when the tears are starting?
  Why must a word so sweet bring only pain?
Our love seems all sufficient till the parting,
  And then we feel it impotent and vain.
     "May God be with you."

Oh! may He guide, and bless, and keep you ever,
  He who is strong to battle with your foes;
Whoever fails, His love can fail you never,
  And all you need He in His wisdom knows.
     "May God be with you."

Better than earthly presence, e'en the dearest,
  Is the great blessing that our partings bring,
For in the loneliest moments God is nearest,
  And from our sorrows heavenly comforts spring.
     If God be with us.

Good bye, good bye, with latest breath we say it,
  A legacy of hope and faith and love;
Parting must come, we cannot long delay it,
  But one in Him we hope to meet above,
     If God be with us.

Good bye! 'Tis all we have for one another,
  Our love, more strong than death, is helpless still,
For none can take the burden from his brother,
  Or shield, except by prayer, from any ill.
     "May God be with you."

Consolation for the Bereaved.

VARIOUS AGES AND CONDITIONS CONSIDERED.

Though He cause grief, yet will He have compassion according to the multitude of His mercies.—*Lam. iii., 33.*

MUTUAL RECOGNITION IN HEAVEN.

Rev. George Smith, D.D.

THE hope of reunion in a future state of being has been prevalent amongst devout and thoughtful persons in all ages of time, and under the various dispensations of divine truth which have passed over men. Some glimmerings of this expectation have visited communities and individuals unblest with the light of a written revelation, but who probably derived their impressions from traditionary recollections of a primitive faith. A definite and ever-brightening impression of the truth has been obtained under the Patriarchal, the Jewish and the Christian economies. This hope has been a great comfort to mourners in seasons of bereavement. They have felt as did the monarch of Israel, who, when lamenting the decease of his child, encouraged his heart by uttering the well-known words, "I shall go to him, but he shall not return to me." . . .

By many of those who receive the kingdom of God as little children, this consoling doctrine is admitted without gainsaying, and is almost intuitively perceived. Not very long since, an aged disciple, a highly valued relative of mine, fell asleep in Jesus at the advanced age of eighty-one years. On hearing of the event, his sister, more aged than he, said, "How glad my dear mother will be to see her darling boy again!" When the tidings of death reached my home, a grandchild of the departed saint, my own youngest boy, Richard Morley, being then only in his fifth year, exclaimed, "How delighted grandmamma will be to see him again!" Thus youth and age, both taught of God, testified to a glorious truth. They have both since then passed into the world of light; the child after a few weeks only, and they are doubtless reunited to the loved ones of whom they believingly spoke.

This subject is adapted to comfort the orphan deprived of parental support, and cast on the fatherhood of God. It is equally suited to bind up the wounds of parents who mourn, like Rachel, over their children, because they are not. Nor is it less fitted to support the mind of others who are deprived of companions in labor, and sorrow, and joy. We can follow them by faith within the veil, and behold their ever-increasing happiness. We can listen to the voice of revelation, which assures us that they without us cannot be perfect; and we can look forward with hope to the time when, knowing as we are known, we shall rejoin them in the climes of bliss, and with them place the crown of redemption at the feet of the Redeemer. With Richard Baxter, the eloquent discourser on "The Saint's Everlasting Rest," we may say, addressing the Captain of our salvation—

> "As for my friends, they are not lost;
> The different vessels of Thy fleet
> Though parted now, by tempests tost,
> At length shall in the haven meet."

GRIEF NOT FORGOTTEN.

Rev. William Blair, M.A.

WHEN God sends grief to any of His children, He has a two-fold purpose in view: to awaken thought in them at the time, and to lay up for them a store of instruction and profit for the future. The immediate effect of God's visitations to us by the death of dear babes is preparatory to the higher end and ultimate effect. *Grief*, as the word literally signifies, is *heaviness*, and therefore not "joyous." But the heaviness " must needs be" to create anything like a real, deep impression in the soul. If adversity is to afford "sweet uses," the bitter must be tasted first. No permanent benefit will result from a superficial contact with sorrow. What the poet sings of "a little learning" is equally applicable to our experience of grief: we must "drink deep or taste not," if we would enjoy the outcome of genuine tribulation. It depends very much on the entertainment we give to impressions of sorrow whether the future will bring a blessing back to our bosom. The world's way is to shut down grief as it shuts down the coffin lid on the dead, to let the waves of worldliness rush in as they do behind the keel that has parted them asunder. In plain words, the world's remedy is oblivion, utter extinction of the sight or sound of the objects of buried affection and hope. Nor is that fatalistic way of submitting to sorrow as an inevitable necessity, as devotees beneath the wheels of inexorable destiny, one whit more Christian or childlike than the sullen forgetfulness of the worldling. The virtues of submission, of holy resignation to God's will, of softened and sanctified experience, will never grow on such wild olives. Very significant are Paul's words of warning, neither to "despise the chastening of the Lord, nor faint when we are rebuked of Him." Those who grow hard in the fire affect to "despise" grief as a thing unmanly, womanish, weak, and unworthy of being cherished in the memory or the heart. And, to some extent they are right, when we analyze the kind of grief they indulge.

It is grief as a *sentiment* that is weak and "shallow," not as a motive power in the soul. Let sentimental, sensational grief be unremembered, for it is no better than noisy laughter. It touches only the surface: it has no power to stir the depths of our nature. It weaves its *immortelles,* and hangs them around the tomb, and straightway forgets what manner of man it once was. But genuine, real grief is not forgetful nor empty. It is a fruitful bough by a well whose branches run over the wall. It is a full rounded cluster wherein is the wine of life; "destroy it not, for there is a blessing in it." Keep alive the memory of your grief, the hallowed associations with which it is entwined, the nearness of your soul to God when heaven seemed to let down to earth to take from you the best of earth to heaven, the reality of prayer then offered, and of the answer received, and the rapture of heavenly joy in which you walked when your home was "the valley of the shadow of death." Cherish the memory, freshen the sense you have of your grief, not to throw shadows athwart your pathway, but to brighten it with light from heaven. Visit in thought the chamber where the strife of death was waged, and the church-yard corner where you deposited the precious dust, and think of the transfiguration, now that the decease has been accomplished, and the new link to bind your heart to the unseen, and the grand reunion coming nearer every day, and then the untold happiness not of "months in the New Jerusalem," but of "forever with the Lord," and with all you have loved and lost, but found again when you shall be found of Christ at His coming.

Lord Monboddo lost a beloved daughter, and grieved after a worldly sort over her. Her picture on the wall only reminded him of his misery. A friend drew a curtain over that picture: upon which the sad father said, "That is kind: come now, and let us read Herodotus." Miserable comforter, that romancing father of Greek history to a grieving father! Seek not so to bury your sorrow. "Go and tell Jesus," as John's disciples did when their master was taken away. That is the way to get your grief assuaged, to have it transfigured so that the *carte* in the album, or the bust on the wall, or the head-stone at the grave, will bring no shade of gloom around your brow; but each remembrance of your little one may prove a beckoning light up through the darkness to the light that is inaccessible and full of glory. That is the way to get the breach healed. It may be that in the first outburst of your sorrow, when your sons and daughters rose up to comfort you, you put aside their ministry of consolation, and, like Jacob, said, "I will go down into the grave unto my son mourning." But, in the end of the days when parting words are spoken, Benoni, the son of sorrow, has become Benjamin, the son of my right hand, and the crowning benediction rests on the head of him that was separate from his brethren. Then, in the light of Heaven, every shadow of earth's darkness will flee away, every Gethsemane become an Olivet, every step in the vale of tears a step in your ascension to the everlasting Kingdom.

RECOMPENSE.

How many things are clear to us to-day,
That yesterday we saw through mists of tears;
How many things are better than our fears;
What sunbeams through our self-wrought shadows
    play.
Not one fair, earnest hope is laid away
Within its shroud of weary wasted years,
But from the tangled grass above it peers,
Full soon, some blossom redolent of May.
We stretch beseeching hands to Heaven and pray
That this, or that, be granted, whilst we plead;
We turn with empty hands from prayer and say
"We are unheard, forgotten, lost indeed!"
When lo! within our reach some priceless gift,
For which imploring palms we dared not lift.

HARRIET E. PRITCHARD.

BEREAVEMENT is a dispensation of God; what He gives in His goodness He has a right to take away in His wisdom.

DR. H. F. BURDER.

THE SYMPATHY OF CHRIST.

Professor John Cairns, D.D.

"For we have not an high priest which cannot be touched with the feeling of our infirmities, but was in all points tempted like as we are, yet without sin."—Heb. iv. 15.

WE have Christ's sympathy in these pregnant words exhibited in *two* points of view—as an effect and as a cause. As an effect, it is due to training and experience; and as a cause, it influences the whole exercise of His priestly office.

Christ's sympathy is presented as the *effect* of training and experience in the latter half of this sentence, which comes first in the order of nature and history. He "was in all points tempted like as we are, yet without sin." Hence His sympathy: He "can be touched with the feeling of our infirmities." Sympathy as a state of mind involves three exercises. There is, *first*, the entering into the case of another, so as to take it up, to conceive distinctly all the painful feelings by which another is agitated, and to read his very heart when torn and darkened by grief. This, however, is not yet the distinctive working of sympathy, for a great poet may be able thus to enter into and describe the workings of distress, without feeling them as a friend. Nay, a tyrant may enter into and gloat over the sufferings of his victim. Still, this is a help to sympathy; and wherever the latter is, this has gone before. The *next* element in sympathy, and the most vital, is the feeling of pain in our breast when we realize another's woe. It is not only the conceiving of what he suffers, but a suffering along with him, such a suffering as amounts to a positive unhappiness, and as is due entirely to his grief being by sympathy made our own. And the *third* element in sympathy is the desire or impulse to relieve the sufferer, which is not merely, or at all, the selfish wish to get rid of our own reflected pain (for this we might do in other ways), but to remove the burden from him who bears it, for his own sake, or at least to soothe and assuage, by any means, his trouble. When we ascribe sympathy, then, to our blessed Saviour, we ascribe to Him these three things—His entering into our case—His feeling our woe—and His impulse and desire to relieve. It might seem, indeed, as if the second of these experiences, a feeling of our woe, could not belong to the Redeemer in His state of exaltation, because it would involve Him in all our misery, and that in proportion to His own tenderness. There is no doubt a mystery here which we cannot fathom. But the language of Scripture is so express that we dare not deny to our exalted Saviour this element of sympathy. We must bring in another great law by which the capacity of sympathy is governed; and that law we may call the law of training or experience.

It is the fact that those who have suffered any form of evil have more sympathy with sufferers from the same evil than those whose experience has spared them this trial. One who has endured the keen pangs of hunger has more sympathy with the poor in their want of daily food than those who have fared sumptuously every day. A shipwrecked mariner has most sympathy with the shipwrecked—a widow with widows—a heart-broken father with another exclaiming over some ill-fated youth, "O Absalom, my son, my son!" The nearer our experience of danger, suffering, sorrow, or evil of any kind, comes to that of those whom we see or hear of as undergoing the same calamities, the more entire is our sympathy with them, and that in all the three elements which I have already spoken of; for we take up more easily their case for its resemblance to our own; we feel more keenly afflicted in their woe; and, as a consequence, we have a stronger impulse to help and succor them. He can sympathize with the poor, for his whole life was one of poverty, of labor, of dependence, and, even in His public ministry, of homelessness; and few of the poor can repeat His words—"Foxes have holes, and the birds of the air have nests; but the Son of Man hath not where to lay His head." The meanest pauper who is carried out at the expense of others can think of Him who was anointed against the day of His burial, and laid in a borrowed grave. He was also an hungered and athirst, and wearied with work and travel; so that all who suffer on the side of physical want and exhaustion may think of Him who fasted in the wilderness, who sat tired by Jacob's well, and who was overpowered by sleep even amidst the storm. The innumerable host of the victims of pain may turn to Him who bled in Gethsemane and agonized on Calvary; and "the noble army of martyrs" may dwell on His tortures by the scourge, the thorny crown, and the cross, as the precursors of their own.

He suffered every kind of opposition, beginning

life amidst persecution and exile, and ending it amidst the rejection and cruelty of a violent death. He suffered every kind of reproach, being charged with ignorance, with pride, with falsehood, with intemperance, with insanity, with sedition, with blasphemy, with alliance with Satan. He suffered every form of ingratitude, being despised as well as rejected by those whom he stooped to save; being betrayed, denied and forsaken by His own disciples; and being nailed to the cross by the very sinners whom He came to ransom from death. All these wounds had in them the bitter sting of sin, as well as of unkindness; and where he was not suffering from the sins of others He was suffering from their sorrows, as when He touched the bier of the widow's son, or wept at the grave of Lazarus. Every affection was in turn wounded—His social, when He sighed over the people fainting as sheep without a shepherd—His domestic, when from the cross He looked down on His mother with her pierced heart—His patriotic, when He mourned over Jerusalem's approaching end.

Aside from our Saviour's sympathy as an effect due to His training and experience, we must consider His intercession.

First, Christ's intercession procures our pardon. No sinner is pardoned simply because Christ died. There must be a personal application, and a personal introduction of each applicant for the Divine clemency, on the footing of the Saviour's death. And it is the office of Jesus to introduce each penitent and conscience-stricken applicant, and in that awful hour to plead on his behalf for mercy. Is it possible then, that, when the Saviour sees the transgressor at

His feet, like Saul of Tarsus, trembling and astonished, wrung at once with fear and with remorse, and lifting the new-born cry for pardon and safety, His heart should not yearn over the sinner who thus becomes a suppliant, and that recalling His own agony and bloody sweat, and all that He has endured for the ransom of the guilty, He should not second his prayer with a deeper tenderness in His own breast, and a more melting earnestness in His own utterance before the eternal throne? Hence it is that every sinner may draw near with fullest confidence, encouraged by those representations which set forth the Saviour in heaven as a Lamb that had been slain, and as clothed with a vesture dipped in blood; for this is but the assurance that the sympathies of Calvary are transferred to Paradise, and that He still remembers the penitent for whom He suffered when He is come into His kingdom. Nor is it only when the sinner first appeals to the loving heart of this well-tried Advocate that He is succored; but after every fall and backsliding the Saviour yearns over him, and remembering all that He suffered in seeking and saving the lost, pleads for him still, and secures for him pardon and recovery through His own blood.

Secondly, Christ's intercession procures our help in trouble. He looks down on all our afflictions with a tried and experienced eye. Every form of trouble that gathers around us touches some chord in His heart. We cannot in our hours of deepest and darkest sadness go beyond the circle of His experience. In truth, we are only in the shallows where He was in the depths; and His sympathy as much outreaches our case as His gracious power. We may well believe, then, that this fathomless spring gives movement and impulse to all the streams of intercession that flow from it, and that to the very uttermost He is able to help and save. In the beautiful words of a much-tried friend, now for years removed from earthly trouble, "If the head of the Republic of Science, Letters, and Arts, should be the greatest professor of these, who should be the Head of the sympathies, the affections, the deep-seated yearnings of the heart, but the one only sinless, perfect Man, the sympathizing High Priest, the mighty Intercessor, and the all-prevailing Redeemer? Without Him all earthly love is precarious and transitory; with Him the dreariest heart knows a peaceful sunshine."

Thirdly, Christ's intercession procures our succor in death. The heathen anticipated death with deep gloom of spirit, or with a kind of mournful resignation almost more affecting. It was a night that had to fall—an impenetrable shade into which they had to go. Those who are strangers to Christian hope are still in the same "horror of great darkness." But, O what a light has arisen through the advent of Him who is the Resurrection and the Life! One has died, and has returned, not with a message of terror, but of peace. He returns as the Victor, the Deliverer, the Head of a conquering host, gathering in His train, and marching on to immortality. To Him the battle is past, but to them it is yet future. Hopeful as they are, they are not without misgiving; and many a wistful look is directed to the last scene of conflict. What a solace, then, to think that their Guide knows the way, and remembers the path that leads through strife and pain to certain victory! And what an inspiration to catch from His now triumphant voice the signal, "Fear not; I am He that liveth, and was dead; and, behold, I am alive for evermore, Amen; and have the keys of hell and of death!" Let us hear the call thus descending from the exalted seat of His interceding love and care; and let us, inwardly strong and glad, respond, "Lead on, incarnate, dying, risen Lord; through darkness and through death we follow Thee! Thanks be unto God, who giveth us the victory through our Lord Jesus Christ."

Let those who mourn rehearse these lessons of immortal consolation beside the grave! Our dead in Christ have not perished. To believe it were to falsify every article of Christianity and to resign all its dearest hopes. It were to re-instate the fallen King of Terrors, and to revive the dead and buried paganism over which Christ has set up his throne. Let us not be guilty of such disloyalty to our reigning Lord, who ever lives to comfort His redeemed. By the memory of all that is mightiest in His death and tenderest in His intercession—by the efficacy of His blood and the sacredness of His sympathy—let every Christian mourner, lamenting the dead that sleep in Jesus, refrain his eyes from tears; and in so far as they are the tears of an unbelieving and unpermitted sorrow, seek to have them wiped away!

And may the sympathy of Him who forbids oppressive grief, grant also the grace to rise above it to His own glory and to hasten on the day when, in a heaven of re-union and recognition, the eyes that, like His own have wept their last tears, shall be made exceeding glad with the light of his countenance.

THE DAY OF DEATH BETTER THAN THE DAY OF BIRTH.

Rev. Principal Caird, D.D.

"A GOOD name," it is written, "is better than precious ointment; and the day of death than the day of one's birth." The idea in the first clause of this verse may be, that the love and honor that follow departed worth are a better embalming than all the preparations and perfumes that steal the body from decay. The latter succeed only in preserving for a little what is at best a ghastly semblance of the outward form of the man. The former seizes hold of the spirit or essence of his inward being, the central principle of his life, and suffuses that with the fragrance of sweet and tender memories, the preservative of human respect and love. It is well when death has claimed his own, to let him do his worst to that which alone it is in his power to touch; enough for us to feel that there is an immortality which love confers on which he cannot lay his destroying hand. When we have looked our last on the dear old face, calm with the changeless peace of death; or when the great or good man, at the close of an honored life, is carried to the grave, true affection shrinks from any miserable attempt to confer a spectral show of life on that which is our friend no more. But embalm him in the heart. Let the idea of his life rest in the sanctuary of imagination. Open for him in the inmost shrine of the living temple a place where the name and memory of our noblest and dearest are treasured; and gather round him there the myrrh and frankincense, the sweet spices and fragrant ointment of loving thoughts and tender recollections, of sympathy and reverence for all in him that was noble, and honorable, and good;—so will you obtain a better triumph over death, and more truly arrest the progress of decay; for "a good name is better than precious ointment."

The day of a Christian's death is better than that of his birth, because, rightly viewed, his death-day is but a better birth-day. It is the day of his entrance with a nobler nature into a grander world. "Our birth," it has been said in well-known words,

> " is but a sleep and a forgetting;
> The soul that rises with us, our life's star,
> Hath elsewhere had its setting,
> And cometh from afar:
> Not in entire forgetfulness,
> And not in utter nakedness,
> But trailing clouds of glory do we come
> From God, who is our home."

But that which a poetical imagination sees in the infant's birth, the eye of faith and hope discerns more truly in the Christian's death. What, seen from one side of death, is the setting, from the other is but the rising of the soul on a world more glorious far than this. Nor does it pass in forgetfulness or nakedness to Him who is its eternal home. He who has lived nobly loses not in death any one of the best results of life—the treasures of learning with which years of study and thought have enriched the mind, the wisdom and experience gained by long converse with men and things, the ripe judgment, the cultured taste, the exquisite susceptibility to all that is beautiful and noble in nature and life, the affections and sympathies expanding and deepening, growing in tenderness and purity to the last; above all, the high qualities that give dignity and greatness to man's moral nature—generosity, truthfulness, unselfishness, gentleness, humility, reverence, piety. Nothing of all this is lost in the transition from time to eternity. Rich with all this accumulated spiritual wealth, does the soul enter on its new career. God has uses for it all. It is all precious to Him. He will not suffer one atom of it to be lost when he recalls the spirit to Himself.

The sentimentalist may sigh over the brevity and vanity of human existence, and speak of all that is great and noble in man and in human life as created only to become the prey of death. Struck by some instance of what we call untimely death, the premature extinction of some great and gifted mind, we are disposed sometimes to wonder at this strange squandering of what is so rare and invaluable. All this learning and experience, all this acuteness and polish of intellect, this slowly-gathered wisdom, this ardor for truth and goodness, from which the world might so much have benefited—how sad and unaccountable that by one seemingly arbitrary stroke it should be destroyed! What mockery of human exertions that man should toil passionately and painfully for long years to gain that which, ere it has well begun to be used or enjoyed, is in one instant wantonly swept away! But does not this so common moralizing betray, after all, a miserable narrowness and impiety? Why should we talk as if our little world were co-extensive with the universe, as if there might not be other and grander spheres of effort, other and greater work to be done in regions and worlds unknown, to which our Father, when He has need of them, calls our best and bravest-hearted away? Important though the world's work may be, do we not greatly exaggerate when we speak as if in the measureless order of the universe, in the carrying on of the affairs and destinies of His boundless government, God might not have, for the highest minds, places of trust to be filled, plans and schemes to be developed, high and holy achievements to be performed, work to be done affording wider, grander scope for wisdom and energy and ardor, than this world's most momentous business and affairs? There is no waste of power when an able and gifted man is called from some obscure sphere to a position of dignity and responsibility. So, surely, there is no waste, no annihilation of what is most precious, no frustration of the long education of life, when, in the very midst of their years and their usefulness, God calls away the best and wisest of the sons of men to play their part on a wider, grander stage. The very fact that they are the best and wisest may be the reason why they are earliest called. God cannot spare them longer from the greater destinies that await them. So, not seldom "the good die young, while they whose hearts are dry as summer's dust burn to the socket." And even the hour in which we mourn over their untimely fall, is that in which they have attained their grandest exaltation—while we talk of their sun as having gone down when it was yet day, already they have begun to shine as the stars for ever and ever. Death here is birth into immortality.

Compare, then, the two days spoken of, and say which is the "better." The day when a great and good man dies is like the day of his birth, that on which he enters on a new existence. But the first birth was in feebleness and unconsciousness and ignorance; the second is in the noble maturity of powers ripened by the discipline of years. The first was the birth of a nature possessed at best of the negative innocence and guilelessness of infancy; the second is that of a nature purified by a trial, strong with the strength of conquest, attired in raiment that has been "washed and made white in the blood of the lamb." The former birthday beheld a weeping child clinging in blind instinct to the mother's breast, the latter witnesses a redeemed and glorified spirit, enfolded, in the ineffable consciousness of love and life, in the everlasting arms. An earthly home and a little circle of earthly friends welcomed at the first the new entrant on life; the glorious society of heaven, angels and spirits of the just made perfect, hail the coming of another brother born to immortality. The first birth was into a world whose beauty had been marred by sins and strife and care and crime; the second ushers the soul into the home of eternal purity,—a world on which the faintest shadow of evil can never rest,— the new heavens and earth wherein dwelleth righteousness. Who, then, if this all be so, can doubt that "the day of a man's death" may be "better than the day of his birth?"

THE SAVIOUR'S SYMPATHY WITH THE AFFLICTED.

Rev. John Eadie, D.D.

IT is in the period of suffering and bereavement that the soul is brought into nearer contact with God, and knows Him, not from what it believes, but from what it enjoys—not from what it has been taught, but from what it has experienced. We are all aware that our Lord is named the "Man of Sorrows," and we are taught that He is "touched with the feeling of our infirmities;" but we do not adequately comprehend the truth, till, under the pressure of infirmity, we enjoy His sympathy; and then we can say, now we know it for we have felt it. There is truly a sublime meaning in the words which He spoke to Martha, "I am the Resurrection and the Life;" but only those circumstanced as she was—the grave having closed over her brother—can really enter into their nobility and triumph. He who has never felt the pang or desolation of bereavement—whose heart has never been pierced by the barbed and mortal shaft—who has never gazed on the corpse of parent, brother, or child, and seen it closed up from view—who has never made one of the group of weeping mourners that stand, inexpressible solemnity! by the grave, and feel a sad sinking of heart as they leave behind them, in dust and darkness, that form which they shall not see again till Christ descend and the trumpet sound—such a scatheless and untried believer cannot, though he would, unfold to himself the sweetness and comfort of the saying, "I am the Resurrection and the Life." There is no Christian heart that does not hold by the pledge, "My grace is sufficient for thee;" but it is only when "weakness" overpowers it, that it can really find that His "strength is made perfect." Without affliction, the purest and closest knowledge of God could never be acquired; a veil would still seem to lie upon Him. The glory that surrounds Him might dazzle us; but we should still be comparative strangers to the tenderness and love of His heart. Still at a distance from Him, we would indeed trust Him; but when He lays His hand upon us and brings us nearer Him, then do we acquaint ourselves with His loving-kindness, no longer by report, but by tasting it. You may have seen the solar beam thrown back in yellow splendor from the crystal rocks, as they glistened with gold, but now you have found and gathered the precious ore. It is one thing to admire the beauty of His pavilion, and another thing to be in it; one thing to know Him from what He has said, and another to know Him in what He has done. Surely experimental intimacy far excels theoretic information; but it is gained only in the school of affliction.

Did, therefore, the friendship of Christ secure us against suffering, it would shade from our view these prime and happy lessons. But Christ is anxious that we learn them, and therefore, though he loves us, He permits us to suffer, that we may yearn for a fuller sense of this presence, and penetrating into His heart, know, because we feel, the love and power of our Beloved and Friend.

SORROW FOR THE DEAD.

John Tulloch, D.D.

THE New Testament teaches us to think of our dead ones as "asleep." "Them also which sleep in Jesus will God bring with him." (1 Thess. iv. 14). They are gone from us, but they rest in the Lord. And when they awake, they will be still with Him. Why, then, should we weep for those who, now calmly resting in Christ, await a joyful resurrection?

As "sleep is to waking, so is death to the resurrection." It is the dawn of a Resurrection morning which gives its full force to the image. In death there is rest from care and sorrow, and all the ills which make life painful; and so far it is like to sleep, when we lie down and put from us, in unconscious slumber, the cares of the day, the sorrows that may have vexed us, or other ills that may have pained or wearied us. But it requires the assurance of an awakening to complete the analogy. It were little to say to men, as Socrates said long ago, that death is a "great gain," even if we only think of it as a "deep sleep in which one has had no dream." Insensibility is better than pain or toil. But to the Christian the sleep of death is only the prelude to a joyful day. The sleeper awakes refreshed and strengthened to a "mightier power of life." The believer sinks to rest in the grave that he may rise again on the Resurrection morning in new and more glorious being. "For if we believe that Jesus died and rose again, even so them also which sleep in Jesus will God bring with Him."

It was this view of death of which the heathen knew nothing. They might think of their dead ones as resting in the dust. Their Philosophers might discourse of a dreamless sleep; and their Poets sing of a long night of perpetual slumber towards which they were hastening; but they knew nothing of the Morning that was to break on their long sleep —of the Resurrection to which it was destined. Even the ancient Hebrews saw this but dimly, and therefore they cried, "The living, the living, he shall praise Thee. For the grave cannot praise Thee; death cannot celebrate Thee: they that go down into the pit cannot hope for Thy truth." (Isaiah xxxviii. 18, 19.) "In death there is no remembrance of Thee: in the grave who shall give Thee thanks?" (Psa. vi. 5.) "The dead praise not the Lord, neither any that go down in silence." (Psa. cxv. 17.) Prophet and Psalmist had at the best but a feeble hold of the doctrine of Resurrection to Eternal Life. They saw before them the darkness; they felt, with something of horror, the silence of the tomb, but the eye of faith did not pierce steadily beyond the voiceless gloom. Life and immortality have only been brought clearly to light in the Gospel, in Him who hath Himself risen "the first-fruits of them that sleep." And hence, the Christian alone looks with cheerful hopefulness in death. Others may face it with steadfastness or calm: he alone lies down to sleep in hope. Not only without fear, but in joy he enters the dark valley, and friends lay him in the narrow prison-house, "dust to dust, in the hope of a joyful Resurrection." "For this corruptible must put on incorruption, and this mortal must put on immortality. . . . Then shall be brought to pass the saying that is written: Death is swallowed up in victory. O death, where is thy sting? O grave, where is thy victory? The sting of death is sin, and the strength of sin is the law. But thanks be to God, which giveth us the victory, through our Lord Jesus Christ." (1 Cor. xv. 53-27.)

It is this fact of Resurrection which leads the apostle to say that we who remain alive should not sorrow for our dead ones, "even as others which have no hope." (1 Thess. iv. 13.) Why, indeed, should we thus sorrow, who believe that as "Jesus died and rose again, even so them also who sleep in Jesus will God bring with Him?" (1 Thess. iv. 14.) They who had no such faith, might well weep as they buried their Dead out of sight and knew not whether they should evermore see the light of life. But why should we hopelessly weep for those who are resting with the Lord—who have gone before to be for ever with Him? Why, indeed, but for the faintness of our hearts and the weakness of our flesh? Let us sorrow rather for ourselves, that our sight is so dim and our faith so dull—that we are so little able to look beyond things which are "seen and temporal" to those which are "unseen and eternal!" The living, rather than the Dead, may have a claim upon our sorrowful regard. For the Dead have gone beyond our anxiety. They have entered into their rest. They are asleep in Jesus; while the living, who are around us, and with us, may be wandering far away from Him, may be wounding Him by their sins, may be "crucifying Him afresh and putting Him to an open shame." It is as if we were to weep for the child resting in its father's bosom, sheltered in a happy home, rather than for the child who has gone astray in darkness, and cannot find its homeward way. It is as if we were to sorrow for the mariner who has found a safe harbor, and rests in peace, rather than for the storm-tossed sailor in the open main, around whom the billows may be heaving high, and over whom the sky may be darkening to his doom. No, brethren, let us not sorrow for those who are with God, safe in a Father's house, sheltered in the haven of eternal rest. But let us be anxious and careful for the Living, that we may help them, and guide them by God's blessing in a right way; and for ourselves, that we may "know the things which belong unto our peace before they are hid from our eyes."

Weep not for those whom the veil of the tomb
In life's happy morning hath hid from our eyes,
Ere sin threw a blight o'er the spirit's young bloom,
Or earth had profaned what was born for the skies.
Death chilled the fair fountain ere sorrow had stain'd
    it,
'Twas frozen in all the pure light of its course,
And but sleeps till the sunshine of heaven has un-
    chain'd it,
To water that Eden where first was its source.
THOMAS MOORE.

Grief and joy look out of the same window.
J. T. HEADLEY.

"HOW ARE THE DEAD RAISED UP, AND WITH WHAT BODY DO THEY COME?"

Professor Islay Burns, D.D.

"BUT how are the dead raised up, and with what body do they come?" The question will still recur, not on the suggestion only of a wistful curiosity, but under the pressure of these doubts which the physical difficulties of the case now, as in the Apostle's days, awaken. How shall it be possible even for Omnipotence itself to gather together again from the sepulchres of all the ages the dust of each of His saints, so long since dissolved, dispersed, blown about the world, mixed up with other organisms, taken up in the very blood and flesh of other animals and other men in the long succession of ages? How shall each reclaim his own, when the same substance, the same identical particles have belonged successively to many? Can Omnipotence itself overcome the natural impossibility of the same atom being in two places and forming a part of two distinct material organisms at once? Surely if the immortal spirits of men are again to be invested with a material form, it cannot be the same identical body which they laid aside at death, and which they left behind them in the grave.

The objection is specious, but not solid. It is founded altogether, not on the difficulties of the doctrine itself, but on an erroneous and superficial understanding of the doctrine. The identity of animal organisms is an identity, not of particles, but of form and structure and continuous sentient life.

Even during our present state of existence, while the organic identity of our bodies remains, their material substance is incessantly changing; so that in the course of a very few years every single atom of their present framework shall have passed away and given place to others. Thus, in this sense, the body of the child is different from the body of the boy, and the body of the boy from that of the man, and the substance of which we are composed at our birth is not the same, but wholly other than that which we shall lay in the tomb. It is not in this, then, that our true identity consists, seeing that amid all the incessant change that in this respect takes place, that identity remains all the while unaffected. There is no individuality in atoms; each one, so far as we know, is like another, and can contribute nothing therefore to the distinctive peculiarity or differentia of the bodies which they compose. I am what I am, not because I am composed of such and such particles, but because out of such particles I have been moulded by the plastic hand of God into that distinctive form and type of organic substance which belongs to me, as an individual, and which is mine and not another's. Even if, by a miracle, every atom of my bodily substance were in an instant eliminated and substituted by others, I would still remain, as to everything which constitutes my true identity, alike in body as in soul, totally unchanged. In this sense, then—that is to say, in the sense, not of an atomic but of an organic and vital identity—the body of our resurrection shall be the same with the body of our burial. As the body of our birth is the same with the body of our death; so shall be the body of our death with the body of our immortality. It will be changed, and yet the same, —changed in its conditions, properties, powers; the same in individual form of type, in its characteristic style and physiognomy, in the proportion of its parts, and its special adaptation to the uses of that one particular soul to which it inalienably belongs; so truly the same that both we ourselves shall be sure of it, and all who knew us before in the flesh shall recognize and know us again. It will be the same, though raised now to the full predestined perfection of its nature, conformed to its true ideal, even as its type was cast in the eternal thought of God from the first,—bright, beautiful, glorious, each according to its own individual style and fashion of brightness, beauty, glory, as every true work of God is and must be. It was thus that the Apostle, in his own grand way, solved the difficulty: "Thou fool, that which thou sowest is not quickened, except it die: and that which thou sowest, thou sowest not that body that shall be, but bare grain, it may chance of wheat, or of some other grain; But God giveth it a body as it hath pleased Him; and to every seed his own body. . . So also is the resurrection of the dead. It is sown in corruption: it is raised in incorruption; it is sown in dishonor: it is raised in glory; it is sown in weakness: it is raised in power; it is sown a natural body: it is raised a spiritual body. . . So when this corruptible shall have put on incorruption, and this mortal shall have put on immortality, then shall be brought to pass the saying that is written, Death is swallowed up in victory." (1 Cor. xv. 36-54.)

Here, then, we must pause. With this glimpse of the glory to be revealed, grand, but undefined, we must rest satisfied. Other questions manifold, and to the thoughtful spirit of deepest interest, we might ask, but cannot answer. What precisely shall be the new conditions, capacities, powers of our resurrection life? In what respect shall it be the same, and in what unlike our present earthly state? What new avenues of knowledge shall we possess, what new organs of perception, what new spheres of activity, and springs of enjoyment? Shall there be music, poetry, art, science, deepening research, and advancing knowledge of the works and ways of God, in heaven, even as here? Where shall the final seat of the blessed be? or shall they be confined, as now, to any exclusive spot—to any one single orb in the immensity of God's universe; or shall they not rather roam at large through all its wide domains, tread free and unrestrained through all the streets of the illimitable city of God? Shall we still, then as now, only scan from afar, the course of the planetary orbs, and the twinkle of the distant Pleiades, or shall we be permitted to visit them, and know all about them, and be at home in them, as in so many chambers of the one Father's house? In what form or stage of their development shall the bodies of the blessed rise,—as in youth, or in manhood, or in ripe majestic age? Shall the child of this world be still a child in heaven; or expand all at once in that wondrous transfiguration moment into the fulness of its stature and perfection of its powers? and shall the old man be still an old man for ever; or shall he not rather, by that great regenerative baptism, be brought back to all the freshness and strength of his manly prime? Shall we, in short, appear then, just as we were when death took us; and not rather as we were or might have been, at our best? Shall the great Architect of that new creation realize the true and perfect ideal of the life of His saints: or the restoration only, though in a glorified state, of their actual form here below? We cannot tell. We know not what we shall be. Enough, that God knoweth, and that He planneth and doeth all things well. Enough, that however high our conceptions of the unseen world, and sublime our aspirations in regard to it, it will still be something higher and grander far than we dream; for "eye hath not seen, nor ear heard, neither have entered into the heart of man, the things which God hath prepared for them that love Him." Enough, that there shall be a new heaven, and a new earth, and that we shall be made perfectly meet to possess and to enjoy it. Enough, and above all that Christ shall be there, and that "when He shall appear, we shall be like Him; for we shall see Him as He is."

————————

    O! JESUS, bring us to that rest
      Where all the ransomed shall be found,
    In thine eternal fulness blest,
      While ages roll their cycles round.
WILLIAM LEGGETT.

————————

THOUGH it be not in our power to make affliction no affliction, yet it is in our power to take off the edge of it, by a steady view of those divine joys prepared for us in another state.
REV. F. ATTERBURY.

BLESSED ARE THEY THAT MOURN.

WILLIAM CULLEN BRYANT.

OH, deem not they are blest alone
    Whose lives a peaceful tenor keep,
The power who pities man, has shown
    A blessing for the eyes that weep.

The light of smiles shall fill again
    The lids that overflow with tears,
And weary hours of woe and pain
    Are promises of happier years.

There is a day of sunny rest
    For every dark and troubled night;
And grief may bide an evening guest,
    But joy shall come with early light.

And thou, who o'er thy friend's low bier
    Dost shed the bitter drops like rain,
Hope that a brighter, happier sphere
    Will give him to thy arms again.

Nor let the good man's trust depart,
    Though life its common gifts deny,—
Though with a pierced and bleeding heart,
    And spurned of men he goes to die.

For God hath marked each sorrowing day
    And numbered every secret tear,
And heaven's long age of bliss shall pay
    For all His children suffer here.

A LOVELY LIFE—ITS CLOSING SCENE.

REV. GEORGE GILFILLAN.

THERE was one event in my domestic history at this time which cast a deep shadow on my soul, and weakened me for the contest with my spiritual foes. This was the death of a dear little girl who was connected with me, and whom I regarded as a daughter. I am guilty of no conscious exaggeration when I call my Agnes all that Mrs. Stowe has since represented in Eva—one of the rarest specimens of the workmanship of Heaven. In her simple yet profound nature was united a wisdom beyond her years to the most bewitching artlessness. Playful yet serious; quick in feeling; buoyant in spirits; fond of books and of solitude to a degree which is rarely to be found in one so utterly a child; affectionate and open-hearted, she wielded a gentle fascination which was felt beyond her own little circle, and attested by the tears which the news of her loss drew from many to whom she was but partially known. Her face was one of those which, without being perfectly regular in their beauty, win their way still more beseechingly to the heart. Its leading characters were transparent openness—every feature obeying the motions of the mind within, promply and fully as the wave receives the sunbeam; great flexibility and intelligence of expression; and that indescribable something which *naïveté* and heart unite in stamping on the countenance. Her brow was prominent, pale as marble, and nobly expanded; her eyes—

> "O! speak not of her eyes—they were
> Twin mirrors of the Scottish summer heaven;"

her chin Grecian, as if chiselled by Phidias; her cheek, in exercise or emotion, often flushing up through its paleness into a rich and roseate hue; her voice clear, sweet, none the less for its Norland accent, and predicting a beautiful singer; and her step light, airy, and swift as a "roe or a young hart upon the mountains." Disease—it was severe whooping-cough—changed her countenance ere it sent her away, spreading a fearful pallor over the whole, protruding the fine eye into a stare of anguish, and choking up the music of her voice, which, inarticulate, became unable to express her thickening thoughts and wants; but death restored her to herself, and almost all her former beauty clustered round her corpse. Death is often a ghastly disguise, a dread mask, reminding you of an ill-executed picture. But *she* was so calmly beautiful, so spiritually still, so smilingly radiant amidst her marble coldness, that but for the heart-heard whisper—how stilly low!—"It is for ever," and the shudder springing from the touch of the icy brow, you would have said, "The maid is not dead; she only sleepeth." Death seemed forced to smile out the news of immortality from her dear cold countenance. It was solemn beyond expression to see friend after friend coming in on tiptoe, raising the covering, looking and leaning over the face, and with sighs or tears, or aspect of withered unweeping woe, turning away. It was inexpressibly touching, too, to see the immediate relatives taking their last look ere the lid of the coffin was closed, amid bursting sobs, and all the other irrepressible signs of sorrow—suddenly brought under the sense of an eternal separation; one parent the while looking not—daring not to look—but patting the dear brown head once more, and hurrying away. In a sweet southerly side of the beautiful kirkyard of Fettercairn, beside the bones of her grandfather (and now of her father, who loved her so fondly), under the clear blue sky of the north, and in the expectation of the coming, to this sunlit vale of tears, of Jesus Christ with His holy angels, repose, and have for twenty-five years reposed, the remains of one who never gave a pang to a friend's heart, nor armed with a rod a father's hand; whose memory shall be cherished, and her sweetest name repeated, and the spot where lies her virgin dust visited and watered with tears, while there lives one of those who really knew her, or felt how insipid in comparison was all love beside what *she* inspired—of one who in the brief business of her existence exhibited the affection of the amiable child, the ardor of the docile scholar, the liveliness of the fearless girl, and the graces of the saint sanctified from the womb. She was my play-fellow when cheerful, my comforter when sad; her artless yet piercing prattle at once smoothed and roused my mind; and assuredly, amid all the "chambers of my imagery," I have never had an idol like her, whose premature loss I continued bitterly, yet submissively, to deplore.

Not so submissive were my feelings at the time. How my heart bled, and what dark, unhappy thoughts crossed my soul, as I saw this good and beautiful young being writhing in anguish, and weeping with her fearful pain, till there came at last a wild and merciful delirium, and gave her partial forgetfulness! And it was not till I saw the child I loved so dearly fairly committed to the grave, and had leaned a long time in anguish over a tombstone which was casting its shadow on the little spot, and, looking up to the sun shining so bright and cold in the spring sky, had said within myself, as Scott cried at the burial of one of his friends, "There shall be less sunshine for me henceforth," that tears came to my relief, and a rainbow of resignation, if not of hope, seemed to smile through these bitter yet blessed tears.

We train our children; but it is no less true that our children train us. They are meant by God as a means and occasion of much discipline for heaven. How they call out our purest and most unselfish affections! what new tenderness they pour into our hearts! how they humanize and soften the roughest nature! And when taken from us, are they not like magnets to draw our hearts to the things that are above? There are fathers and mothers who seem to see, when they look up into the deep blue of heaven, a dimpled hand that beckons to them, and to hear a silver voice that whispers from the skies, "Come up higher." To very many, this theme—the removal of children—can not be out of season.

Rev. John R. Macduff, D.D.

There is no grief which time does not lessen and soften.

Cicero.

THE BELIEVER'S CONFIDENCE.

REV. JAMES PARSONS.

NOTWITHSTANDING the dissolution that awaited him, — "*in my flesh,*" exclaimed the patriarch Job, "I shall see God:" and it is now plain that he recognized and delighted in the mystery of the resurrection of the body to which we have already adverted—that grand truth, on which Christianity has shed the light of its full disclosure. Here was, moreover, an anticipation, not only of a resurrection, but of that glorious resurrection,—that "resurrection unto life,"—which is to be the exclusive portion and privilege of the redeemed people of God. It is the subject of emphatic promise, that at the sounding of the trumpet which shall announce the second coming of Jesus, "the dead in Christ shall rise," beautiful and lovely from their graves, and assume a perfected nature before the throne. As to the mode, and many of the circumstances, of that blessed restoration, there is an impenetrable mystery; yet we know that wonderful will be the change. With what ecstatic delight must our bosoms glow, when we meditate on the record that proclaims it! Listen, believer, and rejoice! "It is sown in corruption; it is raised in incorruption: it is sown in weakness: it is raised in power: it is sown in dishonor; it is raised in glory: it is sown a natural body; it is raised a spiritual body. As we have borne the image of the earthly, we shall also bear the image of the heavenly." "The Saviour shall change our vile body, that it may be fashioned like unto his glorious body, according to the working whereby he is able even to subdue all things unto himself." (1 Cor. xv. 42-49. Phil. iii. 21.)

And is it not indeed animating to the soul, when it can look forward to the arrival of the day to be signalized, for the saints of the Lord, by an exaltation like this? Multitudes have already gone from the abodes of the living; the worm has preyed upon them, and their bones have mouldered. Generation after generation yet shall pass away. Some may sleep in the graves of their fathers, and in an assemblage of holy dust; some may have their tombs dug by foreign hands, in foreign climes, where is no friend to mourn; some may have their ashes scattered to the winds of heaven; or perhaps the unfathomed ocean may be made their funeral bed, and there they may lie beneath the heaving billow, "unknelled, uncoffined, and unknown." But what matters it where lie the Christian's remains, and what matters it how he may be tenanted in the regions of death? That vast variety of disposal shall terminate at the shout of Him who is the "Resurrection and the Life." Not one then shall be left in the desolate slumber. All, from every clime and period, shall be clothed afresh, and arise, and gather, bright and splendid in heavenly radiance, into one vast assembly, the inheritors of everlasting joy. What inspiration is in the prospect! Who feels not already a triumph over death? and whose spirit, eager and panting for the destined majesty, does not unite in the cry of the ransomed church,—"WE WAIT FOR THE ADOPTION, TO WIT, THE REDEMPTION OF THE BODY?"

"RESIGNATION."

H. W. LONGFELLOW.

THERE is no flock, however watched and tended,
    But one dead lamb is there!
  There is no fireside, howsoe'er defended,
    But has one vacant chair!

The air is full of farewells to the dying,
    And mournings for the dead;
The heart of Rachel, for her children crying,
    Will not be comforted.

Let us be patient! these severe afflictions
    Not from the ground arise,
But oftentimes celestial benedictions
    Assume this dark disguise.

We see but dimly through the mists and vapors
    Amid these earthly damps;
What seem to us but sad, funereal tapers,
    May be Heaven's distant lamps.

There is no Death! what seems so is transition:
    This life of mortal breath
Is but a suburb of the life elysian,
    Whose portal we call Death.

She is not dead—the child of our affection—
    But gone into that school
Where she no longer needs our poor protection,
    And Christ Himself doth rule.

In that great cloister's stillness and seclusion,
　By guardian angels led,
Safe from temptation, safe from sin's pollution,
　She lives whom we call *dead*.

Day after day we think what she is doing,
　In those bright realms of air;
Year after year, her tender steps pursuing,
　Behold her grown more fair.

Thus do we walk with her, and keep unbroken
　The bond which nature gives,
Thinking that our remembrance, though unspoken,
　May reach her where she lives.

Not as a child shall we again behold her;
　For when with raptures wild
In our embraces we again enfold her,
　She will not be a child;

But a fair maiden, in her Father's mansion,
　Clothed with celestial grace;
And beautiful with all the soul's expansion
　Shall we behold her face.

And though at times, impetuous with emotion
　And anguish long suppressed,
The swelling heart heaves moaning like the ocean
　That cannot be at rest—

We will be patient, and assuage the feeling
　We cannot wholly stay;
By silence sanctifying, not concealing,
　The grief that must have way.

　　　　　........................

　But patience was willing to wait.

　　　　　　　　　　　　　J. Bunyan.

HEAVEN A VAST AND HAPPY SOCIETY.

Rev. Wm. Morley Punshon, D.D.

THE question of the recognition of departed friends in heaven, and special and intimate reunion with them, Scripture and reason enable us to infer with almost certain persuasion. It is implied in the fact that the resurrection is a resurrection of individuals; that it is *this* mortal that shall put on immortality. It is implied in the fact that heaven is a vast and happy society; and it is implied in the fact that there is no unclothing of the nature that we now possess, only a clothing upon it with the garments of a brighter and more glorious immortality. Take comfort, then, those of you in whose history the dearest charities of life have been severed by the rude hand of the spoiler; those whom you have thought about as lost are not lost, except to present sight. Perhaps even now they are angel watchers, screened by a kindly providence of forgetfulness from everything about you that would give them pain; but if you and they are alike in Jesus, and remain faithful unto the end, doubt not that you shall know them again. It were strange—don't you think?—if amid the multitudes of the heavenly hosts, the multitudes of earth's ransomed ones that we are to see in heaven, we should see all but those we most fondly and fervently long to see. Strange, if in some of our walks along the golden streets we never happened to light upon them! Strange, if we did not hear some heaven-song learned on earth trilled by some clear ringing voice that we have often heard before! Oh, depend upon it, in a realm of perfect happiness this element of happiness will not be absent, to know and love again what we have known and loved below.

"The resurrection and the life." Oh, what heart is not thrilled by the preciousness of the promise? Whose does not throb the more joyously as he recognizes the Redeemer who brings him life? "The resurrection and the life?" Enjoyed recompense, recovered friends, these are our hopes above. Ah! but nearer still and dearer still, enhancing each of these a thousand-fold as every true and loyal believer thinks with Jesus there! So shall it be in heaven, and with glad eye and with beating heart will each ransomed spirit break from its own private joy to fasten gratefully its gaze upon the Master who has purchased it, and to hear again in a pronounced immortality of comfort and of bliss, "I am the resurrection and the life."

CONSOLATION DERIVED FROM THE HOPE OF IMMORTALITY.

ROBERT HALL, D.D.

IF the Scripture doctrine of immortality is entitled to weight in the regulation of *life*, its influence is not less sovereign in dispelling the terrors of *death*, and consoling us under the loss of our dearest friends and relatives. "I would not have you be ignorant, brethren, concerning them which are asleep, that ye sorrow not as others who have no hope; for if we believe that Jesus died and rose again, even so them also which sleep in Jesus will God bring with him. For the Lord himself shall descend from heaven with a shout, with the voice of the archangel, and the trump of God. Then we which are alive, and remain, shall be caught up together with them in the clouds, to meet the Lord in the air; so shall we be ever with the Lord. Wherefore, comfort one another with these words." And who can fail being penetrated with the divine consolation they afford? If ever Christianity appears in its power, it is when it erects its trophies on the *tomb;* when it takes up its votaries where the world leaves them, and fills the breast with immortal hopes in dying moments.

Nor are the words I have quoted adapted to support the mind of a Christian in the view of his own dissolution only; they administer the firmest support amidst the breaches which death is continually making in the church of Christ. A degree of sorrow on such occasions, nature compels us to feel, and religion does not condemn. At the decease of Lazarus, while his sisters were lamenting his loss, "Jesus wept." But the sorrow which a Christian feels in such situations is mingled with hope. By the light of faith he traces his deceased friends into an eternal world. Instead of considering them as lost or extinct, he beholds them under the eye of Divine Providence. The period of their trial is closed; they have entered into rest, where, sheltered from the storms of life and the dangers of temptation, their happiness is forever fixed and unalterable. Their separation is neither final nor complete. The pious living and the pious dead are still one family, under one head; and when He " who is their life shall appear, they shall appear together with Him in glory."

OH, WHERE SHALL REST BE FOUND?

James Montgomery.

OH, where shall rest be found,
    Rest for the weary soul?
'Twere vain the ocean depths to sound,
    Or pierce to either pole;
The world can never give
    The bliss for which we sigh;
'Tis not the whole of life to live,
    Nor all of death to die.

Beyond this vale of tears,
    There is a life above,
Unmeasured by the flight of years,
    And all that life is love:
There is a death whose pang
    Outlasts the fleeting breath;
Oh, what eternal horrors hang
    Around the second death!

Lord God of truth and grace,
    Teach us that death to shun,
Lest we be banished from thy face,
    And evermore undone;
Here would we end our quest;
    Alone are found in thee,
The life of perfect love, the rest
    Of immortality!

THE HOPE OF A RESURRECTION.

JOHN FLAVEL.

LET those mourn without measure, who mourn without hope. The husbandman does not mourn, when he casts his seed into the ground. He expects to receive it again, and more. The same hope have we, respecting our friends who have died in faith. "I would not have you ignorant," says Paul, "concerning them who are asleep, that ye sorrow not as others who have no hope; for if we believe that Jesus died and rose again, even so them also who sleep in Jesus will God bring with him." He seems to say, "Look not on the dead as lost. They are not annihilated. Indeed, they are not *dead*. They only sleep; and they sleep to awake again." You do not lament over your children or friends, while slumbering on their beds. Consider death as a longer sleep, from which they shall certainly awake. Even a heathen philosopher could say, that he enjoyed his friends, expecting to part with them; and parted with them, expecting to see them again. And shall a heathen excel a Christian in bearing affliction with cheerfulness? If you have a well-grounded hope that your deceased friend was interested in Christ, ponder, I entreat you, the precious supports afforded by the doctrine of the Resurrection of the Just.

RECOGNITION AFTER THE RESURRECTION.

REV. WM. ANDERSON, D.D.

HOW different in character will be the meeting after the resurrection! when that grave, feared as a destroyer, shall be demonstrated, as made of Christ, the regenerator of our friends—rendering back in incorruption that which it received in corruption, in glory that which it received in dishonor, in power that which it received in weakness, a spiritual body, fit as a tabernacle for the glorified soul, that which it received a natural body, an impediment to its exercises. Hosannah to the Lord of Resurrection for this blessed hope! Yea, so overwhelming is its glory, that it is like to obscure our faith. How shall the mother recognize her son, who departed from her an emaciated infant, in yonder angelic form in the vigor and brilliancy of resurrection manhood? And how shall the father, who wept bitter tears in secret over his daughter's decrepitude, distinguish her in yonder seraph of celestial grace? What mean you, friends? You surely cannot wish to meet your children in that plight of wretchedness in which you bade them farewell, so that, unassisted, you could of yourselves recognize them. The Lord will provide; but methinks it will, probably, be a busy day for those good angels who ministered to us on earth, finding us out for one another, and introducing us. Remembering how they had seen us grieve for one another, how sympathetically they will enjoy the scene, as we stand amazed for a while at one another's glory before we embrace!

How many parents there are, who have almost entirely forgotten those of their children who died in infancy; and who, being inquired at about the number of their family, will, so unlike that sweet faithful child who so resolutely maintained "We are seven," give account only of those who live—the least worthy of being reckoned! Faithless father and mother, that you are! amid all your rapture, how ashamed you shall be of your forgetfulness, when these neglected ones are restored to you, so beautiful and glorious; and especially when, under that angel-guidance, they hasten with such excitement to meet with those of whom they are told, that under the Creator they were the authors of their existence! Nor will it be with little excitement that they hasten to meet *you*, their brothers and sisters, with whom they may associate and worship, as being more of their own nature than any others to be found in all the kingdom. The whole of you—brothers and sisters, as well as parents, meditate on them; the thought is most sanctifying: it endears the Redeemer with peculiar attraction to a tender heart; and, remember, there are no hearts great which are not tender.

'Tis the sunset of life gives me mystical lore,
And coming events cast their shadows before.
CAMPBELL.

MY FIRST HOUSEHOLD GRIEF.

HUGH MILLER.

IN the spring of 1839, a sad bereavement darkened my household, and for a time left me little heart to pursue my wonted amusements, literary or scientific. We had been visited, ten months after our marriage, by a little girl, whose presence had added not a little to our happiness; home became more emphatically such from the presence of the child, that in a few months had learned so well to know its mother, and in a few more to take its stand in the nurse's arms, at an upper window that commanded the street, and to recognize and make signs to its father as he approached the house. Its few little words, too, had a fascinating interest to our ears; —our own names, lisped in a language of its own, every time we approached; and the simple Scotch vocable, "awa, awa," which it knew how to employ in such plaintive tones as we retired, and that used to come back upon us in recollection, like an echo from the grave, when, its brief visit over, it had left us for ever, and its fair face and silken hair lay in darkness amid the clods of the churchyard. In how short a time had it laid hold of our affections! Two brief years before, and we knew it not; and now it seemed as if the void which it left in our hearts the whole world could not fill. We buried it beside the old chapel of St. Regulus, with the deep rich woods all around, save where an opening in front commands the distant land and the blue sea; and where the daisies, which it had learned to love, mottled, starlike, the mossy mounds; and where birds, whose songs its ear had become skilful enough to distinguish, pour their notes over its little grave.

FOR A BEREAVED MOTHER.

CHARLES SPRAGUE.

YOUNG mother! what can feeble friendship say,
To soothe the anguish of this mournful day?
They, they alone, whose hearts like thine have bled
Know how the living sorrow for the dead.
Each tutored voice, that seeks such grief to cheer,
Strikes cold upon the weeping parents' ear;
I've felt it all,—alas! too well I know
How vain all earthly power to hush thy woe!
God cheer thee, childless mother! 'tis not given
For man to ward the blow that falls from heaven.

I've felt it all—as thou art feeling now;
Like thee, with stricken heart and aching brow,
I've sat and watched by dying beauty's bed,
And burning tears of hopeless anguish shed;
I've gazed upon the sweet, but pallid face,
And vainly tried some comfort there to trace;
I've listened to the short and struggling breath;
I've seen the cherub eye grow dim in death;
Like thee, I've veiled my head in speechless gloom,
And laid my first-born in the silent tomb.

THE DYING MOTHER AND HER CHILD.

ROBERT POLLOK, A.M.

OUR sighs were numerous, and profuse our tears;
   For she we lost was lovely, and we loved
   Her much. Fresh in our memory, as fresh
As yesterday, is yet the day she died.
It was an April day; and blithely all
The youth of Nature leaped beneath the sun,
And promised glorious manhood: and our hearts
Were glad, and round them danced the lightsome
    blood,
In healthy merriment, when tidings came
A child was born: and tidings came again
That she who gave it birth was sick to death.
So swift trode sorrow on the heels of joy!
We gathered round her bed, and bent our knees
In fervent supplication to the Throne
Of Mercy, and perfumed our prayers with sighs
Sincere, and penitential tears, and looks
Of self-abasement; but we sought to stay
An angel on the earth, a spirit ripe
For heaven; and Mercy, in her love, refused:
Most merciful, as oft, when seeming least!
Most gracious when she seemed the most to frown!
The room I well remember, and the bed
On which she lay, and all the faces, too,
That crowded dark and mournfully around.
Her father there, and mother, bending, stood;

And down their aged cheeks fell many drops
Of bitterness. Her husband, too, was there
And brothers, and they wept; her sisters, too,
Did weep and sorrow, comfortless; and I
Too wept, though not to weeping given: and all
Within the house was dolorous and sad.
This I remember well; but better still
I do remember, and will ne'er forget,
The dying eye! That eye alone was bright,
And brighter grew as nearer death approached:
As I have seen the gentle little flower
Look fairest in the silver beam which fell
Reflected from the thunder-cloud, that soon
Came down, and o'er the desert scattered far
And wide its loveliness. She made a sign
To bring her babe—'twas brought, and by her placed.
She looked upon its face, that neither smiled
Nor wept, nor knew who gazed upon't; and laid
Her hand upon its little breast, and sought
For it, with look that seem'd to penetrate
The heavens, unutterable blessings, such
As God to dying parents only granted,
For infants left behind them in the world.
"God keep my child!" we heard her say, and heard
No more. The Angel of the Covenant
Was come, and, faithful to His promise, stood
Prepared to walk with her through death's dark vale.
And now her eyes grew bright, and brighter still,
Too bright for ours to look upon, suffused
With many tears, and closed without a cloud.
They set, as sets the morning star, which goes
Not down behind the darkened west, nor hides
Obscured among the tempests of the sky,
But melts away into the light of heaven.

RESIGNED IN HOPE.

WILLIAM T. M'AUSLANE.

OUR little boy is gone!
   His gladsome voice, whose music lately filled
  Our homes and hearts, is now for ever stilled!
How changed his looks! Closed are his bright eyes
     now;
Pale is his cheek, as marble cold his brow;
Those limbs, before so active, are at rest,
The spring is broken, motionless the breast,
    Life, light, and joy are flown!

    Oh, earthly hopes, how vain!
Frail is the fabric, fair though it appear,
Which on uncertain human life we rear;
Before some sudden storm it yields away,
A ruin lies, and sinks into decay.
So have our hopes of what, in future days,
Our boy might prove, crumbled before our gaze,
    Ne'er to revive again!

    But why should we repine?
Our darling child was only ours in loan,
God, when he lent him, lent what was His own.
And shall we feel displeased He now should come
To claim and take him to the Heavenly Home?
Oh, rather let us, though 'tis sad to part,
Yield up the loved one, and, with thankful heart,
    Bow to the will Divine!

> Then let our tearful eyes
> Turn from the little tenement of clay
> From which the ransom'd soul has passed away;
> Let us behold, by faith, that land so fair,
> Now dearer to us that our boy is there.
> And may we seek to join him on that shore
> Where, when we meet, we meet to part no more,
> But dwell beyond the skies.

THE GATHERED LILIES.

Rev. Ebenezer Erskine.

UPON the 7th day of December, my dear, sweet, and pleasant child, Isabel, died. I got freedom during her sickness, particularly the same afternoon, before she died, to present her before the Lord, and to plead His covenant on her behalf. The Lord enabled me to quit her freely to Him, on this account, that He had a far better title to her than I. She was mine, only as her earthly father; she is His by creation, preservation, by dedication to Him in baptism, and His also, I hope, by covenant and redemption, and therefore, I am persuaded, she is now His by glorification; and that she is with the Lord Jesus, and with her dear mother, triumphing with God in glory. I had a particular affection for the child, and doted but too much upon her, because she was nearer like her mother than any of the children, both as to her countenance and disposition. But I see that the Lord will not allow me to have any idols, but will have the whole of my heart to Himself. And, Lord, let it be so! Amen, and amen.

She died pleasantly, without any visible pang or throe; her soul, I hope, being carried by angels into Abraham's bosom, and her body buried by her mother's side in her brother's grave. I take it kindly that the Lord comes to my family to gather lilies wherewith to garnish the upper sanctuary! "for of such is the kingdom of heaven." And oh, it sometimes affords me a pleasing prospect, to think I have so much *plenishing* in heaven before me; and that, when I enter the gates of glory, I shall not only be welcomed by the whole general assembly of saints and angels, but that my wife and four pleasant babes will, in a particular manner, welcome me to those regions of glory, and that I shall join in the hallelujahs of the Higher House, which shall never have an end.

FROM SHADOW INTO SUNSHINE AT LAST.

> There he waits for his release,
> There in God finds perfect peace;
> Till the long years end at last,
> And he too at length has past
> From the sorrows and the fears,
> From the anguish and the tears,
> From the desolate distress
> Of this world's great loneliness.
> From its withering and its blight,
> From the shadows of its night,
> Into God's pure sunshine bright.
>
> Richard Chenevix Trench.

He that would avoid trouble must avoid the world. Eusebius.

HOME IN OUR FATHER'S HOUSE.

Rev. Newman Hall, D.D.

AFFLICTED believers, your sorrows are only for a little season; your weeping is for a brief night; joy cometh in the morning, the morning of an everlasting day. A Christian's trials are but the discomforts of a journey, each stage of which, however rough the road and wild the weather, brings him nearer the home of his heart. The darkness is only that of the tunnel through which we are hurrying at express speed. The speck of light at the end is nearing and brightening as we speed onward to the sunshine of eternal day.

Our Lord allayed the heart trouble of His disciples by assuring them that in His Father's house were many mansions, and that the parting which caused them sorrow was for their good; that though He was going from them, it was to prepare a place for them, and that He would surely return to receive them to Himself that they might abide with Him for ever.

Our Lord speaks of heaven as home, "My Father's house." What a contrast to the gorgeous imagery employed by servants is this sublimely simple familiarity of the child. It is as if a poor cottager, after visiting a royal palace, tried to describe the unimagined splendors of a place which members of the royal family simply knew as home. How in harmony with the high claims of Deity asserted by and for Him! The disciples were not to be troubled on His account. Although betrayed, condemned, crucified, He was going home. "Let not your heart be troubled." And because of their intimate union, they were not to be troubled for themselves.

If heaven is Christ's home it is ours also. He is our Elder Brother. "He is not ashamed to call us brethren." He said, "I ascend to my Father and your Father." We are "joint heirs with Jesus Christ." His Father's home is ours also. What hallowed associations are suggested by the word! Most persons of all conditions, whatever scenes of grandeur they may visit, feel, "There's no place like home." Love makes home.

Home promises rest. There the wearied limbs or wearied brain repose after the day's toil. So, amid the multiplied cares and labors of the present life, we look forward to "the rest that remaineth for the children of God." There will be occupation, but no painful toil. "Blessed are the dead that die in the Lord; they rest from their labors."

Home suggests fidelity. There is no true home without it. We may suspect deceit and treachery outside, but we can cast off all reserve, all distrust, at home. Home suggests sympathy. There may be coldness outside, no interest in what deeply concerns us, no response to our warmest feelings, but at home we are always sure of a listening ear, a kindling eye, a responsive hand-grasp, a heart-expressive kiss. There may be curiosity outside, openly avowed or suspiciously concealed; and even friends may sometimes prove forgetful, selfish, and unkind. But home, true home, is the palace of love,

"Where hearts are of each other sure."

But the purest and brightest of earthly homes are but faint types of the home above. There every heart is wholly true to every other, being wholly true to God. No suspicion lurks there, no envy at other's gifts, no cherished ill-will, no antipathy, no mere calculating kindness, but true, hearty, genuine, expressive, warmly-manifested love. Whatever in this world hinders true intercourse among Christians will have been left behind. "We shall all be changed" in this respect, and the unloveliness which more or less clings to believers and interferes with fellowship here will disappear, when the bride of Christ will be "without spot or wrinkle or any such thing."

It is a permanent home. There are mansions yonder, abiding places, not movable tents, but a fixed, enduring habitation. We know that when this earthly tabernacle is dissolved, we have a building of God. How unlike the uncertainty and perishableness of earthly things! The lake, so calm, reflecting from its unruffled surface the sky and stars, may, in one short hour, be wild with storms. The stream which oft refreshed us, suddenly becomes dry. The fairest flowers droop and die even as we gaze on them. The loveliest and most loving homes are quickly broken up. No locks and bolts can shut out sickness, sorrow and death. But as the home above is everlasting, so its pleasures are for evermore. The sunshine will never be overcast by one fleeting thought of change or death.

And there is abundance of supply. There are "many mansions." The Jewish temple was a place not merely for worship but for residence, and had around its courts a variety of chambers for priests of various degree. So the heavenly Jerusalem has habitations for all whom Jesus consecrates "kings and priests unto God;" and these consist of all who are washed from their sins by his blood. The Father's house is large enough for all his children. The preparation is vast as the heart of God. Holy angels are there, and saints of all ages, "a great multitude whom no man can number, out of all kindreds and tribes and peoples." But still there is room. The Father is bringing not a few but "many sons unto glory." There are multitudes unknown to men, but known to God, who have not bowed their knees unto Baal. Heathen nations are pressing into the kingdom, and the day is not far distant when all shall know the Saviour from the least to the greatest. There is room for them all. There is room for us. There is room for every mourner; "Let not your heart be troubled." Number implies variety. The mansions are not of uniform size and arrangement, though all are perfect in beauty. They are fitted and prepared for dwellers of varied capacity and degree. Mansions for children and for young men, for the weak and the strong, for babes in Christ and for those of full age. None need fear that because they are inferior to others there will be no place for them above. There will be no seclusion of classes, no barriers of separation, but there will be variety of degrees of glory, suited to the meetness for the inheritance, and thus the very lowest in attainment, if a sincere believer in Christ, may be sure of a home among the many mansions. Let not your heart be troubled. Those gates shall open for *you*. *You* shall drink of the river, clear as crystal, and *you* shall eat of the Tree of Life, and find a home in the many mansions of our Father's house.

THE RAINBOW OF PROMISES AS SEEN THROUGH TEARS.

Bishop Wm. Bacon Stevens, D.D.

AS a token of God's gracious assurance the bow in the cloud is peculiarly suggestive. It never appears but at the time when the rain is falling, and hence, viewed in itself, is rather a ground of apprehension than of peace. But God has chosen that to be a pledge of our security, which is, in itself, an intimation of our danger, that our trust might be, not in any change of terrestrial arrangements, but in the simple word of God, a pledge repeated to us by each new-born rainbow as it carries our thoughts back to the days of Noah, and the covenant token then first pointed out. Look then upon the rainbow, whenever it appears in its parti-colored glory, and praise Him who set it in the clouds as the perpetual token of His covenant of love. "Very beautiful is it in the brightness thereof, it compasseth the whole heaven with glory, and the hands of the Most High have bended it."

The rainbow is made up of seven colors, caused by the different angles at which the light is refracted and reflected from the falling drops of rain. The conditions under which it can be seen are, that there must be rain falling at the time; that there must be sunlight at the time; and that the beholder must be between the two. Let us look, then, if we can see on the dark and showery cloud of sorrow the rays of the Sun of Righteousness so refracted as to form the iris of mercy, at once inspiring hope and exciting thanksgiving. We turn to Isaiah, the evangelical prophet, and find the first of these prismatic promises in the comforting words, "But now thus saith the Lord that created thee, O Jacob, and he that formed thee, O Israel, Fear not for I have redeemed thee, I have called thee by thy name; thou art mine. When thou passest through the waters I will be with thee; and through the rivers they shall not overflow thee; when thou walkest through the fire thou shalt not be burned, neither shall the flame kindle upon thee. For I am the Lord, thy God, the Holy One of Israel, thy Saviour." How much and how beautiful the light refracted from this glowing passage! As if God had said, Fear not, for He who created thee out of nothing, He who formed thee in the shape and fashion of humanity, He who redeemed thee from the dominion of death, He who so knows thee as to call thee by name, and to grave thee on the palms of His hands, and to make thee unto him a chosen peculiar people, will not forsake thee in any emergency or trial; but "when thou passest through the waters" of affliction, "I, the Lord thy God, the Holy One of Israel, thy Saviour," will not suffer thee to burn, but will protect thee from the fiery trial. What wide promises, what divine assurance! How full of hope and comfort to the sorrowful and the persecuted!

A few pages on, and we find another promise for our covenant bow; one, too, that has specific relations to the rainbow of the deluge, for that token was evidently present to the mind of God when the words were uttered: "For a small moment," says Jehovah, speaking to His ancient people, "for a small moment have I forsaken thee, but with great mercies will I gather thee. In a little wrath I hid my face from thee for a moment: but with everlasting kindness will I have mercy on thee, saith the Lord thy Redeemer." "For," he continues, "this is as the waters of Noah unto me: for as I have sworn that the waters of Noah should no more go over the earth, so have I sworn that I would not be wroth with thee, nor rebuke thee, for the mountains shall depart and the hills be removed, but my kindness shall not depart from thee, neither shall the covenant of my peace be removed, saith the Lord that hath mercy on thee."

Sitting with our Saviour upon the grassy mount, and listening to the sermon he delivered there, we find another tinted promise of a dye so heavenly that it at once finds its place as one of the septenary colors in this rainbow of hope. The words are few but condensed, the promise is brief but of intensive force, of infinite expansibility—it is the verse "Blessed are they that mourn, for they shall be comforted." But how comforted? Not with earthly sympathy, for that gives but little solace; not with worldly succor, for the world has no balm for a broken heart; but comforted with the choice blessings of the Divine Comforter, by which strength is imparted to the weak, light to the darkened, joy to the saddened, peace to the troubled, and hope to the sinking spirit.

But our Saviour furnishes another prismatic color for our covenant arch in the invitation, "Come unto me, all ye that labor and are heavy laden, and I will give you rest." There is here no restriction as to the persons invited, none as to the rest promised.

Whether then you labor under the cares, trials, and perplexities of life; whether you are burdened by the crushing weight of poverty, sorrow and sickness; whether you labor under the sharp convictions of sin from which you struggle to free yourself, or whether you are burdened by a sense of weighty guilt and a conscious deserving of eternal woe; in each case you are invited to Jesus with the promise of heavenly rest.

In the last interview of our Saviour with the apostles before His crucifixion, He gave them many and peculiar consolations in view of His near removal from them. Among the many thrilling sentences uttered on that memorable night there is one so terse, so full of thought, so rich in comfort, that we may well claim for it a place in Mercy's triumphal arch.

It is the passage, "I will not leave you comfortless, I will come unto you." I will come to you—come to you in the cheering influences of my love; come to you in the precious outpourings of my spirit; come to you in the imparted strength and comfort of the Holy Ghost; come to you in sickness, in suffering, in sorrow; come to you with the oil and wine of gospel truth; come to you in the light of my own countenance, making your dark soul radiant with joy, and painting upon the lowering vapor whose showers have but just discharged themselves upon your head, the overarching bow of covenant peace and hope. The sixth color of this "bow in the cloud" is added by the pencil of St. Paul. His words are, "Our light affliction, which is but for a moment, worketh for us a far more exceeding and eternal weight of glory; while we look not at the things which are seen, but at the things which are not seen; for the things which are seen are temporal, but the things which are not seen are eternal."

The "AFFLICTION," light as to its character; "but for a moment" as to its duration; while the "GLORY" has "weight" as being heavy with blessing; is "eternal" as to its permanence; is "exceeding," as passing human conception; is "far more exceeding" as expressive of its unspeakable excellence. So intense was the feeling of the Apostle here, that the usual superlatives could not body forth his thought, and he was forced to make a new word to give utterance to his emotion, it is glory, it is a weight of glory, it is an eternal weight of glory, it is a far more exceeding and eternal weight of glory. What a climax! like the rainbow, its foot indeed rests on earth, but it arches upward to heaven, spanning the dark cloud of affliction with a bond of beauty. The last color in this prismatic arch is furnished by "the Beloved Disciple," and is drawn from a revelation to him of some of these very "things which are unseen and eternal." The Apostle, in his vision at Patmos, had "beheld, and, lo, a great multitude which no man could number, of all nations, and kindreds, and people, and tongues, stood before the throne and before the Lamb, clothed with white robes, and palms in their hands." While he listened to their ascriptions of praise, one of the celestial host approached and asked him, by way of calling his attention to the scene, "Who are these which are arrayed in white robes? and whence came they?" The surprised Apostle answered, "Sir, thou knowest." In reply to this the heavenly visitant said unto him, "These are they which came out of great tribulation, and have washed their robes and made them white in the blood of the lamb. Therefore are they before the throne of God, and serve Him day and night in His temple; and He that sitteth on the throne shall dwell among them. They shall hunger no more, neither thirst any more, neither shall the sun light on them, nor any heat, for the lamb which is in the midst of the throne shall feed them, and shall lead them unto living fountains of waters, and God shall wipe away all tears from their eyes."

And now we have laid side by side seven rich and precious promises as the seven colors of the rainbow, each lovely in itself, but combined, forming that arch of covenant glory which God has equally "set in the cloud" of sorrow on earth, and "around the throne" in heaven. Behold it in its varied but exquisite hues! Is it not beautiful as it springs upward—as it swells heavenward—as it bends downward, curving over our sorrow-drenched hearts, with assurance of present sunshine and of future bliss? Many are the passages in the Bible which represent Christ as the light of the world, and Malachi especially designates him as the "Sun of Righteousness." He shines out from the zenith of the spiritual firmament, and there is no going down of His light—no evening to shroud his departed rays. Once shining—forever shining—without a shadow—without an eclipse—without a sunset. Such is the Sun whose refracted rays paint the iris of hope on the cloud of sorrow. But when through the sovereign grace of God we receive this "adoption of sons," then is it our peculiar privilege to see God's love in every dispensation of His hand, and to see His bow of covenant promise in every cloud of sorrow.

SORROW SUCCEEDED BY JOY.

REV. THEODORE L. CUYLER, D.D.

SORROW is represented by the Psalmist as only a lodger for a night, to be succeeded by joy at the sunrising. This is a truthful picture of most frequent experiences; it is full of comfort to God's people, and it points on to the glorious dawn of heaven's eternal day, when the night-watch of life is over. Sorrow is often the precursor of joy; sometimes it is so needful, that unless we endure the one we cannot have the other. Some of us have known what it is to have severe sickness lodge in our bodily tent, when every nerve became a tormentor and every muscle a highway for pain to course over. We lay on our beds conquered and helpless.

But the longest night has its dawn. At length returning health began to steal in upon us, like the earliest gleams of morning light through the window shutters. Never did food taste so delicious as the first meal of which we partook at our own table. Never did the sunbeams fall so sweet and golden as on the first Sabbath when we ventured out to church; and no discourse ever tasted so like heavenly manna as the one our pastor poured into our hungry ears that day. We sang the thirtieth psalm with melody in the heart, and no verse more gratefully than this one, "Sorrow may endure for a night, but joy cometh in the morning."

The history of every discovery, of every enterprise of benevolence, of every Christian reform, is the history of toil and watching through long discouragements. I love to read the narrative of Palissy the potter, of his painful struggles with adversity, of his gropings after the scientific truth he was seeking, and of his final victory. Sorrow and poverty and trial lodged with that brave spirit for many a weary month, but at length came singing and shouting. All Galileos and Keplers and Newtons have had this experience. All the Luthers and Wesleys who have pioneered great reformations, and all the missionaries of Christ who have ever invaded the darkness of paganism, have had to endure nightwork and watching before the hand of God opened to them the gates of the "dayspring from on high." God tests His people before He blesses them. The night is mother of the day; trust through the dark brings triumph in the dawn.

THE MOUNT OF HAPPINESS.

To banish sorrow's tear, to speak a kind
    Word to the friendless, and to feed
The hungry, lift the fallen, and to find
    Thy time most spent in giving heed,
In love, to all such as are in distress,—
    Herein is true joy understood,
And thou made it glad--The Mount of Happiness
    Is only gained in doing good.

                      GEORGE NEWELL LOVEJOY.

CHRIST A MAN OF SORROWS.

Edward Payson, D.D.

IT has been supposed by many that the sufferings of our Lord were rather apparent than real; or at least that His abundant consolations, and His knowledge of the happy consequences which would result from His death, rendered His sorrows comparatively light, and almost converted them to joys; but never was supposition more erroneous. Jesus Christ was as truly a man as either of us, and, as man, He was really susceptible of grief, as keenly alive to pain and reproach, and as much averse from shame and suffering as any of the descendants of Adam. As to divine consolations and supports, they were at all times bestowed on Him in a very sparing manner, and in the season of His greatest extremity entirely withheld; and though a knowledge of the happy consequences which would result from His sufferings rendered Him willing to endure them, it did not, in the smallest degree, take off their edge, or render Him insensible to pain. No, His sufferings, instead of being less, were incomparably greater than they appeared to be. No finite mind can conceive of their extent; nor was any of the human race ever so well entitled to the appellation of the Man of Sorrows as the man Christ Jesus. His sufferings began with His birth, and ended but with His life. It must have been extremely painful to such a person as Christ, to live in a world like this. He was perfectly holy, harmless and undefiled. Of course, He could not look on sin but with the deepest abhorrence. It is that abominable thing which His soul hates. Yet during the whole period of His residence on earth, He was continually surrounded by it, and His feelings were every moment tortured with the hateful sight of human depravity. How much sorrow the sight occasioned Him, we may in some measure learn from the bitter complaints which similar causes extorted from David, Jeremiah, and other ancient saints. But the sufferings of Christ from this cause were incomparably greater than theirs.

Another circumstance which contributed to render our Saviour a man of sorrows, and His life a life of grief, was the reception He met with from those whom He came to save. Had they received Him with that gratitude and respect which He deserved, and permitted Him to rescue them from their miseries, it would have been some alleviation of His sorrows. To see Himself despised, slandered, and persecuted with implacable malice, by the very beings whom He was laboring to save; to see all His endeavors to save them frustrated by their own incorrigible folly and wickedness; to see them by rejecting Him filling up to the brim their cup of criminality and wrath, and sinking into eternal perdition within reach of His vainly offered hand,—to see this, must have been distressing indeed. Yet this Christ saw.

Another circumstance that threw a shade of gloom and melancholy over our Saviour's life, was His clear view and constant anticipation of the dreadful agonies in which it was to terminate. He was not ignorant, as we happily are, of the miseries which were before Him. He could not hope, as we do, when wretched to-day, to be happier to-morrow. Every night, when He lay down to rest, the scourge, the crown of thorns, and the cross, were present to His mind; and on these dreadful objects He every morning opened His eyes, and every morning saw them nearer than before. Every day was to Him like the day of His death, of such a death too as no one ever suffered before or since. How deeply the prospect affected Him is evident from His own language, "I have a baptism to be baptized with, and how am I straitened till it be accomplished!" What was our Saviour's conduct under the pressure of these sorrows? "He was oppressed and afflicted, yet He opened not His mouth. He was brought as a lamb to the slaughter, and as a sheep before her shearers is dumb, so He opened not His mouth."

Was Christ a man of sorrows and acquainted with grief? Then we need not be surprised or offended if we are often called to drink of the cup of sorrows; if we find the world a vale of tears. This is one of the ways in which we must be conformed to our glorious Head. Indeed, His example has sanctified grief, and almost made it pleasant to mourn. One would think that Christians could scarcely wish to go rejoicing through a world which their Master passed through mourning. The path in which we follow Him is bedewed with His tears and stained with His blood. It is true, that from the ground thus watered and fertilized many rich flowers and fruits of paradise spring up to refresh us, in which we may and ought to rejoice. But still our joy should be softened and sanctified by godly sorrow.

When we are partaking of the banquet which His love has spread for us, we should never forget how dearly it was purchased.

> "There's not a gift His hand bestows,
> But cost His heart a groan."

The joy, the honor, the glory through eternity shall be ours; but the sorrows, the sufferings, the agonies which purchased them were all His own.

Was Christ wounded for our transgressions; were the iniquities of all His people laid upon Him; then, surely, our iniquities shall never be laid upon us. He has borne and carried them away. He was made sin for us, that we might be made the righteousness of God in Him. Away then with all guilty unbelieving fears. Whatever your sorrows or trials may be, He knows by experience how to sympathize with you. Has your Heavenly Father forsaken you, so that you walk in darkness and see no light? He well remembers what He felt, when He cried, "My God, my God, why hast thou forsaken me?" Has Satan wounded you with His fiery darts? He remembers how sorely His own heart was bruised when He wrestled with principalities and powers, and crushed the head of the prince of darkness. Are you pressed down with a complication of sorrows, so as to despair even of life? The soul of Christ was once exceeding sorrowful, even unto death. Are you mourning for the danger of unbelieving friends? Christ's own brethren did not believe in Him. Does the world persecute and despise you, or are your enemies those of your own household? Christ was despised and rejected of men, and His own relations stigmatized Him as a madman. Are you suffering under slanderous and unjust accusations? Christ was called a man gluttonous, and a wine-bibber, a friend of publicans and sinners. Are you struggling with the evils of poverty? Jesus had not where to lay His head. Do Christian friends forsake or treat you unkindly? Christ was denied and forsaken by His own disciples. Are you distressed with fears of death? Christ has entered the dark valley that He might destroy death. O, then, banish all your fears. Look at your merciful High Priest who is passed unto the heavens, and triumphantly exclaim with the apostle, Who shall separate us from the love of Christ?

THE DIVINE SYMPATHY.

JOHN R. MACDUFF, D.D.

HERE are God's own words, "I know their sorrows."—Exod. iii. 7. Man cannot say so. There are many sensitive fibres in the soul the best and tenderest *human* sympathy cannot touch. But the PRINCE OF SUFFERERS, He who led the way in the path of sorrow, "knoweth our frame." When crushing bereavement lies like ice on the heart—when the dearest earthly friend cannot enter into the peculiarities of our grief, JESUS *can*, JESUS *does!* He who once bore my *sins* also carried my *sorrows*. That eye, now on the throne, was once dim with weeping! I can think in all my afflictions, "He was afflicted;" in all my tears, "JESUS WEPT."

Israel had long groaned under bondage. God appeared *not* to "*know*" it. He seemed, like Baal, "asleep;" yet at that very moment was His pitying eye wistfully beholding His enslaved people. It was *then* He said, "*I* KNOW *their sorrows!*"

He may *seem* at times thus to forget and forsake us;—leaving us to utter the plaintive cry, "Hath God forgotten to be gracious," when all the while He is bending over us in tenderest love. He often suffers our needs to attain their extremity—that He may stretch forth His succoring hand, and reveal the plenitude of His Grace! "*Ye have seen the end of the Lord, that the Lord is very pitiful and of tender mercy*" (James v. 11).

And "*knowing*" our sorrows, is a blessed guarantee that none will be sent but what He sees to be needful. "I will not," says He, "make a full end of thee, but *I will correct thee* IN MEASURE" (Jer. xxx. 11). All He sends is precisely meted out—wisely apportioned. There is nothing accidental or fortuitous:—no redundant thorn—no superfluous pang. He "*putteth our tears into His bottle*" (Ps. lvi 8). Each one is *counted*—drop by drop—tear by tear;—they are sacred things among the treasures of God!

Suffering believer, the iron may have entered deeply into thy soul; yet rejoice! Great is thine honor—thou art partaker with Christ in His sufferings. Look upwards to this bright Bow encircling thy dark sky! JESUS, a sorrowing, sympathizing Jesus, "knows" thine aching pangs and burning tears, and He will "*come down to deliver thee!*"

And of this divine sympathy we are also assured in the New Testament—"We have not an high priest which cannot be touched with the feeling of our infirmities."—Heb. iv. 15. What an elevating truth. *The Sympathy of the God-Man-Mediator* (the true Bow in the cloud)—*Jesus* in our *sorrows!* What a source of exalted joy to the stript and desolate heart!—what a green pasture to lie down upon, amid the windy storm and tempest, or in the dark and cloudy day.

The sympathy of man is cheering and comforting; but "thus far shalt thou go, and no farther." It is finite—limited—often selfish. There are nameless and numberless sorrows on earth, beyond the reach of all human alleviation.

The sympathy of *Jesus* is alone exalted—pure—infinite—removed from all taint of selfishness. He has Himself passed through every experience of woe. There are no depths of sorrow or anguish into which I can be plunged but His everlasting arms are lower still. He has been called "The great sympathetic nerve of His Church, over which the afflictions and oppressions, and sufferings of His people continually pass." Child of Sorrow! a Human heart beats on the Throne! and He has *thy* name written on that heart. He cares for thee as if none other claimed His regard. As the Great High Priest, He walketh in the midst of his Temple lamps—(His golden candlesticks),—plenishing them, at times, with oil;—trimming them, if need be, at others;—but *all* in order that they may burn with a steadier and purer lustre.

"*He was* IN ALL POINTS *tempted.*" Blessed assurance!—I never can know the sorrow into which the "Man of Sorrow" cannot enter. Ah rather, in the midst of earth's most lacerating trials, let me listen to the unanswerable challenge from the lips of a suffering Saviour—" *Was there ever any sorrow like unto* My *sorrow?*" Yet He refused not to drink the cup of wrath! He shrunk not back from the appointed cross! "He set His face steadfastly to go to Jerusalem;"—and even when He hung upon the bitter tree, He refused the vinegar that would have assuaged the rage of thirst and mitigated physical suffering. Are we tempted at times to murmur under God's afflicting hand? "CONSIDER HIM *that endured, lest ye be weary and faint in your minds...*" Shall we hesitate to bear any trial our Lord and Master sees meet to lay upon us, when we think of the infinitely weightier Cross He so meekly and unrepiningly carried for *us?*

Afflicted one! Have thine eye on this radiant Bow in thy cloud of Sorrow—thou mayest, like the disciples on the Transfiguration-mount, "*fear to enter the cloud*"—but hear the voice issuing from it —"*This is my Beloved Son: hear* HIM."

Jesus speaks through these clouds! He tells us *our* cares are *His* cares; *our* sorrows *His* sorrows. He has some wise and gracious end in every mysterious chastisement. His language is—"*Hear ye the rod and who hath appointed it*" (Micah vi. 9). He has too kind and loving a heart to cause us one needless or superfluous pang.

Oh that we may indeed *hear* the voice out of the cloud, and seek that the trials He sends in love may be greatly sanctified. Let us not dream that affliction of itself is a pathway to Heaven. Clouds do not form the material rainbow. These glorious hues come from the sunbeams alone. Without the latter, we could discern nothing but blackened heavens and dismal rain torrents. It is not because those clad in "white robes" had "come out of *great tribulation*" that they were enjoying the Beatific Presence; but because they had "*washed their robes, and made them white in the blood of the Lamb*" (Rev. vii. 14.) We have only reason to glory in affliction when it has been the means of bringing us nearer the Saviour, and leading us to the opened Fountain.

"Jesus! my only hope Thou art,
Strength of my failing flesh and heart;
Oh! could I catch a smile from Thee,
And drop into Eternity!"

"IF I am asked what is the remedy for the deeper sorrows of the human heart—what a man should chiefly look to in his progress through life as the power to sustain him under trials and enable him manfully to confront his afflictions—I must point to something which in a well-known hymn is called, 'The old, old story,' told in an old, old book, and taught with an old, old teaching, which is the greatest and best gift ever given to mankind."

WM. EWART GLADSTONE.

"WHEN this passing world is done,
When has sunk yon glaring sun,
When we stand with Christ in glory,
Looking o'er life's finished story,
Then, Lord, shall I fully know,
Not till then, how much I owe."

IT is by affliction chiefly that the heart of man is purified and that the thoughts are fixed on a better state.

DR. JOHNSON.

COMFORT FOR THE POOR.

Rev. James Smith, D.D.

"Hearken, my beloved brethren, hath not God chosen the poor of this world rich in faith, and heirs of the kingdom which he hath promised to them that love him?"—James ii. 5.

POVERTY is not spirituality; but sanctified poverty is a great friend to it. Poverty is no sin; but it is sometimes a preventive to sin. Poverty has its temptations; but it has also its consolations. The poor ought not to repine at poverty, because God in his infinite wisdom has appointed it, and is able to render it the greatest blessing. God's chosen are generally found among the poor. Not that he chose them because they were poor; but choosing them in Christ, He appointed them to be poor as the best thing for them. His enemies have their portion in this life: here they have their good things. Not so his children: here they have their evil things, and the best things are to come. The poor Christian has a rich Father in whom to trust; the fullness of Jesus to which to look; the precious promises on which to depend; the Holy Spirit in whom to confide; and a glorious inheritance to anticipate and prepare for. "The kingdom"—grace here and glory hereafter. "The kingdom"—in which Jesus will reign, and where they will be princes, yea, kings and priests. "The kingdom"—prepared for them from the foundation of the world.

My poor brother—my poor sister! look up, look forward. The cottage will soon be exchanged for a mansion, sickness for health, poverty for wealth, sin for holiness, earth for heaven. You will not always be poor; you will not be poor long. Jesus will soon come; and then the meek, the spiritual poor, shall inherit the earth. For you an inheritance is reserved in heaven; for you a mansion is being prepared; for you glory, honor, immortality, even eternal life, are in reserve.

"God hath chosen the foolish things of this world to confound the wise; and God hath chosen the weak things of the world to confound the things which are mighty."—1 Cor. i. 27.

TO A BROTHER DEPARTED.

UNKNOWN.

THOU art gone to thy rest, brother!
   We will not weep for thee;
  For thou art now where oft on earth
   Thy spirit longed to be.

Thou art gone to thy rest, brother!
   Thy toils and cares are o'er,
And sorrow, pain, and suff'ring now
   Shall ne'er distress thee more.

Thou art gone to thy rest, brother!
   Thy sins are all forgiven;
And saints in light have welcomed thee.
   To share the joys of heaven.

Thou art gone to thy rest, brother!
   Death had no sting for thee,
Thy dear Redeemer's might had gained
   For thee the victory.

COMFORT FOR THE WIDOW.

Rev. James Smith, D.D.

"A father of the fatherless, and a judge of the widows, is God in his holy habitation."—Ps. lxviii. 5.

THE widow often feels destitute and desolate; and when she most needs the sympathy of man, she often experiences it least. The God of Israel is the widow's God. He offers to be her husband; to fill the husband's place, and perform the father's part. He says, "*Let thy widows trust in Me.*" As if He had said, "I am able to supply all the widow's needs, to crush all the widow's foes, to sanctify all the widow's sorrows, and to fill the widow's heart with comfort and peace. Let her ask me to do so; let her trust me to do so; let her expect me to do so." My widowed sister! carry all that pains thy heart or depresses thy spirit to Jesus; look to Jesus through thy tears, and for the supply of all thy needs. And if enemies arise, if man would oppress thee, go to Jesus as the judge: He will listen to thee, take the case in hand, carry thy cause for thee, and even turn man's curse into a blessing. Take thy poor fatherless children to Him: put them into His hands, ask Him to adopt them for His own, to manage them for thee, and make them holy, honorable, and useful—a comfort to thee and a blessing to others. You cannot ask too much of Jesus, nor expect too much from Jesus. He will love to hear thee; He will kindly listen to thee; He will value thy confidence; He will crown and reward thy faith. Fret not, fear not: but put Jesus in thy husband's place, and expect Him to do a husband's part. Believe these precious words: "Thy Maker is thy husband; the Lord of hosts is His name: and thy Redeemer the Holy One of Israel; the God of the whole earth shall He be called." Jesus loves to hear the widow's voice, to sympathize with the widow's sorrows, and to answer the widow's prayers.

"Ye shall not afflict any widow or fatherless child. If thou afflict them in any wise, and they cry at all unto me, I will surely hear their cry."—Exod. xxii. 22, 23.

A PARENT'S DEATH.—The death of a parent has been useful. His expiring charge has never been forgotten. The thought of separation forever from one so loved and valued has awakened in the son a salutary fear. Returning from a father's grave, he has met with God, saying, "Wilt thou not from this time cry unto me, My Father! thou art the guide of my youth?" And the death of the parent has proved the life of the child.

WILLIAM JAY.

Look not mournfully into the past—
It comes not back again;
Wisely improve the present—it is thine.
Go forth to meet the shadowy future
Without fear and with a manly heart.

H. W. LONGFELLOW.

A WORD OF WARNING TO MOTHERS.

Rev. Dr. Wm. Anderson.

THE Psalmist says of God, "There is none upon earth that I desire beside Thee," evidently speaking comparatively, and signifying that among many objects desired, God received the supreme place. This is a subject of familiar illustration. But David said something before that: "Whom have I *in heaven* but Thee?" Ah, let the bereaved mother be admonished. If the vision of her child in heaven be more frequent and more endeared to her heart than the vision of the child's Saviour; and much more, if the vision of the former so engross her heart as to exclude the vision of the latter altogether,—I must assure her that heavenly-mindedness such as this will not promote that heavenly meeting on which her hope is set. Her first object of admiring contemplation in heaven must be *her own* Saviour; and her great hope must be, meeting with Him, and seeing Him in His glory, before any meditation on the present happiness of her deceased child be of a sanctifying character; and before any hope of meeting again with that child in heavenly bliss be a hope not to be disappointed. I would express myself tenderly, when it is a bereaved mother's heart which is addressed; but would it be genuine tenderness if it were delusive, flattering unfaithfulness? Hope first in Christ for yourself, and then hope, not for your child's salvation (that is secure), but that you shall enjoy companionship with Him in glory.

THE SHADOW.

Rev. J. S. Meissner.

WE have known what it is to mourn over the loss of beloved children, having accompanied two to their resting-place during our service in this distant land. I was once standing by the grave of my departed children, under a brilliant sun and cloudless sky, when suddenly a light shadow passed over the green turf. Looking up for the cause, I beheld a snow-white gull winging her lofty flight through the air. The thought immediately struck me—Thus it is with the dear objects of my mournful remembrance. Here indeed lies the shadow, but above is the living principle. Nor was the reflection without comfort to my wounded spirit, since of such is the kingdom of heaven.

....

"THY WILL BE DONE."

Rev. Henry Alford, D.D.

I SUPPOSE, when we say every day "Thy will be done," in our Lord's prayer, we mean, "Here I am, dispose of me as Thou wilt." And doubtless such a general feeling is a good and salutary one, an excellent introduction to our daily duties and trials. It may be well, however, to put it sometimes more to the test, and question it somewhat more closely than Christians usually do. Have we reflected, when we thus say, that our heavenly Father's will evidently is, that we should become perfect, as our Saviour did, through *suffering?* Have we made our account, that health and strength, fortune and friends, are all in His hand, suspended in the balance with our eternal welfare? that our Father's care over us is such, that if one of them is seen by Him to outweigh and interfere with our soul's health, He will surely interpose and take it from us? Have we borne in mind that the very day in whose opening hour we kneel in our closets and say, "Thy will be done," may see our whole life's bitterest and dreariest passage,—may behold us stricken down by our Father's judgment, may make the strong man a miserable wreck, the rich man a poor bankrupt, the social man a solitary in the world's wilderness? Do those whose souls are knit in one by love's closest tie of God's own sanctioning, reflect, when they say these words together in the morning, that one may be taken before the evening, and the other left, to try how deep the resignation to God's will really was? Does it ever cross the mother's mind, as she teaches the blessed prayer to her babe, fresh risen and bright in the morning, that, ere night His will may indeed be done upon both,—that she may be striving to suffer it on earth, while her darling is doing it in heaven? Far be it from me to dash or imbitter the heart's joys, pure and holy like these. But, O brethren, such thoughts as these will not dash nor imbitter joy. Then it is imbittered, when the soul has made her nest and her home here below, has gazed on her beloved object insatiably, and never thought of God—has used the world as if she possessed it—and some hour when all is fair and serene, in the midst of much treasure laid up for many years, comes the fatal stroke, unlooked for, unaccountable, irremediable.

One such record I have seen engraved on the tomb of a beloved child: "The miserable parents ventured their all on this frail bark, and the wreck was total." This is bitterness indeed—but to see all our comforts coming day by day from God's hand—to live in the continual consciousness that He who to-day tries our gratitude by giving them, may to-morrow try our faith by withdrawing them,—this is not to poison joy, but to enhance it tenfold—it is not to blight the fair plant, but to give it strength and endurance, so that it shall flourish not only in the sunshine but in the storm; not only in the morn and promise of life, but amidst disappointment and decay and death.

"Thy will be done." And what if that will be not only afflictive, but dark and mysterious also? What if God be pleased to wound just where we believed we wanted cherishing? What if to the weak and shortsighted eye of sense He even seem as a tyrant, delighting in doing us harm, striking us when we are down, yea, forgetting His own promises and breaking His everlasting covenant? O brethren, I know how hard it is in such cases to feel from the heart this prayer—how the words seem almost to choke us in utterance, and the petition to be more than we ever can really attain to. But let us not, for all that, relinquish our trust in our Father's love and care of us. What He does we know not, we know not now; but we shall know hereafter. I remember, on one of those glorious days of all but cloudless sunshine, with which some of our summers abound, passing in view of a well-known line of bare and majestic downs, then basking in the full beams of noon. But on one face of the hill rested a mass of deep and gloomy shadow. On searching for its cause, I at length discovered one little speck of cloud, bright as light, floating in the clear blue above; this it was which cast on the hill-side that ample track of gloom. And what I saw was an image of Christian sorrow. Dark and cheerless often as it is, and unaccountable as it passes over our earthly path, in heaven its token shall be found; and it shall be known to have been but as a shadow of His brightness, whose name is Love. In this case too, then, His will be done; rest in the Lord, and He shall make it plain. It is good to wait; it lifts men above the world and out of themselves, and they grow in the knowledge of their Father and God, and in ripeness for the day when He shall be revealed.

"WHAT a superlatively grand and consoling idea is that of death! Without this radiant idea, this delightful morning star, indicating that the luminary of eternity is about to rise, life would, to my view, darken into midnight melancholy. Oh! the expectation of living here, and living thus always, would be indeed a prospect of overwhelming despair. But thanks to that fatal decree that dooms us to die; thanks to that gospel which opens up the vista of an endless life; and thanks, above all, to that Saviour Friend who has promised to conduct all the faithful through the sacred trance of death into scenes of Paradise and everlasting delight."

JOHN FOSTER.

A WORD TO PARENTS.

Rev. Henry Allon, D.D.

WHAT a deep religiousness appeals to us in a child! How simply it prays—how implicitly it believes—how reverently it feels! It has to learn to disbelieve. What a lesson to our hard, unspiritual, unbelieving nature is the simple, pure, and beautiful religiousness of a child. Thank God, our seared, battered hearts come day by day into contact with the gentle innocence, purity, and love of children. Thank God, we are all children before we are men and women. Happy is he who is wise enough, and humble enough, to learn the lessons that his child teaches him.

No wonder that Christ himself takes a little child and makes him the exemplar of His new kingdom. While the worldly teacher of a child is ever summoning him to manhood, the spiritual teacher of a man is ever recalling him to childhood. Christ bids us return to the guileless consciousness, the pure feelings of childhood. We must re-live our child-life; reproduce our child consciousness; realize again the sinless and simple experience of childhood; become as we were when little children—humble, docile, pure, believing, prayerful—or we shall be unable to "receive" the kingdom of heaven, and unfitted to "enter" therein.

It is but natural, therefore, that, in the Bible,

children should be represented as the very choicest of God's gifts. They are God's "heritage,"—that which He gives as our very richest portion in life. How enthusiastically the Bible always speaks of them as such! We never meet with a dubious estimate of them, with a faltering congratulation. Everywhere they are spoken of rapturously and exultingly, as the very crown of earthly blessings. Like all life, they come more directly than other things from the hand of God Himself. They are His precious gift—His "heritage."

We do not always so conceive of them. Pure, unselfish, and self-sacrificing as parental love is—the holiest and most perfect of all our human affections—even it is capable of being deteriorated by circumstances, corrupted by wrong and sinful feeling. It is not every parent that receives a child as God's "heritage." A precious thing it may be to him, but not a gift from God. Other feelings of joy it may awaken, and yet not a feeling of religious gratitude; other obligations it may create, and yet not the obligation to learn and to teach religious lessons. We may "take the child and nurse it" for our own parental joy—for our social, or commercial, or ambitious purposes—and yet not "nurse it for God." Every feeling of joy may be awakened by it except religious joy; every sense of obligation except religious obligation. It ought to expel all selfishness, to purify and intensify conjugal love, and to multiply it by a new affection—and yet selfishness may feel a child a restriction upon social pleasure, a tax upon worldly gain. It ought to inspire thoughtfulness and faith;—it is an entrustment so high and holy—a soul to train for God, and heaven, and eternity;—an entrustment accompanied by great promise, connected with the highest joys and with the greatest destinies; —and yet the highest thoughts and purposes inspired by it may be selfish and earthly; or, if pious feeling is excited by it, it may be only misgiving and fear—an unbelieving, godless feeling, that, almost as a matter of course, it will grow up wicked, and need conversion in adult life.

THE little graves, alas! how many they are! The mourners above them, how vast the multitude! Brothers, sisters, I am one with you, I belong to you. Those waxen folded hands, that still breast so often pressed to your own, those sleep-bound eyes which have been so full of love and life, that sweet, unmoving, alabaster face—ah! we have all looked upon them, and they have made us one and made us better. There is no fountain which the angel of healing troubles with his restless and life-giving wings so constantly as the fountain of tears, and only those too lame and bruised to bathe miss the blessed influence.

DR. J. G. HOLLAND.

OUR trials are medicines which our gracious and wise Physician prescribes because *we need* them, and he proportions the frequency and the weight of them to what the case requires. Let us trust in his skill, and thank him for his prescriptions.

JOHN NEWTON.

ONE LESS AT HOME—ONE MORE IN HEAVEN.
Unknown.

   One less at home!
The charmed circle broken—a dear face
Missed day by day from its accustomed place,
But cleansed, and saved, and perfected by grace!
   One more in Heaven!

   One less at home!
One voice of welcome hushed and evermore
One farewell word spoken; on the shore
Where parting comes not, one soul landed more —
   One more in Heaven!

   One more at home!
This is not home, where, cramped in earthly mold,
Our sight of Christ is dim—our love is cold,
But there, where face to face we shall behold,
   Is home and Heaven!

   One less on earth!
Its pain, its sorrow, and its toil to share;
One less the pilgrims daily cross to bear;
One more the crown of ransomed souls to wear,
   At home in Heaven!

   One more in Heaven!
Another thought to brighten cloudy days,
Another theme of thankfulness and praise,
Another link on high our souls to raise
   To home and Heaven!

   One more at home!
That home where separation cannot be,
That home where none are missed eternally,
Lord Jesus, grant us all a place with Thee,
   At home in Heaven!

BENEFICENT DESIGN OF AFFLICTION.

Rev. Robert Trench, M.A.

IN the world in which we dwell trouble and death are no strangers. Few, indeed are the families into which these unwelcome visitors have not found an entrance. However long the beneficent Creator may give them health and prosperity they are none the less exposed to the calamities which others around them have endured. Unexpectedly, the clear and cloudless sky, which gave promise of a beautiful day, may soon be overcast, and a storm suddenly burst forth, leaving destruction everywhere in its track. Without any warning, the untimely frost may nip the young bud and the tender blossom, and our expectations of a fruitful autumn may soon be blasted. Exemption in the past from affliction is no argument that we shall always be exempted in the future. Speedily the child who romped about the household—whose presence shone like a sunbeam through the dwelling—whose rosy cheek and increasing vigor inspired the hope of a long life, may be snatched away by the rude hand of death. The light of our eyes may be extinguished by some sudden darkness, and the children may soon miss the tenderness and soothing love of one whom they can never expect to see again on earth. The anxious father may soon require to commit to the "Husband of the widow, and the

Father of the fatherless," those from whom, in this life, he is about to be separated for ever.

By the majority of families such events do not need to be anticipated. In some form or other, they have already happened. Since, therefore, there is nothing we may more surely expect than "a day of trouble," it is well for us not to disregard the trials of others, that we may not be impatient under our own afflictions, or unsatisfied murmurers when death removes from us the objects of our warmest love.

Trouble and death seize upon us by God's appointment. These are the penalties attached to sin. In His infinite mercy, He seeks to turn them into channels through which spiritual blessings may flow. They are always inflicted not in anger, but in love, and are designed to bring back the unbelieving to the favor of God, and to refine, purify, and prepare His own people for the fellowship of the redeemed in heaven. With regard to the first, in whatever form trials may come, the end the great loving Father has in view is to lead his erring offspring to thoughtfulness, repentance, and reformation. "I smote you with blasting, with mildew, and with hail, in all the labor of your hands; *yet ye turned not to me*, saith the Lord." Tender, yet awful, are words like these! "Turn ye, turn ye," is His earnest entreaty, and when treaty fails, He lifts the rod and strikes. Reader, has your life been spent in sin? Have you been careless in regard to your best interest? Have you been selfish and self-indulgent—caring nothing for the God of love? Have you been living without Christ—a stranger to His brotherly sympathy, and a despiser of His mercy?

Do not wonder, then that God has lifted His rod and smitten you. Do not imagine that He *hates* you because He has sent trouble and death into your domestic circle. You are mourning—perhaps you are murmuring—perhaps you are saying, "Such things must happen; we must yield; we cannot help ourselves." O see the mercy of God in your trials! He is seeking to redeem you from neglect of your eternal interests, and from indifference to His honor and glory. He seeks your highest well-being. He is watching with intense interest the effect produced upon your mind and heart by these severe and crushing blows, and upon your first motion towards Him to express regret for the past, He will run to meet you; clasp you in the arms of His love; clothe you with the best robe; put a ring on your hand, and shoes on your feet, and make you a partaker of all the honors and privileges which the members of His family enjoy. Here, then, is *your* consolation. Your trials have been sent in mercy. See that they do not harden your heart and drive you further from God. Return to the great loving-hearted Father, and you shall never cease to rejoice that you have been brought back, even though it has been through a fiery furnace. "Call upon me in the day of trouble; I will deliver thee, and thou shalt glorify me."

As to His own people, God deals with them not merely in mercy, but with the greatest parental love. They are His children, and accordingly He addresses them: "My son, despise not thou the chastening of the Lord, nor faint when thou art rebuked of Him: for whom the Lord *loveth* He chasteneth, and scourgeth every son whom He receiveth." Purification, refinement, elevation of the spiritual faculties, are the ends He seeks when He sends trouble and death upon them. Reader, have you met with worldly losses? Have your children been swept away by the pestilence? Or have they drooped, and withered, and died? Have you had severe domestic trials in which "living griefs" were worse to bear than even the ravages of death? Do not think God has forsaken you because of these things. You may have been severely afflicted. The billows may have passed over your soul. The very flames of the fire may have kindled upon you. What then? Perhaps you were becoming too worldly and needed all you have endured to enable you to set your affections on things above. You may rest assured that whatever may have been your trials, however severe and difficult to bear, the one grand end your Father has in view is to draw you nearer to himself; to make you wiser and happier, and better qualified for the purity of the heavenly home. You may not soon or easily perceive either the goodness or wisdom of His procedure in these troubles and bereavements; but for the present you must "walk by faith not by sight." Patiently wait and you shall see the glory of God. Call upon Him in your "day of trouble," and He will disclose to you in due time, His great purposes, both in regard to yourself and your loved ones. Remember, infinite wisdom is at work on your behalf. Can you then murmur or question God's plan of operation? Remember, also, infinite goodness is at work on your behalf. Can you then imagine that God hates you, and is plotting your ruin? Remember, still further, that infinite power is at work on your behalf. How, then, can any real harm befall you?

When you reflect that all these divine attributes are exerted on your behalf, how can you doubt that your highest good will be secured?

Listen to His voice while He speaks to you through these afflictions, and drink at this well of consolation—"Fear not; for I have redeemed thee, I have called thee by name; thou art mine. When thou passest through the waters I will be with thee; when thou walkest through the fire, thou shalt not be burnt; neither shall the flame kindle upon thee. For I am the Lord thy God, the Holy One of Israel, thy Saviour."

....

OUR EVENING STAR IN HEAVEN AFAR.

"CHRISTIAN TREASURY."

SHE was "the evening star" I thought would shine
 Upon my path, as I, with years decline—
Thought I should watch its lustre softer glow,
Cheering my weary pilgrimage below;
But God hast my bright and gentle star
    In heaven afar.

She was my flower: the sad pathway of life,
So full, to sinful man, of care and strife,
Was by her presence stripped of many a thorn,
Making my trials easier to be borne.
My flower is now in realms of holy light,
    In glory bright.

Yes, she is there; for, while on earth in pain,
She loved supremely her Redeemer's name;

Now she is with Him, near His throne she stands,
Rests in His arms, one of His folded lambs.
Soon shall we meet before that glorious throne
                My little one.

Yes, there's my child; I see, with eye of faith,
Her happy spirit free from sin and death;
She is a jewel on her Saviour's brow;
Low at His feet her crown she loves to throw;
While He, enthroned in love and mercy mild,
                Smiles on my child.

Shall I then grieve, my precious one is where
She doth the golden crown and white robe wear?
No; rather would I joy that she is free,
And wait my Father's summons patiently,
To join with her the heavenly blessed throng,
                In glorious song.

THE MOTHER'S COMFORT.

Miss Jessie Blevin.

SOME day, O lonely mother,
  You will find the child you miss,
  And your heart will feel the rapture
  Of touch and voice and kiss;
And when mid fields of glory,
  You greet your child once more,
Earth-shadows will have vanished
  In the light of that blest shore.

HOME BEREAVEMENTS.

Henry Ward Beecher.*

WE are joined together, many of us, by a common experience. Many of us have met in each others' houses and in each others' company on just such errands of grief and sympathy and Christian triumph as this. How many of us have sent children forward; and how many of us feel to-day that all things are for our sakes; and that those things which for the present are not joyous but grievous, nevertheless work in us the peaceable fruit of righteousness! So we stand in what may be called a relationship of grief. We are knit together and brought into each other's company by the ministration of grief, made Christian and blessed.

To be sure, if we were to ask this life what would be best, there is no father, there is no mother, who would not plead with all the strength which lies in natural affection, "Spare me, and spare mine." For the outward man this is reasonable and unrebukable; and yet, if it be overruled by Him who loves us even better than He loves His own life, then there comes the revelation of another truth: namely, that the things which are seen are the unreal things, and that the real things are the things which are invisible.

---

* Remarks made at the funeral of a child in Plymouth Church, Brooklyn.

When our children that are so dear to us are plucked out of our arms, and carried away, we feel, for the time being, that we have lost them, because our body does not triumph; but are they taken from our inward man? Are they taken from that which is to be saved—the spiritual man? Are they taken from memory? Are they taken from love? Are they taken from the scope and reach of the imagination, which, in its sanctified form, is only another name of faith? Do we not sometimes dwell with them more intimately than we did when they were with us on earth? The care of them is no longer ours, that love-burden we bear no longer, since they are with the angels of God and with God; and we shed tears over what seems to be our loss; but do they not hover in the air over our heads? And to-day could the room hold them all?

As you recollect, the background of the Sistine Madonna, at Dresden (in some respects the most wonderful picture of maternal love which exists in the world), for a long time was merely dark; and an artist, in making some repairs, discovered a cherub's face in the grime of that dark background; and being led to suspect that the picture had been overlaid by time and neglect, commenced cleansing it; and as he went on, cherub after cherub appeared, until it was found that the Madonna was on a background made up wholly of little heavenly cherubs.

Now, by nature motherhood stands against a dark background; but that background being cleaned by the touch of God, and by the cleansing hand of faith, we see that the whole heaven is full of little cherub faces. And to-day it is not this little child alone that we look at, which we see only in the outward guise; we look upon a background of children innumerable, each one as sweet to its mother's heart as this child has been to its mother's heart, each one as dear to the clasping arms of its father as this child has been to the clasping arms of its father; and it is in good company. It is in a spring-land. It is in a summer-world. It is with God. You have given it back to Him who lent it to you.

Now, the giving back is very hard, but you cannot give back to God all that you received with your child. You cannot give back to God those springs of new and deeper affection which were awakened by the coming of the little one. You cannot give back to God the experiences which you have had in dwelling with your darling. You cannot give back to God the hours which, when you look upon them now, seem like one golden chain of linked happiness. You are better, you are riper, you are richer, even in this hour of bereavement, than you were. God gave; and he has not taken away except in outward form. He holds, he keeps, he reserves, he watches, he loves. You shall have again that which you have given back to him only outwardly.

Meanwhile the key is in your hand; and it is not a black iron key; it is a golden key of faith and love. This little child has taught you to follow it. There will not be a sunrise or a sunset when you will not in imagination go through the gate of heaven after it. There is no door so fast that a mother's love and a father's love will not open it and follow a beloved child. And so, by its ministration, this child will guide you a thousand times into a realization of the great spirit-land, and into a faith of the invisible, which will make you as much larger as it makes you less dependent on the body, and more rich in the fruitage of the spirit.

To-day, then, we have an errand of thanksgiving. We thank God for sending this little gift into this household. We thank God for the light which he kindled here, and which burned with so pure a flame, and taught so sweet a lesson. And we thank God, that, when this child was to go to a better place, it walked so few steps, for so few hours, through pain. Men who look on the dark side shake the head, and say, "Oh, how sudden!" but I say, Since it was to go God be thanked that it was permitted to pass through so brief a period of suffering; that there were no long weeks or months of gradual decay and then a final extinction; that out of the fullness of health it dropped into the fullness of heaven, leaving its body as it lies before you to-day, a thing of beauty. Blessed be God for such mercy in the ministration of sickness and of departure.

I appreciate your sorrow, having myself often gone through this experience; and I can say there is no other experience which throws such a light upon the storm cloud. We are never ripe till we have been made so by suffering. We belong to those fruits which must be touched by frost before they lose their sourness and come to their sweetness. I see the goodness of God in this dispensation as pointing us toward heaven and immortality. In this bereavement there is cause for rejoicing; for such it is that you and your child shall meet again never to be separated.

THE DEAD ARE WITH US.

Rev. S. Irenæus Prime, D.D.

MILLIONS of spiritual beings walk the earth unseen, both when we wake and when we sleep. And we believe, with many others, that if we were suddenly divested of this mortal, we should find ourselves in a vast amphitheatre reaching to the throne of God, filled with spirits, the unseen witnesses, the cloud of witnesses of which we are encompassed continually. There is a place where the Most High dwells in light that no man can approach, where the darkness of excessive brightness hangs over and around his throne, making *Heaven*, as Heaven is not elsewhere in the Universe of God. But neither time nor place may with propriety be affirmed of spiritual existence. * * It is, therefore, scriptural and rational to suppose that the spirits of our departed friends are around by day and night; not away from God; His presence fills immensity; He is everywhere present. If an angel or the soul should take the wings of the morning, and dwell in the uttermost part of the sea, there to be with us or with those we love, even there the gracious presence of God would dwell, and the sanctified would find Heaven as blessed and glorious as in the temple of which the Lamb is the Light.

ONE LINK GONE.

UNKNOWN.

TAKE the pillows from the cradle
  Where the little sufferer lay;
Draw the curtain, close the shutters,
  Shut out every beam of day.

Spread the pall upon the table,
  Place the lifeless body there;
Back from off the marble features
  Lay the auburn curls with care.

With its little blue-veined fingers
  Crossed upon its sinless breast,
Free from care, and pain, and anguish,
  Let the infant cherub rest.

Smooth its little shroud about it;
  Pick the toys from off the floor,
They, with all their sparkling beauty,
  Ne'er can charm their owner more.

Take the little shoes and stockings
  From the doting mother's sight;
Pattering feet no more will need them,
  Walking in the fields of light.

Parents, faint and worn with watching
  Through the long, dark night of grief,
Dry your tears and soothe your sighing—
  Gain a respite of relief.

Mother, care is no more needed
  To allay the rising moan;
And though you perchance may leave it,
  It can never be alone.

Angels bright will watch beside it
  In its quiet, holy slumber
Till the morning, then awake it
  To a place among their number.

Thus a golden link is broken
  In the chain of earthly bliss,
Thus the distance shorter making
  'Twixt the brighter world and this.

HEAVEN IS OUR HOME.

E. L. Bulwer.

HAPPY, thrice happy, he who relies on the eternity of the soul; who believes, as the loved fall one after one from his side, that they have returned to their native country; who feels that each treasure of knowledge he attains, he carries with him through illimitable being; who sees in virtue the essence and the element of the world he is to inherit. He comforts his weariness amid the storms of time, by seeing, far across the melancholy seas, the heaven he will reach at last; he deems that every struggle has its assured reward, and every sorrow has its balm; he knows, however forsaken or bereaved below, that he never can be alone, and never deserted; that above him is the protection of eternal power, and the mercy of eternal love! Ah, well said the dreamer of philosophy, "How much HE knew of the human heart, who first called God our Father!"

TO A FATHER BEREFT OF A SON.

RALPH ERSKINE.

I CANNOT, I dare not say, weep not. Jesus wept at the grave of Lazarus, and surely, he allows you to weep; surely, there is a "needs be" that you feel a heaviness under such a trial. But O, let hope and joy mitigate your heaviness. I know not how this, or a former trial, shall work for your good, but it is enough that God knows. He that said, "All things shall work together for good to them that love God," excepts not from this promise the sorest trial. You devoted your son to God; you cannot doubt that he accepted the surrender. If he has been hid in the chamber of the grave from the evil of sin, and from the evil of suffering, let not your eye be evil, when God is good. What you chiefly wished for him, and prayed on his behalf, was spiritual and heavenly blessings. If the greatest thing you wished for is accomplished, at the season and in the manner Infinite Wisdom saw best, refuse not to be comforted; you know not what work and joy have been waiting for him in that world, where God's "servants shall serve him." Should you sorrow immoderately when you have such ground of hope that he, and his other parent, are rejoicing in what you lament? I know that nature will feel; and I believe suppressing its emotions in such cases is not profitable, either to soul or body; but I trust, though you mourn, God will keep you from murmuring, and that you shall have to glory in your tribulation and infirmity, while the power of Christ is manifested thereby.

WEEP NOT FOR HER!

D. M. Moir.

WEEP not for her!—Oh she was far too fair,
    Too pure to dwell on this guilt-tainted
      earth!
The sinless glory, and the golden air
    Of Zion, seemed to claim her from her birth—
A spirit wandering from its native zone:
    Which soon discov'ring took her for its own,
                Weep not for her!

Weep not for her!—her span was like the sky;
    Whose thousand stars shine beautiful and bright;
Like flowers that know not what it is to die!
    Like long-link'd shadeless months of Polar light;
Like music floating o'er a waveless lake,
    While Echo answers from the flowery brake,
                Weep not for her!

Weep not for her!—She died in early youth,
    Ere hope had lost its rich romantic hues;
When human bosoms seem'd the homes of truth,
    And earth still gleam'd with beauty's radiant
      dews,
Her summer prime waned not to days that freeze,
    Her wine of life was run not to the lees:
                Weep not for her!

Weep not for her!—By fleet or slow decay,
    It never griev'd her bosom's core to mark
The playmates of her childhood wane away,
    Her prospects wither, or her hopes grow dark:—

Translated by her God with spirits shriven,
    She passed as 'twere in smiles from earth to heaven:
                Weep not for her!

Weep not for her!—It was not hers to feel
    The miseries that corrode amassing years,
'Gainst dreams of baffled bliss the heart to steel,
    To wander sad down Age's vale of tears,
As whirl the wither'd leaves from Friendship's tree,
    And on earth's wintry world alone to be:
                Weep not for her!

Weep not for her!—She is an angel now,
    And treads the sapphire floors of Paradise,—
All darkness wiped from her refulgent brow,
    Sin, sorrow, suffering, banished from her eyes;
Victorious over death, to her appear
    The vista'd joys of Heaven's eternal year:
                Weep not for her!

Weep not for her!—Her memory is the shrine.
    Of pleasing thoughts, soft as the scent of flowers,
Calm as on windless eve the sun's decline,
    Sweet as the song of birds among the bowers,
Rich as a rainbow with its hues of light,
    Pure as the moonshine of an autumn night:
                Weep not for her!

Weep not for her! There is no cause for woe;
    But rather nerve the spirit, that it walk
Unshrinking o'er the thorny paths below,
    And from earth's low defilements keep thee back:
So, when a few fleet severing years have flown,
    She'll meet thee at Heaven's gate, and lead thee on!
                Weep not for her!

CONSOLATION FOR THE LONELY.

Mary Howitt.

THERE is a land where beauty cannot fade,
    Nor sorrow dim the eye;
  Where true love shall not droop, nor be dismayed,
    And none shall ever die!
    Where is that land, O where?
    For I would hasten there!
    Tell me,—I fain would go,
For I am wearied with a heavy woe!
The beautiful have left me all alone;
The true, the tender from my path are gone!
    O, guide me with thy hand,
    If thou dost know that land,
For I am burdened with oppressive care,
And I am weak and fearful with despair!
    Where is it? tell me where.

Friend, thou must trust in Him who trod before
    The desolate paths of life;
Must bear in meekness, as He meekly bore,
    Sorrow, and pain, and strife!
    Think how the Son of God
    These thorny paths hath trod;
    Think how He longed to go,
Yet tarried out for thee the appointed woe:
Think of His weariness in places dim,
When no man comforted or cared for Him!

Think of the blood, like sweat,
    With which His brow was wet,
Yet how He prayed, unaided and alone,
In that great agony, "Thy will be done!"
    Friend, do not thou despair,
Christ from His heaven of heavens will hear thy
        prayer!

ON THE DEATH OF A YOUNG GIRL.

WILLIAM H. BURLEIGH.

SHE hath gone in the spring-time of life,
    Ere her sky had been dimmed by a cloud,
    While her heart with the rapture of love was
        yet rife,
And the hopes of her youth were unbowed—
From the lovely, who loved her too well;
    From the heart that had grown to her own;
From the sorrow which late o'er her young spirit fell,
    Like a dream of the night she hath flown;
And the earth hath received to its bosom its trust—
    Ashes to ashes, and dust unto dust.

The spring, in its loveliness dressed,
    Will return with its music-winged hours,
And, kissed by the breath of the sweet southwest,
    The buds shall burst out in flowers;
And the flowers her grave-sod above,
    Though the sleeper recks it not,
Shall thickly be strown by the hand of Love,
    To cover with beauty the spot—
Meet emblems are they of the pure one and bright,
    Who faded and fell with so early a blight.

Ay, the spring will return—but the blossom
  That bloomed in our presence the sweetest,
By the spoiler is borne from the cherishing bosom,
  The loveliest of all and the fleetest!
The music of stream and of bird
  Shall come back when the winter is o'er;
But the voice that was dearest to us shall be heard
  In our desolate chamber no more!
The sunlight of May on the waters shall quiver,
  The light of her eye hath departed forever!

As the bird to its sheltering nest,
  When the storm on the hills is abroad,
So her spirit hath flown from this world of unrest
  To repose on the bosom of God!
Where the sorrows of earth never more
  May fling o'er its brightness a stain;
Where in rapture and love, it shall never adore,
  With a gladness unmingled with pain;
And its thirst shall be slaked by the waters which
      spring
  Like a river of light, from the throne of the King!

There is weeping on earth for the lost!
  There is bowing in grief to the ground!
But rejoicing and praise 'mid the sanctified host,
  For a spirit in paradise found!
Though brightness hath passed from the earth,
  Yet a star is new-born in the sky,
And a soul hath gone home to the land of its birth,
  Where are pleasures and fullness of joy!
And a new harp is strung, and a new song is given
  To the breezes that float o'er the gardens of heaven.

ON THE DEATH OF A SON.

ARCHBISHOP FENELON.

THE great loss which you have sustained escapes not my sight; but God has taken what belonged to him, and not to us. Who dare say to Him, Why hast thou done thus? This language is far from you. You know He is not accountable for what He doeth. His good pleasure is the supreme reason; besides, we may always see, in the most severe strokes of His fatherly hand, a secret design of mercy. He takes away in a happy hour certain weak men, whom, perhaps, the delusions of the world might have caused to err. He is hasted away to prevent a miserable fall. O what wonders shall we see in the next world, that escape us in this! then shall we sing the song of joy and everlasting thanks, for events that made us weep here. Alas! in the present darkness, we know not what is really good for us, or really evil. If God should do what pleases us, all would be lost. He saves us, by breaking our chains, and making us sorrowful. The same stroke that saves him we love, by taking him from the midst of iniquity, prepares us by his death for our own. What can we desire for ourselves and our friends in this vain and corrupted world? If it be true that faith and love constitute the life of our soul, can we weep because God loves us better than we know how to love ourselves; shall we lament His taking out of temptation and sin, those that are dear to us? Does He hurt us, by contracting the days of misery? Do we desire a continuance of danger, and greater temptations? We would have every thing that flatters self-love, in order to make us forget ourselves in this place of exile. Your son was prosperous in the midst of a corrupted world; it is this afflicts you, in the loss of him. But his success was, perhaps, the cause that the thread of his life was cut short by a design replete with mercy, both for him and his friends. Let us, then, adore God, and be silent. Nothing but prayer can comfort us. As soon as we are with God, by an union of heart in the simple view of faith, we are in prayer. And every occupation, even in the most holy things, that does not place us in this presence, and this society of love, is rather a study than a prayer. At this time nothing but the society of the true Comforter can comfort us. Let us, then, rest in silence; He will comfort us, and we shall find all in Him alone. Blessed are those who desire no other comfort! This is pure and inexhaustible.

JESUS IS DRAWING.

WILLIAM LUFF.

STRAYING and playing, our journey delaying,
   Often we linger for blossoms of gold:
   In danger of falling, while Jesus is calling,
Craving and seeking each flower we behold.

Is our heart breaking. to find Jesus taking
   All the sweet bloom we have plucked by the way?
Is he alluring—our laggard steps curing?
   Let us come nearer as fadeth the day.

DEATH OF THE FIRST-BORN.

WILLIS GAYLORD CLARK.

YOUNG mother, he is gone!
    His dimpled cheek no more will touch
        thy breast;
  No more the music-tone
Float from his lips, to thine all fondly pressed;
His smiles and happy laugh are lost to thee;
Earth must his mother and his pillow be.

    His was the morning hour,
And he hath passed in beauty from the day,
    A bud, not yet a flower,
Torn, in its sweetness, from the parent's spray;
The death-wind swept him to his soft repose,
As frost, in spring-time, blights the early rose.

    Never on earth again
Will his rich accents charm thy listening ear,
    Like some Æolian strain,
Breathing at eventide serene and clear;
His voice is choked in dust, and on his eyes
The unbroken seal of peace and silence lies.

    And from thy yearning heart,
Whose inmost core was warm with love for him,
    A gladness must depart,
And those kind eyes with many tears be dim;
While lonely memories, an unceasing train,
Will turn the raptures of the past to pain.

Yet, mourner, while the day
Rolls like the darkness of a funeral by,
And hope forbids one ray
To stream athwart the grief-discolored sky;
There breaks upon thy sorrow's evening gloom
A trembling lustre from beyond the tomb.

'Tis from the better land!
There, bathed in radiance that around them springs,
Thy loved one's wings expand;
As with the choiring cherubim he sings,
And all the glory of God can see,
Who said, on earth, to children, "Come to me."

Mother, thy child is blessed:
And though his presence may be lost to thee,
And vacant leave thy breast,
And missed, a sweet load from thy parent knee;
Though tones familiar from thine ear have passed,
Thou'lt meet thy first-born with his Lord at last.

THE MOURNING MOTHER.

BISHOP DOANE.

O WHO shall tell what fearful pangs
That mother's heart are rending,
As o'er her infant's little grave
Her wasted form is bending;
From many an eye that weeps to-day
Delight may beam to-morrow;
But she—her precious babe is not!
And what remains but sorrow?

Bereavèd one! I may not chide
    Thy tears and bitter sobbing,—
Weep on! 'twill cool that burning brow,
    And still that bosom's throbbing:
Be not thine such grief as theirs
    To whom no hope is given,—
Snatched from the world, its sins and snares,
    Thy infant rests in heaven.

THE DEPARTED WIFE.

JOHN NEWTON.

YES, she is absent! she who was to me the light and music of my happy home. It was her smile that made this house so gay, her voice that made it eloquent with joy. Her very tread had life and gladness in it. But 'tis gone, and silence fills her place, and solitude spreads like a shadow over the very walls. Not a place, chair, or book, is what it was when she was here. Alas! how fondly do we concentrate our happiness in one beloved form! a human form so perishably frail! On that one form we staked our earthly joy. In that one life we lived. It was our world; that gone, our sun is darkened, and the scene, of late so full of beauty, is rife with desolation. From the dark ruins of our withered love, methinks there comes a voice in unison with thine, eternal Father! "*Set your affections upon things above*, lay up your treasure *there!*" and not beneath: earth is too treacherous for so vast a trust!

ON THE DEATH OF A SON.

W. B. O. PEABODY.

I NEVER trusted to have lived
    To bid farewell to thee,
And almost said, in agony,
    It ought not so to be;
I hoped that thou within the grave
    My weary head shouldst lay,
And live beloved, when I was gone,
    For many a happy day.

With trembling hand, I vainly tried
    Thy dying eyes to close;
And almost envied, in that hour,
    Thy calm and deep repose;
For I was left in loneliness,
    With pain and grief oppressed,
And thou wast with the sainted,
    Where the weary are at rest.

Yes, I am sad and weary now,
    But let me not repine,
Because a spirit, loved so well,
    Is earlier blessed than mine;
My faith may darken as it will,
    I shall not much deplore,
Since *thou art where the ills of life*
    Can never reach thee more.

MOURN NOT THE DEAD.

Eliza Cook.

Mourn not the dead—shed not a tear
    Above the moss-stained sculptured stone,
  But weep for those whose living woes,
    Still yield the bitter, rending groan.
Grieve not to see the eyelids close
  In rest that has no fevered start,
Wish not to break the deep repose
  That curtains round the pulseless heart.
But keep thy pity for the eyes
  That pray for night, yet fear to sleep,
Lest wilder, sadder visions rise
  Than those o'er which they waking weep.
Mourn not the dead—'tis they alone
  Who are the peaceful and the free;
The purest olive branch is known
  To twine about the cypress tree.
Crime, pride, and passion hold no more
  The willing or the struggling slave;
The throbbing pangs of earth are o'er,
  And hatred dwells not in the grave.
The world may pour its venomed blame
  And fiercely spurn the shroud-wrapped bier,
Some few may call upon the name,
  And sigh to meet a "dull, cold ear."
But vain the scorn that would offend,
  In vain the lips that would beguile;

The coldest foe, the warmest friend,
   Are mocked by Death's unchanging smile.
The only watchword that can tell
   Of peace and freedom won by all,
Is echoed by the rolling bell,
   And traced upon the sable pall.

GRIEF WAS SENT THEE FOR THY GOOD.
T. H. Bayley.

SOME there are who seem exempted
   From the doom incurred by all;
Are they not more sorely tempted?
Are they not the first to fall?
As a mother's firm denial
Checks her infant's wayward mood,
   Wisdom lurks in every trial—
   Grief was sent thee for thy good.
In the scenes of former pleasure,
Present anguish hast thou felt?
   O'er thy fond heart's dearest treasure,
As a mourner hast thou knelt?
In the hour of deep affliction,
Let no impious thought intrude—
   Meekly bow with this conviction,
   Grief was sent thee for thy good.

THE Lord blows off the blossoms of our hopes in this life, and lops the branches of our worldly joys to the very root, on purpose that they should not thrive. Lord, spoil my fool's heaven for this life that I may be saved forever.

Rutherford.

COMFORTED.

Rev. P. T. Pockman.

"**B**LESSED are they that mourn: for they shall be comforted." So our Saviour instructed His disciples of old, and so we have declared to many of His children in our day upon His authority. Grief is the forerunner of the blessing. Sorrow is the condition upon which we inherit this promise. Before we enter the deep waters we wonder *how* the comfort will be given, through what channels it will come, and who will speak the word that will do us most good. We also wonder what will be the *occasion* of our mourning, and what the time.

Few ever care to anticipate this blessing because it costs so much of heartache, and is so frequently accompanied by earthly desolation. None know the beauty and power of it, except those who have experienced the separation which is never atoned for by a reunion in this life. The company of those who mourn is very great, and hence the blessing is in constant demand. It is administered freely and is just what the dear Lord said it would be—a blessing of *comfort*.

We speak from experience. We were precipitated into mourning by a few clicks of the telegraph. Two days previous we left the darling well and strong. When next we saw her cherub face she had been sixteen hours in the arms of Jesus. Dear little saint, how we loved her! The Spirit brought many tender words of the Saviour to our remembrance and opened up a hitherto sealed revelation. Christian friends, in every direction, sent words of love and cheer until our hearts were made to rejoice with the thought that we had been *honored* by this visitation. Confidence and resignation, like twin sisters, composed themselves at the thought advanced by one of the Lord's true pastors, as, stretching forth the hand of sympathy, he said: "The hand of the Lord is upon you: but it is the hand of the Lord." Others said: "God knows best." "He doth not afflict willingly." "He has done it for some wise purpose." "He does it in love." These, and many more, magnified our heavenly Father, who loans us these treasures to enjoy until He wants them on high; and a dear friend writes: "This morning you were remembered at our family altar, when we besought 'the God of all comfort' that He would comfort your hearts."

Some made mention of the Saviour and of His loving care for the tender lambs in strains that were most beautiful and helpful. A number said: "Jesus doeth all things well," and "She is safe in the arms of Jesus." One chord was touched when a kind mother in her "In Memoriam" penned the words:

> "Away He bore thee in His arms
> To shield thee from all earthly harm,
> From sorrow, sickness, sin and pain,—
> *Our* loss is your unending gain."

Another chord was touched when a younger

mother, who had passed through the first trying ordeal of parting with her only child—her first-born son—declared, "It was sweet to give him to Jesus." Still another chord thrilled us when the voice of the preacher uttered in his prayer, "The dear Saviour has laid His hand upon this little child and *blessed* her, and said suffer her to come unto me." And thus the Lord Jesus was magnified.

Others brought consolation by speaking of the preferment given to the *child*. "What trouble she is spared!" "She is in heaven, where there is no sin." "She will be supremely happy forever." "If we love little ones more for what they will become than for what they are, then your first one taken is your most precious now."

"She is not *dead*—
The child of your affections,
But gone into that school. . .
Where Christ Himself doth rule."

Just think of it—"A life just opening here and expanding there all unstained by sin."

Our troubled hearts were pacified. A great calm set in, for we knew it was well with the child.

Some would soothe our anguish by referring to parental exaltation through bereavement. "You have become the father and mother of an angel." "This 'little child' will lead you nearer, and into deeper, sweeter knowledge than you have yet been led, as you look up and see the heaven open and Jesus calling little children unto Him." "The little white-robed angel will await your coming and welcome you with greatest joy." You will find, dear friends, "It has the sweetest lesson of all, the lessons living is bringing us."

The experience is one which will fit you for some higher duty in the world. It comes within the province of your calling "to comfort;" now you can do it more efficiently.

To offset the thought of the "empty crib" came a "Tract," with the message:

> "One less at home!
> The charmed circle broken—a dear face
> Missed day by day from its accustomed place,
> But cleansed and saved and perfected by grace!
> One more in heaven!
>
> "One more in heaven!
> Another thought to brighten cloudy days,
> Another theme of thankfulness and praise,
> Another link on high our souls to raise
> To home and heaven!
>
> "One more at Home!
> That home where separation cannot be,
> That home where none are missed eternally.
> Lord Jesus, grant us all a place with Thee,
> At home in heaven!"

In addition to all the foregoing, the suggestion of Dr. Bridgman brought its measure of solace. "A family lives but a half-life until it has sent its forerunners into the heavenly world, until those who linger here in thought can cross the river and fold a transfigured, glorious form in the embrace of their human love." The blessing is ours. By these means the great Sympathizer has given "a garland for ashes, the oil of joy for mourning, the garment of praise for the spirit of heaviness."

FRIENDS GONE BEFORE.

L. W. WARD.

AS I sit all alone, at the close of the day,
    I muse on the years that are fled
    And I think of the friends that are far, far away,
And of those that have long since been dead.

And my thoughts wander on to the sweet by-and-by,
    And I fancy I'm with them again,
And we roam through the land where the saints never die,
    And never know sorrow or pain.

They have passed from my sight. Oft I fancy I hear
    Their sweet voices calling me home;
And I long to depart from this wilderness drear,
    With them, and in glory, to roam.

Sweet music, sweet music, falls soft on my ear,
    As it floats through the portals above,
And it speaks to my soul words of comfort and cheer,
    And whispers of mercy and love.

WERE there a common bank made of all men's troubles, most men would choose rather to take those they brought than venture on a new dividend, and think it best to sit down with their own.

SOCRATES.

THE SILVER LINING.

Unknown.

THERE'S never a day so sunny
  But a little cloud appears;
 There's never a life so happy
  But has its time of tears;
Yet the sun shines out the brighter
  Whenever the tempest clears.

There's never a garden growing
  With roses in every plot;
There's never a heart so hardened
  But it has one tender spot;
We have only to prune the border
  To find the forget-me-not.

There's never a sun that rises
  But we know 'twill set at night;
The tints that gleam in the morning
  At evening are just as bright,
And the hour that is the sweetest
  Is between the dark and light.

There's never a dream so happy
  But the waking makes us sad;
There's never a dream of sorrow
  But the waking makes us glad;
We shall look some day with wonder
  At the troubles we have had.

TRUE SYMPATHY.

UNKNOWN.

IF you have a friend worth loving,
    Love him—yes, and let him know
  That you love him, ere life's evening
 Tinge his brow with sunset glow.
    Why should good words ne'er be said
    Of a friend till he is dead?

If you hear a song that thrills you,
  Sung by any child of song,
Praise it—do not let the singer
  Wait deservèd praises long.
    Why should one that thrills your heart
    Lack the joy you may impart?

If you hear a prayer that moves you
  By its humble, pleading tone,
Join it—do not let the seeker
  Bow before his God alone.
    Why should not your brother share
    The strength of two or three in prayer?

If you see the hot tears falling,
  Falling from a brother's eyes,
Share them—and thus by the sharing
  Own your kinship with the skies.
    Why should any one be glad
    When a brother's heart is sad?

THE COMPENSATIONS OF LIFE.

Rev. John Philip, M.A.

THE law of compensation is one of the most beautiful and beneficent in God's kingdom. It is most wonderful, too, in its operation, and crops out in so many unlooked-for ways, that it gives man a sweet surprise to those who carefully study it. There is, perhaps, no study that will more deeply interest us, or more richly reward us.

That there are many bitternesses and burdens and problems in life no one can fail to see; and yet there are so many counter-balancing sweets and uplooks, and upliftings, that those who duly mark these providences, are made to feel that life is very different from what it would otherwise be. A quiet, cultured, observant eye, a calm reflective spirit, will discover threads of gold interlacing the homespun sombre web of life, and green spots dotting the dreary wilderness, where others would see only dull monotony and everlasting sameness.

And thus, amid the dullness and monotony, or even the sadness and sorrowfulness, that often seem to characterize life in general; there are many relieving sights and cheering sounds and counterbalancing joys, which steal in upon the wakeful and sympathetic mind, and which, although trifling in themselves, yet in the aggregate may do much to sweeten life, and to render it not only tolerable, but even enjoyable.

God's law of compensation is all-embracing in its manifoldness and extent. It runs through all the seasons of the year, all the stages of human life, and all the varieties of individual experience.

The same beneficent law that rules the succesion of the seasons, each one being, so to speak, the complement of the other, we see operating also in the alternation of day and night, the rest and repose of the night recruiting the wasted energies of the day, and the rest and refreshment of the holy Sabbath fitting in with and following after the toils of the week.

This law of compensation, too, is seen pervading all the different ages and stages of human life: Childhood, youth, manhood, and old age, have each their joys and sorrows, their lights and shadows.

When we come down to the details of individual experience, to one's own personal history, how many striking illustrations we find of the law of compensation running through life!

How true it is that God hath set the day of prosperity over against the day of adversity! The ups and downs of life, like the hills and valleys in nature, border on each other, and as it were arise out of each other. Our temporary depressions are met by corresponding elevations. The days of gladness are intended as a foil and relief to the days of sadness. Although the latter may score a deeper mark on the mind and memory, yet how many are our days of gladness, and what sweet and seasonable surprises they often give us!

> "For every cloud, a silvery light:
>   God wills it so,
> For every vale, a shining height,
> A glorious morn for every night,
>   And birth for labor's throe.

> "For snow's white wing, a verdant field;
>   A gain for loss.
> For buried seed, the harvest yield;
> For pain, a strength, a joy revealed;
>   A crown for every cross."

The means and measure of happiness are far more equally distributed than many are willing to allow. It is even within the reach and at the command of all who seek it and will take the trouble to find it. The inequalities of life are often more apparent than real. Happiness is far less dependent on mere externals than many suppose. It is much more closely linked to the world within than to the world without.

On one occasion, when some friends were condoling with an old man regarding the many troubles of his long and chequered pilgrimage, he remarked, "What you say is too true. I have been surrounded with troubles all my life long; but there is a curious thing about them—nine-tenths of them never happened!" Another genial spirit said, "Some people are always finding fault with nature for putting thorns on roses; I always thank her for putting roses on thorns."

A London city missionary calling on a poor woman, who lived in a garret on two and sixpence a week, and observed a strawberry plant growing in a pot in the room, remarked that she would soon have some fruit from it. She replied, "It is not for fruit I keep it; but because when I see it growing, I know no power but God's could cause it to grow, and as He makes it grow, I know that God is near—that's why I keep it."

But not only in cases of poverty and want, but also in many other very trying circumstances, as under the privation of some bodily or even mental faculty, do we see the law of compensation manifestly at work. How often do we find the loss of one faculty, as of sight or hearing, compensated for by the sharpening of another, or by the infusion of such a spirit of contentment, or even of cheerfulness, as might well put to the blush any grumblers among those who have all their senses and faculties unimpaired. In the case of the deaf, the power of vision and observation is sometimes wonderfully quickened, as with the well-known John Kitto, whose Bible illustrations will remain a standing monument, not only of his learning, but also of his wide observation and patient research. In the case of the blind, too, the senses of hearing and of touch often become very acute; and notwithstanding the blank expression of their sightless eyeballs you will often see a smile of quiet, contented joy lighting up their countenance, as if some secret spring of happiness had been revealed to them that was denied to others, as if—

"Some heaven were opening on their sightless eyes,
And airs from Paradise refreshed their brow."

Dr. Moon, the noted blind philanthropist, has recorded the following remarkable testimony: "On my blindness would I ever have this inscribed, and through eternity my song of praise shall be, 'He hath done all things well.' When I think of the honored instrument He has made me, enabling me to put portions of the Word of Life into 251 languages and dialects, and when thousands of the blind have borne the testimony that these precious truths have been made a blessing and salvation to their souls, I feel that it would more than compensate for a thousand eyes had I them to give."

Perhaps the operation of the law of compensation, in the way of making up for heavy losses and hard trials, was never more signally illustrated than in the case of one who lived in a little village, and who, when eighteen years old, met with a terrible accident in a mine, whereby her spine was broken in three places, and five ribs also, two on one side and three on the other. And at the time he wrote she had been in this state forty-five years, without any feeling below her waist, and one leg bent completely under her. An old sister, over seventy years, who was both deaf and dumb, and could not read, waited upon her. And truly wonderful was it to see the two together—they were so fond of each other. The sick one was turned from her back to her chest by this sister who understood a little by means of signs. And notwithstanding her long and sore affliction, this poor invalid was yet the brightest of Christians. She was full of rejoicing and gratitude, and remarked one day to a lady who went to see her, "How good it is of the Lord to let the sun shine in at my little window!"

Such examples as have been given of the law of compensation might be multiplied indefinitely. That law, we might say, runs through every man's life. Is it not matter of observation how daily wants are met with daily supplies, reverses followed by successes, sorrows lustred with joys, losses turned into gains, and even crosses into crowns?

There is a wonderful balancing of opposite forces in every one's life, a most wise adjustment of seemingly conflicting providences. And we find not only the loss often issuing in gain, but also the gain far exceeding the loss; it may be spiritual and eternal results flowing out of physical pain and temporal losses.

Even in cases where it might seem the loss was irreparable, as in some heart-crushing bereavement, still the law may be traced in its benign and blessed operation. Against the loss sustained by the bereaved must be set the gain of the departed, if he has fallen asleep in Jesus; and his gain is also theirs. Then the hallowed memories that often creep into the chamber of the imagination! Does it not often happen that the departed seems more nearly and dearly present than before.

But while the law of compensation thus, more or less, obtains everywhere, it is only the Gospel that can enable us to read it aright, or to turn it to proper account. And indeed the Gospel itself is the best illustration, as it is the highest embodiment, of that law.

The compensations of life have a new meaning when studied by the light of the Gospel. Thus studied, they may serve to beget and foster that spirit of contentment which is one of the chief factors of the law. Paul said of himself: "I have learned, in whatsoever state I am, therewith to be content." It might help sometimes to silence our murmurs and stir our gratitude to contrast our condition with that of many others, and still more with our own deserts. As one, who was grumbling for want of shoes, felt rebuked on hearing of another who wanted feet.

In studying the law of compensation, everything depends on your standpoint. In surveying a beautiful picture, say of some lovely landscape, you must have it in a proper position, and view it at a proper distance and under proper light. Then you can see the due proportions and true perspective of the different parts, and the wonderful effect of the skillful blendings of the lights and shadows. The shadows are an offset to the sunshine. Thus it is that we can take a right survey and form a right estimate of life only from the standpoint and in the light of the Gospel. Then we can see how beautifully the law of compensation operates and how wisely blended and balanced are the joys and sorrows of life. Then we can see how the sunshine and the shade mutually relieve and illustrate each other. It would not do if life were all sunshine or all shade. The one is as needful as the other, and the presence of the one bespeaks the presence of the other.

> " No shadow, but its sister light
>   Not far away must burn!
> No weary night, but morning light
>   Shall follow in its turn.
>
> " No chilly snow, but safe below
>   A million buds are sleeping;
> No wintry days, but fair spring rays
>   Are swiftly onward sweeping.
>
> ' No note of sorrow, but shall melt
>   In sweetest chord unguessed;
> No labor all too pressing felt,
>   But ends in quiet rest."

The Gospel has shed altogether a new light and given a new interpretation to human life. It brings order out of chaos, and harmony out of discord. Its compensating power will be found more than equal to all the burdens and sufferings and sorrows of time. It offers salvation to the lost, it brings pardon to the guilty, it speaks peace to the troubled, it gives strength to the weak, it breathes patience and submission into the tried, and holds out succor and victory to the tempted. All the other compensations of life are nothing to this. In fact, they are as nothing without this. They are all designed to find their highest fulfillment here.

OUR SAINTED DEAD: LIVING EPISTLES.

ALFRED H. MOMENT, D.D.

IT was no fancy of Chrysostom when he said: "The True Shechinah is Man;" that is, the true representative of God on Earth is the sincere Christian. "We witness," says the author of Ecce Deus, "and are daily called upon to read ever-enlarging editions of the New Testament, in the lives and characters of God's children." Even Paul could say to the members of the Church of Corinth: "*Ye are our Epistle written in our hearts, known and read of all men; being made manifest that ye are an Epistle of Christ, ministered by us, written not with ink, but with the Spirit of the living God; not in tables of stone, but in tables that are hearts of flesh.*" In Christ's own ministry, He recognized the Christian to be his own *open-epistle*, written by, and revealing His own glorious spirit of goodness and love; of the humble, obscure woman of Bethany, who poured upon His head the precious ointment, He said: "*Wheresoever this gospel shall be preached in the whole world, there shall also this, that this woman hath done, be told for a memorial of her."* The act performed demonstrated the divine in man—revealed the real Christ in a human deed--was the Shechinah, not in an effulgent cloud, but in sweet, loving self-sacrificing life.

Jesus, our Lord, does not change. He is still writing enlarged editions of the Gospel with the pen of the Holy Ghost upon fleshly tablets. Our friends and loved ones who have joined the "great majority," and have left behind them long years of toil for the Master, are to-day "Living Epistles" in the which the world may behold Jesus Christ. While here in the flesh they represented God; and all that bemoan them have this glorious consolation, that those who were so like Jesus in the flesh are now with Jesus in the spirit, and are in possession of the fullness of that rich reward inseparable from faithful service and holy love.

In the Saviour, men may indeed find, in the darkest hour of sorrow, and altogether independent of the lives of those for whom they mourn, a solace, calming the troubled heart—illuminating the black cloud of bereavement with "The Bow" of supernal brightness and beauty; and in "the songs in the night," which He giveth to His beloved, even when they mourn without hope as to their dead! But in the death of Christians there is this additional source of true consolation—viz., *the open-living Epistle of Christ,* which their works which follow them exhibit, showing, though imperfectly, Christ's fidelity to human needs—the love and goodness by which the ever-living Saviour is seeking to still the world's tumults, soften its selfishness, and make beautiful and attractive its unsightly parts. *The true believer though dead is still such an open-Epistle.* Death cannot obliterate it. Ink may fade—the record of the diamond pen of the Holy Spirit, *never!* This Epistle the blessed Father would have us read; and, in its jewelled pages of humble service, kindness and sacrifice, He would have us behold "The Bow in the Cloud." In such a life, lived in our own homes, or in the inner circle of our sweetest friendship and purest love, we behold that which we can fully comprehend, having presented to us, in palpable form, one of the strongest and clearest evidences of a glorious immortality and of a coming reunion of all that here are "the true Epistles of God."

The reader may look at these lines under the pressure of an overwhelming bereavement—when life has become a "tear;" when he himself is "a man of sorrows and acquainted with grief," and when he feels an aching heart; yet joy must not be absent—for though there may be a cloud, massive and motionless as it would seem, yet spanning it *is* "The Bow" radiant with light from the throne, in which we read of one who may have remembered His Creator in the days of youth, and whose life was spent in scattering seeds of kindness and fighting battles for God! Next to the witness of the Holy Spirit in the Christian heart and the assurance of Christ's personal love, and the consolations therefrom, is the blessing which the bereaved daily enjoy of such an Epistle of Christ, written, it may be years ago, by the Spirit of the living God, upon a heart which the mourner loved!

Varied Afflictions.

Thou which hast showed me great and sore troubles shalt quicken me again, and shalt bring me up again from the depths of the earth.—*Ps. lxxi.*, 20.

TEMPTATIONS.—THE TRIALS OF OUR FAITH.

John Wesley.

THE first and great end of God's permitting the temptations which bring heaviness on his children is the trial of their faith, which is tried by these even as gold by the fire. Now we know gold tried in the fire is purified thereby, is separated from its dross. And so is faith in the fire of temptation; the more it is tried, the more it is purified. Yea, and not only purified, but also strengthened, confirmed, increased abundantly by so many more proofs of the wisdom and power, the love and faithfulness of God.

When severely tried and tempted there can be no need of darkness, but there may be need of our being in heaviness *for a season*, in order to the end above recited; at least in this sense, as it is a natural result of those manifold temptations which are needful to try and increase our faith, to confirm and enlarge our hope, to purify our hearts from all unholy tempers, and to perfect us in love. And, by consequence, they are needful in order to brighten our crown, and add to our eternal weight of glory. But we cannot say that darkness is needful in order to any of these ends. It is no way conducive to them; the loss of faith, hope, love, is surely neither conducive to holiness, nor to the increase of that reward in heaven which will be in proportion to our holiness on earth.

We ought, therefore, to watch and pray, and use our utmost endeavors to avoid falling into darkness, but we need not be solicitous how to avoid, so much as how to improve by heaviness.

Our great care should be so to behave ourselves under it, so to wait upon the Lord therein, that it may fully answer all the design of his love in permitting it to come upon us, that it may be a means of increasing our faith, of confirming our hope, of perfecting us in all holiness. Whenever it comes, let us have an eye to these gracious ends for which it is permitted, and use all diligence, that we may not "make void the counsel of God against ourselves."

ABIDING IN JESUS.

H. B. Stowe.

ABIDE in Me—o'ershadowed by thy love,
   Each half-born purpose and dark thought of sin,
Quench ere it rise—each selfish low desire,
And keep my soul as thine—calm and divine.
Abide in Me: there have been moments pure,
   When I have seen thy face and felt Thy power;
Then evil lost its grasp, and passion, hushed,
   Owned the divine enchantment of the hour.
These were but seasons beautiful and rare.
   Abide in Me—and they shall ever be;
I pray thee now fulfill my earnest prayer
   Come and abide in Me and I in thee.

THE BIBLE AND PRAYER IN AFFLICTION.

James Buchanan, D.D.

THE Bible opens a spring of comfort for the afflicted by giving them free access to the throne of grace, and inviting them to enjoy the privilege of prayer.

This is, indeed, the Christian's privilege at all seasons; and never will he feel himself to be in a right or comfortable state, whatever may be his outward prosperity, if he allow himself to neglect that blessed ordinance, by which intercourse is maintained betwixt heaven and earth, and fellowship enjoyed by the creature with the Creator. And he who, whether in prosperity or adversity, makes it his daily practice to go to the throne of grace, and in *every thing* by prayer and supplication with thanksgiving, makes his request known unto God, will, from his own experience, bear testimony to the truth of the promise, that "the peace of God which passeth all understanding, shall keep his heart and mind through Christ Jesus." In the day of prosperity, when every want or appetite of our nature is supplied, we may not be conscious of any very strong desire, and are too apt to forget the fact of our dependence, in respect to the supply of our temporal wants; and even in regard to our spiritual necessities, we are prone, when surfeited with worldly prosperity, to become cold and lukewarm in our desires after the communication of divine grace, by which alone they can be supplied. Is there one Christian who has not experienced the deadening effect of uninterrupted prosperity on the spiritual desires and holiest affections of his nature? And if even Christians are too often lulled asleep by its influence, how much more may those be cradled into profound forgetfulness of God, who have never known the necessity, nor made the deliberate choice, of a better and more enduring portion? But when their prosperous course is broken by severe affliction, the minds of both classes are brought into a new state; the Christian is then thrown back on the inward resources of his religion, and will then feel their necessity and value. The most ungodly and careless, when they are suddenly brought into imminent danger, will then *tremble*, and think of God, who cared nothing for religion before. Have we not seen a family, enjoying a long course of prosperity, and as unmindful of God and religion as if they were ignorant that they had a God to worship, and soul to be saved; but when one of their number was suddenly seized by the hand of death, the whole of that gay household were also seized with religious fear, and none more anxious than they to procure the aid of a minister's consolations and a minister's prayers! Have we not known a rude and thoughtless sailor, spending every hour of fair weather and prosperous winds in jovial mirth,— night after night retiring to his cot without thinking of the God above, or of the hell beneath him,—and even, when the first gale arose that was to founder his ship, reckless of the coming storm; but when the crash was heard, and when, from the force of habit, the first word upon his lip was an oath, that oath died away into a prayer, when the foaming waters burst across the deck, and lashed him into the mighty deep! In the 107th Psalm we find the tendency of affliction to produce prayer illustrated by many beautiful examples—as in the case of the Jews wandering in the wilderness, in a solitary way, hungry and thirsty, and their souls fainting within them; or in the case of those who, by reason of personal distress, "sit in darkness and in the shadow of death, being bound in affliction and iron, because they rebelled against the words of God;" or in the case of those who go down to the seas in ships, whole soul is melted because of trouble;—in each case, it is added, "they cried unto the Lord in their trouble, and he delivered them out of their distresses."

In the case of backsliders, too, who have fallen from their first love, and have become conformed to the world, affliction is often sent as the most suitable means of reclaiming them from declension, and restoring them to spiritual health. This it does, by leading them to pray. Oh! how many Christians have had reason to acknowledge the blessed effect of affliction, in renewing their communion with God, and reviving their decayed devotion! Are there not many who can testify, from their own experience, that while they were prosperous the spirit of devotion became imperceptibly more languid in their bosoms; that instead of frequently enjoying prayer as a delightful privilege, they were gradually losing their relish for it, and that when they did observe it, it was observed in a cold and formal manner; and that they were not sensible of the length to which they had proceeded in spiritual declension, till, by some severe stroke of affliction, they were thrown on the resources of a piety too decayed to afford them either support or consolation, and were thus, for the first time, apprised of a danger till then unperceived? Can they not remember what deep humiliation, what earnest desires, and what fervent supplications were produced by that affliction, and the discoveries which it enabled them to make? and are they not sensible that it was in prayer they found their consolation,—when, with their eyes opened to the reality of their condition, they besought the Lord with tears? Indeed, one of the greatest benefits of severe affliction, in the case of God's people, is, that it awakens them to greater ardor and diligence in prayer; and such is the blessedness of communion with God, and such the elevating and sanctifying effect of earnest prayer, that were affliction productive of no other benefit, this alone might well compensate for all the loss which is sustained, and all the pain which is inflicted, even by the severest dispensation of providence.

The impressions that are made during a season of affliction may be the result, in a great measure, of mere natural feeling; but they may, nevertheless, be the means which the Holy Spirit has chosen for the commencement of a saving change; and if they lead the sufferer to pray, they bring him under a new influence, whereby the sentient feelings which at first prompted him, may gradually and imperceptibly rise into gracious and devout affections.

The history of the people of Israel affords many

interesting examples of the effect of prayer in delivering from outward trouble, as well as of the tendency of affliction to impress the most careless with the necessity and value of prayer. These examples are thus beautifully referred to in the 107th Psalm: "O give thanks unto the Lord, for he is good; for his mercy endureth for ever. Let the redeemed of the Lord say so, whom he hath redeemed from the hand of the enemy. They wandered in the wilderness in a solitary way; they found no city to dwell in. Hungry and thirsty, their souls fainted in them. Then they cried unto the Lord in their trouble, and he delivered them out of their distresses. For he satisfieth the longing soul, and filleth the hungry soul with goodness."

LOVE IN CHASTISEMENT.

J. D. Burns, D.D.

THOU, Lord art Love, and everywhere
   Thy name is brightly shown,
   Beneath on earth—thy footstool fair;
  Above in heaven—thy throne.
Thy Chastisements are Love—more deep
  They stamp the seal divine
And by a sweet compulsion keep
  Our spirits nearer Thine.
Thy heaven is the abode of Love!
  O blessed Lord that we
May there, when time's dim shades remove,
  Be gathered home to Thee!

GOD'S LAW OF COMPENSATION.

Rev. Theodore L. Cuyler, D.D.

GOD not only reigns, but He governs His world by a most beautiful law of compensations. He setteth one thing over against another. Faith loves to study the illustrations of this law, notes them in her diary, and rears her pillars of praise for every fresh discovery. I have noticed that the deaf often have an unusual quickness of eyesight; the blind are often gifted with an increased capacity for hearing; and sometimes when the eye is darkened and the ear is closed, the sense of touch becomes so exquisite that we are able to converse with the sufferer through that sense alone. God puts many of His people under a sharp regimen of hardship and burden-bearing in order that they may be sinewed into strength. This law explains the reason why God often sweeps away a Christian's possessions in order that he may become rich in faith, and why He dashes many persons off the track of prosperity where they were running at fifty miles the hour, in order that their pride might be crushed, and that they might seek the safer track of humility and holy living. God's people are never so exalted as when they are brought low, never so enriched as when they are emptied, never so advanced as when they are set back by adversity, never so near the crown as when under the cross. One of the sweetest enjoyments of heaven will be to review our own experiences under this law of compensations, and to see how often affliction worked out for us the exceeding weight of glory.

There is a great want in all God's people who have never had the education of sharp trial. There are so many graces that can only be pricked into us by the puncture of suffering, and so many lessons that can only be learned through tears, that when God leaves a Christian without any trial, He really leaves him to a terrible danger. His heart, unploughed by discipline, will be very apt to run to the tares of selfishness, and worldliness, and pride.

In no direction do we behold more wonderful unfoldings of God than in what we call His Providence. This is a department of God's school in which we are learning fresh lessons every day. In Providence, divine wisdom is married to divine love. All things work together for good to them who love God and trust him. The sceptic jeers at this, but the trusting Christian knows it from actual experience, for some of God's truths are knocked into us by hard blows, and some lessons are spelled out through eyes cleansed with tears. Our perverse mistake is that we demand that God shall explain Himself at every step, instead of waiting for Him to unfold His intricate purposes at His own time and in His own way. Why A—— is set up and good Brother B—— (who seems equally deserving) is cast down; why the only little crib in one Christian home is emptied by death, and the nursery in another home is full of happy voices; why one good enterprise prospers and another one is wrecked—all such perplexing puzzles shake terribly the faith that is not well grounded on the

Rock. To all these pitiable outcries the calm answer of our Heavenly Father is: "Be still and know that I am God. I lead the blind by a way they know not. What I do thou knowest not now, but thou shalt know hereafter." These are the voices of love which come to us from behind the cloud. If we wait patiently, the cloud will break away or part asunder, and our eyes will behold the Rainbow of Mercy over-arching the Throne. God's ways are not our way, but they are infinitely better. The cloud is not so dense but love-rays shine through. In time the revealing "winds shall clear" away the dark and dreadful mystery. Kind words of sympathy steal into the shadowed room of suffering. If Christ does not come in visible form to our Bethanys, He sends His faithful servants and handmaidens with words of warm, tender condolence. The fourteenth chapter of John never gleams with such a celestial brightness as when we read it under the cloud. No cloud can be big enough to shut out heaven if we keep the eye towards the Throne. And when we reach heaven and see the cloud from God's side, it will be blazing and beaming with the illuminations of His love.

THE path of sorrow, and that path alone,
Leads to the land where sorrow is unknown;
No traveller ever reached that blest abode,
Who found not thorns and briars in his road.
                                        WILLIAM COWPER.

THE PILLAR OF CLOUDS.

Edward Paxton Hood, D.D.

BE cheerful beneath the cloud. And if the cloud should come in the daytime, still be cheerful. I recollect once kneeling with familiar friendliness and love around the family altar of a dear friend whom I loved as I believe I loved no other on earth, and he prayed for me that I might know what it was to have the pillar of cloud when the day was too bright, and the pillar of fire when the night was too dark. We need that always, do we not? The pillar of cloud and pillar of fire are needed as much for us as for the Israelites of old. I will mention what I thought as I saw that picture of the German painter some time ago. I could not make out what he meant by it. It was called "cloud-land," and it seemed nothing but cloud on cloud. But what do you think? As I looked, I saw that every cloud turned into an angel or an angel's wing, and the whole picture, that seemed at first only a mass of gloom, looked out upon me with hundreds of angels' eyes and hundreds of angels' wings. So with all clouds; if God comes nigh to us by them, look at them and they turn into angels. They are not desirable in themselves, they are not pleasant; no chastisement, no affliction, no cloud is at present joyous, but grievous. We foolish men would walk always in the day-brightness; we do not want clouds; but the angels know their value, and God too, or he would never send them.

NEEDED BLESSINGS.

WILLIAM HENRY BURLEIGH.

WE ask not that our path be always bright,
   But for Thy aid to walk therein aright;
   That Thou, O Lord, through all its devious way,
Wilt give us strength sufficient to our day.
        For this, for this we pray.

Not for the fleeting joys that earth bestows,
Not for exemption from its many woes;
But that, come joy or woe, come good or ill,
With childlike faith we trust Thy guidance still,
        And do Thy holy will.

Teach us, dear Lord, to find the latent good
That sorrow yields, when rightly understood;
And for the frequent joy that crowns our days
Help us with grateful hearts our hymns to raise,
        Of thankfulness and praise.

Thou knowest all our needs, and will supply:
No veil of darkness hides us from Thine eyes,
Nor vainly from the depths, on Thee we call;
Thy tender love, that breaks the tempter's thrall,
        Folds and encircles all.

Through sorrow and through loss, by toil and prayer,
Saints won the starry crowns which now they wear,

And by the bitter ministry of pain,
Grievous and harsh, but oh, not sent in vain
      Found their eternal gain.

If it be ours, like theirs, to suffer loss,
Give grace, as unto them, to bear our cross,
Till, victors over the besetting sin,
We too Thy perfect peace shall enter in,
      And crowns of glory win.

GRACE PROPORTIONATE TO THE TRIAL.

REV. F. WHITFIELD.

YOU may have yet to pass through many trials, but He will draw close as the night grows darker. He will not let one unneeded thunder-cloud burst over your head, and you shall find the promise true, "He giveth power to the faint and to them that have no might He increaseth strength." When outward things look darkest the peace of God is often fullest in the soul. The Lord gives His people "songs in the night." They rejoice in the midst of sorrow. When the thorn is piercing their song is sweetest, their joy is fullest. So, reader, let it be with you. If trials press sorely, try to praise Him. If the cloud no bigger than a man's hand grow larger and darker, still continue to praise Him. If wants press sorely on every side, carry them to your Heavenly Father and yet mingle your prayers with praises. The Lord will command His lovingkindness in the day time, and in the night His song shall be with you.

LIGHT ON DARK PROVIDENCES.

Rev. Robert F. Sample, D.D.

THE dispensations of Providence are often mysterious. It is true that the relations of sin and suffering may be apparent. As in the cases of Gehazi, Ananias, and Simon Magus, the punishment may tread on the heels of the offense, and although we may be unwilling to admit it to others, we know at what sin the rod points. But in many instances the footsteps of God, as they relate to ourselves, are not known. The people of God are often led by ways that are dark, and the interpretation must be referred to that Sovereignty which embraces the long reach of ages. There are trials that seem to contravene the divine will. They arrest some work to which God had evidently called His servants, where the need was great, and the door widely opened. They involve defeat, suffering, persecution, death. We had not anticipated this. It is not at all as we would have ordered. Unbelief suggests that God is occupied with other interests and has forgotten ours. We limit the Holy One as to His presence and power.

The apostolic Church encountered the opposition of ungodly men, and the fires of persecution girdled them as they pressed their way westward. In the first three centuries three millions of Christians suffered martyrdom; were stoned, sawn asunder, burnt at the stake, torn in pieces by devouring dogs, drowned in the seas, and wrapped in combustible garments and burned like torches in the night.

Then, coming down to a later period, we are reminded of the massacres in the reign of Charles XII., when in the space of a few days seventy thousand Protestants were slain; and we recall the still greater and more protracted cruelties inflicted by Louis XIV., and the slaughter of the saints in Holland, England, Scotland and Ireland. Truly the Church has passed through fires and deep waters, and hard by the gates of hell, on her way to the present. Why was it thus?

Then we raise another question concerning the progress of the truth. Why have its conquests not been more general? Why has darkness followed in the wake of its advance? Why are great empires still enveloped in moral night? Why is error so prevalent, and opposition so strong, and wickedness so defiant in this age, when, for aught we know, the end is drawing nigh? Why does God permit men to trample on His Sabbaths, mutilate His Gospel, obey unrighteousness, open floodgates of iniquity, the heavens meanwhile serene, as if vindictiveness slept and God had ceased to restrain the powers of evil? An answer is sent from His changeless throne, "What I do thou knowest not now." "Be still and know that I am God."

The providences of God are often obscure as they relate to individual believers.

You may think a certain line of action is in accordance with the divine will, and you enter prayerfully upon it. But suddenly some great barrier is thrown across your path, and conscientious effort ends in humiliating defeat. You devote yourself to some form of Christian service, prompted by sense of duty and love to the Master, and on the threshold of a work full of promise you lie down to die. You form relations in life which promise to be helpful, and your confidence is abused, your expectations disappointed, and your faith in men disappears like a dissolving cloud. Or you have prayerfully labored to bring your children to Christ and fit them for usefulness and honorable life. But they reject your instructions, resist your authority, disregard each appeal of parental love, persist in sin and go down under a cloud of shame. Or bereavements occur at what seems the most inopportune time; they come when you need a strong arm on which to lean; when by reason of other trials a loved presence seemed essential to your life; when the son or daughter of your hope promised surcease of sorrow, and the sepulchre is closed with a stone.

There occur to us many illustrations of providences that are uninterpreted as yet, or were once unknown. The first of our race to depart out of life, entering the mysterious beyond along an untravelled passage, was one who feared God and walked trustfully with Him. And yet he fell by the hand of a murderer, and that murderer his own brother. So soon was the throne of empire enveloped in clouds and darkness. And that early martyr had many successors all along the generations, until Stephen was stoned on the margin of a new dispensation. Still later James and Paul were beheaded, and Peter was crucified. Polycarp suffered martyrdom after a long and exceptionally devoted life, and sleeps today under a lone cypress tree. These are representatives of a noble army of martyrs.

Take another class of providences. Luther was confined in the Wartburg, and Latimer in the old London Tower. Harriet Newell departed for the heathen world with the benedictions of weeping parents on her head, and died, ere her voyage was completed, on the Isle of France. Sarah Mateer suddenly fell in the furrow when with joyfulness she anticipated an abundant harvest of souls. Walter Lowrie consecrated the ardor of youth to like service, and slain, by pirates, went to an uneasy grave full many a fathom deep.

There are other experiences darker and sadder than these. The sons of pious Eli defiled themselves, and the news of their sudden taking off proved the father's death. David mourned the filial impiety and wickedness of his son, whose possibilities of honor were great, and in his death, without hope, quite forgot the grave of his own and Bathsheba's child. Why all these forms of suffering? Why do the people of God, especially beloved, God's in covenant, objects of that gentleness that knows our feeble frame, meet these sore trials on their way home? We may find it difficult at times to reconcile all this with our conceptions of the divine character, especially with that love which is its outstanding feature. Desolate homes, buried hopes, broken hearts, the past wrapped in sadness, the future darkened with clouds—what means all this? Is God on our side or is He against us? If He is our Father, though Abraham be ignorant of us, why this long controversy with us? "Joseph is not and Simeon is not, and ye will take Benjamin away; all these things are against us." Ah, let the believer look up and he shall see the outstretched hand of vigilant love beyond the rim of the cloud, and he shall hear a kind voice saying, "What I do thou knowest not now, but thou shalt know hereafter."

Observe, first: Our view of divine providence is necessarily limited. We are finite; God is infinite. We see the little segment of time through which we are passing; God's view embraces eternity. Our thought is engaged with a present event, and we do not see its relations to the future. A given experience seems to terminate on itself, as a completed circle, and to stand motionless, whilst in fact, it is a significant and onward step in history's imperial march. Yonder star by which our Pilgrim Fathers directed their passage across the unknown sea, appears to occupy the very same place in the heavens it occupied then. But there are no fixed stars. The whole universe is moving on, and will never call a halt, and each revolution of our earth is necessary to the measured step and harmony of the whole. So it is in the moral government of God. How little of this we comprehend. We cannot see afar off. And since we do not discern how this experience is to influence another, and to give shape to all the future, we are unable to pass intelligent judgment upon it. "Thou knowest not now."

We are much like those creations of God which live but a single day. How little they know about the world in which they spend a joyous existence whilst the sun is up, and then die with its setting. If they were endowed with intelligence they would conclude as the night gathered that there would never be another day. They would know nothing about the great stretch of earth. They would not know how the chilly rains of April were related to the future harvests and the autumn fruits. They would not understand that by exchange of products the cold North enjoys the wealth of the Southland, and the people along the equatorial line realize the benefits of rigorous climes. Just as true is it that man, although the inspiration of God has given him understanding, cannot measure infinity, or traverse existences out of sight. "Thou knowest not now." Second: We do not know what is real and desirable good. We often crave what it would be an injury to us to possess. We are troubled by its denial. We long to secure wealth, and perchance we pledge ourselves to a faithful stewardship. But instead of riches we are remanded to poverty. We pray for physical strength, and propose to consecrate it to the Master's service. But instead of health we live on in protracted invalidism. Unable to do, we simply endure. God has something better in store for us. The thorn in the flesh will yet prove our crown. Imprisonment in the Bedford jail was to John Bunyan a blessing in disguise. It gave to the world the "Pilgrim's Progress," and to the Bedford tinker a name that shall never die. When Luther was hastened across the moat and the iron door of the old castle closed behind him, it seemed that his life-work was done. But on that secluded height in the Thuringian forest he found time to translate the Bible into the tongue of a great empire, and the banner of the cross still floats above the sombre pines, a prophecy of the latter-day glory of the Church. Thus our defeats are our triumphs, and evil is good.

JOY AFTER SORROW.

Paul Gerhardt, 1659.

COMETH sunshine after rain,
   After mourning joy again,
   After heavy, bitter grief
Dawneth surely sweet relief;
     And my soul, who from her height
     Sank to realms of woe and night,
     Wingeth now to heaven her flight.

He, whom this world dares not face,
Hath refreshed me with His grace,
And His mighty hand unbound
Chains of hell about me wound;
     Quicker, stronger, leaps my blood,
     Since His mercy, like a flood,
     Poured o'er all my heart for good.

Bitter anguish have I borne,
Keen regret my heart hath torn,
Sorrow dimmed my weeping eyes,
Satan blinded me with lies;
     Yet at last am I set free,
     Help, protection, love, to me
     Once more true companions be.

Ne'er was left a helpless prey,
Ne'er with shame was turned away,
He who gave himself to God,
And on Him had cast a load.

Who in God his hope hath placed
Shall not life in pain outwaste,
Fullest joy he yet shall taste.

Though to-day may not fulfill
All thy hopes; have patience still;
For perchance to-morrow's sun
Sees thy happier days begun.
 As God willeth march the hours,
 Bringing joy at last in showers,
 And whate'er we asked is ours.

When my heart was vexed with care,
Filled with fears, well nigh despair;
When with watching many a night
On me fell pale sickness' blight;
 When my courage failed me fast,
 Camest Thou, my God, at last,
 And my woes were quickly past.

Now as long as here I roam,
On this earth have house and home,
Shall this wondrous gleam from Thee
Shine through all my memory.
 To my God I yet will cling
 All my life the praises sing
 That from thankful hearts outspring.

Every sorrow, every smart,
That the eternal Father's heart
Hath appointed me of yore,
Or hath yet for me in store,
 As my life flows on I'll take
 Calmly, gladly for His sake,
 No more faithless murmurs make.

I will meet distress and pain,
I will greet e'en death's dark reign,
I will lay me in the grave,
With a heart still glad and brave.
    Whom the Strongest doth defend,
    Whom the Highest counts His friend,
    Cannot perish in the end.

Translated by Catherine Winkworth, 1855.

THE FUTURE WILL CLEAR UP MANY MYSTERIES.

REV. THEO. L. CUYLER, D.D.

THE future will clear up many a mystery. A few months ago I went into the house of one of the leading merchants, whose beloved daughter had been brought home dead from being run down in the public street. The first word was, "Tell me now why God took away that girl." Said I, "My brother, I have not come here to interpret God's mysteries. I have come here to lead you closer to God's heart. Be still, and know that He who gave takes away. She already knoweth why she is yonder; wait till God clears away the cloud, and thou wilt find that even this was right and well." Do you not remember how the prophet of old once had his eye touched at Dothan, and he beheld the mountains round about him filled with chariots and horsemen? When you and I work in some great cause of reform, and we have met with defiance and discouragement—why, if God were to open the eyes of our faith, and we could see the battle-field as He does, we would find all round about us a great army of God's promises, assuring us of inevitable victory—nothing to do with chariots and horsemen, but simply to stand our ground and fight out the battle, and trust that He will finally clear away the cloud, and the light of His glory shall shine on the banners of truth borne over the field; for by and by shall come the last great day of revelation, when nothing that is right shall be found to have been vanquished, and nothing that is wrong shall be found to have triumphed.

WE SHALL KNOW HEREAFTER.

Rev. Robert F. Sample, D.D.

WHAT is now mysterious in providence will eventually be made plain. "Thou shalt know hereafter."

1. The interpretation may be given in the present world. The generation following may receive it, or it may be granted to ourselves. It may be reserved to the world to come. There was much in old Hebrew history that was not understood until the substance displaced the shadow. Typical men were an enigma until the Christ whom they adumbrated came. The offering of Isaac was a mystery until God's only Son hung on the tree. The hiding of the child in the wicker basket by the water's edge was a mystery, but the anxious parents understood it better when Moses entered Pharaoh's palace, or led Israel through the Red Sea. The same is true of later history. The father of Pericles reproved his boy for wasting his time over an old classic, but

Athens reaped the fruitage of that study when the Olympian orator thundered from the Bema, and reared magnificent temples. John Newton could not conjecture why, when a wicked sailor boy, a rough hand, cut down his hammock and transferred him to another vessel; but when years had passed by he understood it all as he saw Jesus coming across the troubled waters. If men who study the heavens need years of observation to enable them to compute so much as the curve of a planet's orbit, we need not wonder if our intelligence fails to forecast the results of a present joy or sorrow. We do not know the real trend of things. In the expressive language of the Scriptures, we know not how to go to the city. Time will declare it.

Age may interpret the unknown experiences of youth. The old man may see how his early years of permitted sin have magnified the grace of God and made him at last a mighty helper to the outcast and enslaved; or how some domestic sorrow that darkened the morning of life, fitted him to sympathize with other sufferers, and pushed far out the boundary line of useful service. Thus the memory of the sins of youth casts its shadow over all the ministry of the converted Paul, but it made him a more effective preacher of righteousness than he would otherwise have been, and he led the chief of sinners to Christ, who, in their low estate had a feeling of spiritual kinship with Saul of Tarsus. And when he was afterwards persecuted for Christ's sake, defamed, stoned and imprisoned; when he raised psalms of praise with his feet in the stocks, and repeated the sweet evangel when in Rome a chain bound him and the axe gleamed above him, he wrote to Christians in old Corinth, and did it joyfully: "Whether we be afflicted, it is for your consolation and salvation, which is effectual in the enduring of the same sufferings which we also suffer; or whether we be comforted, it is for your consolation and salvation."

When Jacob saw Joseph's wagons, sent to carry him down to Egypt, and learned of the honor which crowned the son he thought dead, he understood for the first time the dreamings and sufferings of his favorite boy, and unravelled the tangled skein of providence which had confounded the long, sad years. By that early sorrow many souls were saved alive, and the sunset of the patriarch's life was without a cloud. Like illustrations might be gathered from all the years. We have found them in our own day. The blood of martyrs has been the seed of the Church. When Harriet Newell died; when Walter Lowrie was drowned; when the Sepoy insurrection startled the world, a multitude arose to fill the vacancies and increase the ranks of the sacramental host. Thus God makes the wrath of man to praise Him, and our eyes may see it ere we depart.

In like manner our personal experiences of sorrow may be interpreted before we go to the better life. Some severe affliction may almost immediately bear the peaceable fruits of righteousness. It may bring increased fitness for the Master's service, an enlargement of our spiritual vision, or sweeter communion with Christ than ever before enjoyed. We are like some plants which the more they are trodden upon the more they grow. In the deep valley, like that near to Chamouni, we see stars by day. So we may obtain new and precious views of Jesus from the low places of human suffering. Well did the holy Rutherford know this, and he was accustomed to say, "Welcome, welcome, Jesus! in whatsoever way Thou comest, if we can but get a glimpse of Thee."

So, too, conversions may quickly succeed some form of suffering. Oftentimes the rough knock of God's hammer has opened the gate of Mercy, and the natural death of one member of the home has brought spiritual life to another. "Before I was afflicted I went astray; but now I have kept Thy word." The hereafter often lies on this side eternity. But if not, then

2. The world to come will reveal what is now hidden.

There our range of vision will be greatly enlarged. From the summits of the heavenly estate we shall survey the earthly life, as from a mountain-top the traveller traces all the windings of the way thither. Much that was inexplicable here will be made plain there. The wisdom and goodness of God will appear written on every passage that was painful, and shall shine in every experience that was dark. We shall see how the varied and oft-recurring trials of life were necessary to keep us humble, to mellow our character, to increase our knowledge of ourselves and of Christ, to enlarge our usefulness, to deliver us from threatening evil, and shut us up to the narrow way. Then our misunderstanding of many events shall be corrected. What we called a *tremolante*, which seemed to sob itself out through the cadences of earth, shall only prove our ears defective, and those very notes prolonged above shall complete the song of the redeemed. Then the wheels of providence that seemed to oppose each other will be viewed in their far-reaching relations, and the perfect harmony of the parts shall awaken grateful praise. Then it shall appear that the trembling descent into the trough of the sea was necessary to the ascent to the crest of the wave, whence we caught our helpful view of the world to come; and that the tacking to the right and to the left, our progress never directly onward, was the only possible means of reaching our desired port. We shall learn how the mystery of providence was necessary to the cultivation of faith, and each experience of trial was fitting us for a higher place in Heaven than we could have attained without it. Then, too, our fears shall, for the first time, be declared wholly groundless, and

> "Out of our stony griefs,
> Bethels we'll raise."

Let us note briefly some of the lessons this subject suggests.

1st. A lesson of trust. We are slow to understand that God intends this life shall be a life of faith. We cannot walk by sight. Much we would like to know is for our good concealed. Only thus can we be shut up to God. And only when we hide ourselves in Him can we put on His beauty, and be prepared for heavenly visions. Faith, and that only, bridges over the gulf that separates worlds, and "all its horrors hides." Hence that discipline which teaches us to trust; that turns our weakness into strength by constraining us to take hold on omnipotence itself; that puts our hands in the hand that is infinitely wise and knows the way to the kingdom, is a discipline we should welcome. This was the lesson the Psalmist learned, though his poor memory sometimes dropped it by the way. "What time I am afraid I will trust in Thee." The pious Cowper, tossed with tempest, the equilibrium of his cultured thought often lost, yet sang himself back to faith when troubles came, and patiently waited for the interpretation which only God could give. In the same spirit Toplady wrote that sweet stanza we should often raise in this house of our pilgrimage:

> "When we in darkness walk,
> Nor feel the heavenly flame,
> Then is the time to trust our Lord,
> And rest upon His name."

The Highlander travelling southward for the first time, when he approached a long, forbidding tunnel, did not leap from the train, but exercised trust in the conveyance that had brought him hither, then calmly plunged into the darkness. Only thus could he enter the historic Edinburg, and join the friend who had gone before him in the home overshadowed by the ancient castle. The trust he exercised along the way brought him to his journey's end. David's hand would not have been bold to contend with the Philistine if he had not trusted God when he fought with the lion and the bear, and slew them. Beloved, let us accept the discipline by which God would cultivate the grace that opens Heaven, and turns earth's discords to undying harmonies on high.

2d. The second is a lesson of patience.

This is a grace which honors God. It rests upon

His word. It trusts His power. It believes that all things are working for good, and that Heaven will more than requite him for all the trials on the way. The connection of the Apostle is suggestive when he couples "rejoicing in hope" with "patience in tribulation." Hope anticipates the sorrowless life, the ever-abounding joy, and Patience says, "I will quietly wait the breaking of the eternal day." So far from seeking to break open its prison doors, Patience watches at the window for the Christ to pass by, assured that He will give release at the appointed time, and wing the soul for its heavenward flight. Surely with such an issue out of all our troubles we should bear them patiently through the "little while" that they stay, then exchange the "light affliction which is but for a moment" for the "far more exceeding and eternal weight of glory." May God help each of us to patiently wait, and no matter what the cross, to say,

> "I will bear it
> With all the tender suffrance of a friend,
> As calmly as the wounded patient bears
> The artist's hand that ministers his cure."

3d. Finally, a lesson of thankfulness.

There never comes an hour to the believer, though every earthly light goes out, that he has not reason for thanksgiving. He should sing songs in prison, and join his hallelujahs with the wailings of the storm. He should be thankful that tribulation worketh patience, and patience experience, and experience hope; that the chisel which is often upon him is fitting him to be a pillar in God's temple; that the weariness by the way is preparing him for a richer enjoyment of the rest that remaineth; that the path of suffering is the path the Saviour trod, and that, with the sweet privilege of putting his feet where Christ's have been, he is going to the Heaven where the King has established His throne, and waits for his coming.

Dearly beloved, let us trust the Heavenly Friend, and with our hands in the Father's hand, whatever the mystery of life, and the painfulness of the road, may we patiently wait the revelations of the life to come; the life just beyond the western hills—assured that Christ will keep His royal word: "Thou shalt know hereafter."

> "God is His own interpreter,
> And He will make it plain."

TRUST GOD IN TRIAL.

PAUL GERHARDT.

TRUST Him to govern, then;
No King can rule like Him:
How wilt thou wonder when
Thine eyes no more are dim.
To see those paths which vexed thee,
How wise they were and meet—
The works which now perplex thee,
How beautiful, complete;
In thy right hand to-morrow,
Thy God shall place the palms;
To Him who chased thy sorrow
How glad will be thy psalms.

BLESSINGS IN DISGUISE.

UNKNOWN.

MISFORTUNES often prove blessings in disguise. It is said that the great European physiologist and natural philosopher, Helmholtz, dates his start in science from an attack of typhoid fever. Strangely enough, this illness put him in possession of a microscope, which he was enabled to purchase, as he tells us himself, " by having spent my autumn vacation in 1841 in the hospital, prostrated by typhoid fever. Being a pupil, I was nursed without charge, and on my recovery I found myself in possession of the savings of my small resources." This fever proved a fortunate illness for Helmholtz and the world, and is a striking instance of a blessing in disguise.

John Bunyan was thrown into a dungeon for preaching the gospel; but while there he wrote " The Pilgrim's Progress " and other books that have blessed the world and immortalized his name. The persecutions which were cruel and severe proved to be real blessings in disguises, for by them he was led into paths of usefulness which he could otherwise never have known. The seeming misfortunes of John Bunyan made him the hero of Bedford jail.

So John Kitto, the eminent writer on biblical subjects, and thousands of others, have been led into paths of distinguished usefulness through some seeming accidental, though no doubt providential occurrence. Many of our most common ills are really blessings in disguise. We shall so see them " when the mists are cleared away." It is well, therefore, to trust God in all things and say, " Thy will be done."

THE BURDEN OF SORROW.

Rev. John Philip, M.A.

THE brotherhood of sorrow is a guild that comprehends all the race. Who has not wept betimes? What human heart is there but has sometimes been riven with sorrow? What bodily frame but has sometimes quivered with pain? No doubt some have a far larger share of sorrow than others. Even God's own children may be corrected when others are let alone. He loves them too well not to correct them. "Whom the Lord loveth He correcteth, and scourgeth every son whom He receiveth." Sonship is not incompatible with scourging, but may rather be attested and approved thereby.

Yet sometimes it is not easy to spell love out of trials. It may be true of God's children, as aforetime, "Now for a season if need be, ye are in heaviness through manifold temptations."

The manifoldness of our relations in life makes us a broader mark for the shafts of sorrow. The more tender our sensibilities the warmer our affections, and the more nearly and closely we touch one another, the oftener and more freely may our hearts be made to bleed. And how often when trouble comes does it seem to double itself! Our bodily and mental troubles, our personal afflictions and relative bereavements, our private and public misfortunes, especially when they come together, like two seas meeting, sometimes make the burden of sorrow a very heavy one. We may feel at such times as if it were heavier than we could bear.

Especially so when it seems as if we must bear the weight all alone. *Human sympathy*, when sincere, is very sweet; 'tis like an oasis in the desert. Yet it is often very powerless to relieve. It may soothe and yet not be able to sustain; it may bend over us with yearning pity, and yet be utterly unable to lift off our load. There are times when we are made to feel how far removed we are beyond the power of human sympathy, and when we realize a terrible isolation and solitariness in our sorrow. Perhaps in our anguish we are ready to cry, "I looked on my right hand, but there was no man that would know me: refuge failed me; no man cared for my soul." Nevertheless, at such times we may be able to add; "I cried unto Thee, O Lord: I said, Thou art my refuge and my portion in the land of the living." Blessed be God there is a great Sorrow-bearer as well as a sin-bearer. He who bare our sins, carried our infirmities. Jesus Christ was indeed "a Man of sorrows and acquainted with grief," and His sinlessness does not impair, but perfects His sympathy; for sin blunts sensibility and deadens feeling. His sympathy is indeed exquisitely tender, as it is thoroughly human; and yet it is all-powerful, for it is Divine. We see the tenderness of His human sympathy on His way to the grave of Lazarus, for "Jesus wept;" and we see also the divinity of His power when He cried, "Lazarus, come forth!"

If it is a great relief to a sorrow-burdened heart to vent its sorrow in the presence of one who is possessed of a large, loving, and sympathizing heart, even when he can do little or nothing to help, how much more should it be to spread out our sorrow before Him whose pity is equalled by His power, who is both infinitely able and willing to do exceedingly abundantly for us above what we ask or think!

If he does not see fit to remove the burden yet He can render our strength equal to bear it. If the thorn is not taken away, yet the promise may be made good, "My grace is sufficient for thee; for My strength is made perfect in weakness!" How often has it been proved that the sorrow that has driven the heart has but cleft a way for the entrance of that word that giveth light. The farther down the ploughshare of sorrow has gone, and the deeper the furrows made in the heart, the more deeply bedded has been the precious seed, and the more abundant the future harvest. "They that sow in tears shall reap in joy."

IN TRIAL.

Sir Robert Grant.

WHEN gathering clouds around I view,
    And days are dark and friends are few,
    On Him I lean who not in vain
Experienced every human pain;
He sees my wants, allays my fears,
And counts and treasures up my tears.

If aught should tempt my soul to stray
From heavenly wisdom's narrow way,

To fly the good I would pursue,
Or do the sin I would not do,
Still He who felt temptation's power
Shall guard me in that dangerous hour.

If wounded love my bosom swell,
Deceived by those I prized too well,
He shall his pitying aid bestow
Who felt on earth severer woe;
At once betrayed, denied, or fled,
By those who shared His daily bread.

If vexing thoughts within me rise,
And sore dismayed my spirit dies,
Still He who once vouchsafed to bear
The sickening anguish of despair
Shall sweetly soothe, shall gently dry,
The throbbing heart, the streaming eye.

When sorrowing o'er some stone I bend,
Which covers what was once a friend,
And from his voice, his hand, his smile,
Divides me for a little while,
Thou, Saviour, mark'st the tears I shed,
For Thou didst weep o'er Lazarus dead!

And O, when I have safely past
Through every conflict but the last,
Still, still unchanging, watch beside
My painful bed, for Thou hast died;
Then point to realms of cloudless day,
And wipe the latest tear away!

It may be that thou art entered into a cloud, which will bring a gentle shower to refresh thy sorrows.—
JEREMY TAYLOR.

VICTORY OVER TEMPTATIONS.

William S. Plumer, D.D.

IT almost startles one to hear the apostle James saying, "My brethren, count it all joy when ye fall into divers temptations. . . Blessed is the man that endureth [patiently endures, with constancy bears up under] temptation." But when we search God's Word, we find the doctrine abundantly supported and illustrated.

Take the case of our Blessed Lord. He was long and sorely tempted of the devil—tempted as no man ever was. Yet see the happy consequences immediately following: "Behold, angels came and ministered unto Him." While His temptation lasted, they stood at a distance to let it appear that Christ could conquer by His own power and holiness. But when the battle was fought and the victory won, they rejoiced in such a Lord; they brought Him food; they comforted Him, as they often strengthen and comfort His tempted people. If Satan was allowed to assail Him, angels were sent to congratulate Him, adore Him, and serve Him. Thus He was prepared and encouraged to go boldly on in His great work of destroying the works of the devil, and in setting up the kingdom of God.

A like result is reached when the saints endure temptation. The trying of their faith worketh patience, constancy, heavenly heroism; and patience worketh experience; and experience hope; and hope maketh not ashamed: because the love of God is shed abroad in our hearts by the Holy Ghost, which is given unto us. So uniformly and so wonderfully does the Lord bless temptation to the edification of His people, that the great and good Luther said: "One Christian well tempted is worth a thousand." Another of his sayings was: "Three things make a good theologian: meditation, temptation, and prayer."

Like testimonies have been borne by others. Fenelon said: "Temptations, as a file, rub off much of the rust of our self-confidence." Dr. Samuel Clarke says: "Bearing up against temptations and prevailing over them, is the very thing wherein the whole life of religion consists. It is the trial which God puts upon us in this world, by which we are to make evidence of our love and obedience to Him, and of our fitness to be made members of His kingdom."

How ill-prepared would David have been for the conflicts of his riper years had he not fought with the lion, and the bear, and the giant of Gath, when young! O, it is good for a man that he bear the yoke in his youth. It makes a man of him. "He sitteth alone and keepeth silence, because he hath borne it upon him. He putteth his mouth in the dust, if so be there may be hope." All great characters are formed more or less in the school of trial — even sharp trial.

The difference between Daniel going into Babylon and Daniel beholding the fall of the Chaldean monarch, was as great as could well be imagined. Hardly any two pious men were less alike than were the young Israelite and the old prophet pronouncing sentence of death on Lucifer, the son of the morning, when he was about to be cast down to hell.

Compare the young Saul of Tarsus, crying, "Lord, what will Thou have me to do?" with such an one as Paul the aged. How great the contrast! What made the difference? Chiefly his experience in trials and afflictions and temptations.

The little child Moses in the rushes, and the old man Moses, with his eye undimmed and his natural force unabated at the age of a hundred and twenty years, were not so unlike in appearance of body as they were in strength and excellence of character.

Everlasting bliss will bear a proportion to what men have endured for Christ and His cause. On earth, Mordecai once wore a crown of gold; and our Saviour once wore a crown of thorns: but in the world to come, the saints shall wear different crowns. "Blessed is the man that endureth temptation; for when he is tried he shall receive the crown of life, which the Lord hath prepared for them that love Him." So spoke James. Paul says: "I am now ready to be offered, and the time of my departure is at hand. I have fought a good fight, I have finished my course, I have kept the faith: henceforth there is laid up for me a crown of righteousness." Peter says: "When the Chief Shepherd shall appear, ye shall receive a crown of glory that fadeth not away." O, what a crowning that will be: life, righteousness, glory — all in one day — all for nothing — all by grace — and all for eternity.

MYSTERIES MADE PLAIN HEREAFTER.

F. C. MONFORT, D.D.

THE eye is a more wonderful instrument than the glasses which men have invented to help it in its work. The ease with which a landscape, or a star, or a companion's face is pictured in it so that we see distinctly, is proof of wider and greater skill than that of man; yet the powers of the eye are limited. There are things within its range too bright for its study. It was not made to look at the sun except through a medium or veil of protection. The direct light of the sun would destroy it.

The mind is more wonderful than the eye. Its range is not limited by distance or time. It discerns not only color and shape and beauty, but reasons and truth. It knows cause and effect, as well as right and wrong. It knows present and past, and searches the earth and the heavens. It makes discoveries, and prides itself on its powers; yet its powers have a limit. There are things which it can no more compass than the unaided eye can study the sun.

The being and character of God are too great for its powers. "No man hath seen God at any time." No man with mortal eyes can see Him. The faintest manifestations of His glory have proved too much for eyes of flesh. Paul, on the way to Damascus, fell to the earth. Neither can the mind endure it. Peter and James and John, when on the Mount of Transfiguration, were bewildered and knew not what they did. A faint earnest of the glory of heaven overcame them.

It is only through a medium that we can know the Infinite—"the only begotten Son, who is in the bosom of the Father; He hath revealed Him." Not in the full majesty of His glory, but only in so far as men are able to bear it.

The mysteries of religion are a study too great for the mind. We look upon things infinite, as one studies the sun through a glass which has been smoked.

The mind is finite, and God's works and providences, though plain to superior intelligences, are a mystery to it. God manifest in the flesh was seen of angels, but men recognized Him only by His works and by the testimony from heaven—things which they could see and understand. The incarnation, the world's great fact, with the whole plan of salvation, is understood in heaven—the angels who sang at the Saviour's birth, who sustained Him and ministered to Him, understand better than we "the great mystery of godliness." The work of God's spirit may be understood by the angels, but it is to us as mysterious as the power which causes the seed to open and the trees to grow. It is not within the range of intellect. We may feel the influence of the Spirit, and be guided and sanctified by Him, but His work is a mystery.

The same is true of the future life. Heaven is the Christian's hope; yet how little he knows of its glory. The Bible promises him a better country, but he can not survey it nor picture its scenery. He is assured of a mansion, but knows not its architecture. Descriptions are given, but they are veiled in human language. The tree and river of life; the gates of precious stones; the light without the sun; continued day; freedom from pain, from sin and death; the throne and the rainbow, and the King in His beauty—though they tell of heaven, are feeble expressions of its glory. They are illustrations suited to our limited capacity. A perfect picture of heaven could not be painted in human language, and would not be intelligible to human minds.

What we know not now we shall know hereafter. Our souls are in their childhood. They will one day understand things which are now hidden. The veil will be removed, and we shall know even as we are known. When we were children we talked and understood as children. We now see that many childish thoughts were foolish. Things are plain which sorely puzzled us. Mysteries have vanished. We have outgrown joys, sorrows, hopes and fears. We have put away childish things. So the soul will put away the things of its childhood. It will understand things now hidden. The being of God, the work of the Spirit, and the joy of heaven, will no longer be veiled and darkened. "Then, face to face," it shall know the full enjoyment of God and of heaven. "What I do (said the Saviour), thou knowest not now; but thou shalt know hereafter."

This is the Christian's hope. It is his comfort in time of trial. It strengthens him against temptation. The world may be dark, but he looks beyond. His life may be a battle with evil, but he sees victory and its reward. His way may be hedged and rough, but he journeys to a sure place—"to a land of which the Lord hath said, I will give thee." Our Saviour, for the joy that was set before Him, endured the cross, despising the shame. So His followers, in the hope of heaven, bear their burdens, counting it a joy that they are allowed to suffer with Him.

Unbelievers may doubt the value of this comfort and strength. They may ask us to demonstrate it and prove its value by figures, as men prove earthly good. So we may ask a child to prove its father's love, or demonstrate the nature of its faith in him. We have no just conception of heaven. No more has a little child a true idea of its country or of liberty. We can only say, We know in whom we believe. We know that God is true. We know that if "our earthly house of this tabernacle were dissolved, we have a building of God; a house not made with hands, eternal in the heavens."

It is not hard to die. It is harder a thousand times to live. To live is to see God through a glass darkly. To die is to see Him face to face. To live is to be one in the ore. To die is to be smelted and come out pure gold. To live is to be in March and November. To die is to find midsummer where there is perfect harmony and perfect beauty.—
Henry Ward Beecher.

Can any man trust a better support under affliction than the friendship of omnipotence, who is both able and willing, and knows how to relieve him?
R. Bentley.

EARTH TO EARTH.

John Hampton Gurney.

EARTH to earth and dust to dust,
   Lord we own the sentence just;
   Head and tongue, and hand and heart,
All in guilt have borne their part;
Righteous is the common doom,
All must moulder in the tomb.

Like the seed in spring-time sown,
Like the leaves in autumn strown,
Low these goodly frames must lie,
All our pomp and glory die;
Soon the spoiler seeks his prey,
Soon he bears us all away.

Yet the seed, upraised again,
Clothes with green the smiling plain;
Onward as the seasons move,
Leaves and blossoms deck the grove;
And shall we forgotten lie,
Lost forever, when we die?

Lord, from Nature's gloomy night
Turn we to the Gospel's light;
Thou didst triumph o'er the grave,
Thou wilt all Thy people save;
Ransomed by Thy blood, the just
Rise immortal from the dust.

IMMORTALITY.

Philip Schaff, D.D., L.L.D.

LIFE, death, eternity—how vast, how deep, how solemn these three words, so familiar to us all! Who can measure, who can fathom their meaning? In the midst of life we are surrounded by death and confronted by eternity, with its boundless prospects of weal and woe. Life on earth ends in death, and death is but the dark door to another life which has no end. Astronomy cannot tell whether this visible universe has boundaries or not, and what lies beyond. Theology cannot determine the locality of that invisible universe from which no traveller returns, nor the direction and length of that lonely passage which carries the disembodied spirit from its present to its future abode. But this we do know—and it is enough for our comfort—that in our Father's house are many mansions, and that our Saviour has prepared a place for all His disciples. There is an abundance of room for all even within the limits of this universe, and for aught we know the spirit world may be very near and round about us. There are exalted moments in our life when we see the heavens open and the angels of God descending and ascending. Life is a mystery, a glorious mystery with a heaven beyond, but a terrible mystery with annihilation or endless punishment in prospect.

The immortality of the soul is a universal instinct and desire of the human race. Like the idea of God, it is implanted in our intellectual and moral constitution. We cannot think backward without reaching an ultimate cause which has no beginning; we cannot think forward without arriving at a result which has no ending. God and eternity precede time and succeed time, and time itself is filled with both. We cannot conceive that a wise Creator should make man in His own image and endow him with the highest faculties without ordaining him for endless existence. He cannot intend the head of His creatures, the master-piece of His hand, to perish like the brute. He cannot allow virtue to suffer and iniquity to flourish without some future adjustment which will give to every one his due and restore the harmony of character and condition. It seems impossible that a rational being filled with infinite longings and capable of endless progress should be suddenly cut off in the beginning of its career, "like the empty fabric of a vision leaving no wreck behind." It seems impossible that the mind, which proves its independence of the body and matures in strength while the body declines, should be dissolved with its material tent. No husband can close the eyes of a beloved wife, no parent can commit a child to the cold grave, no friend can bid farewell to a bosom friend, without the ardent wish of the recovery of the loss and a meeting again in a better world, where tears of parting are unknown. Every consideration of God's goodness, love, and justice, of man's capacities, desires and hopes, and of surrounding nature, with its perennial renovations of seasons and transformations of death itself into new forms of life, forces upon us the belief in the immortality of the human soul.

But after all, philosophy and science can lead us only to the probability of immortality, and there is a vast step from probability to certainty. The starry heavens above and the moral law within may well have filled the great philosopher of the last century with ever-growing reverence and awe; but beyond the starry heavens and behind the moral law lie the sublimer regions of faith, which fill us with deeper reverence and which alone can give us solid comfort in life and in death.

Another profound and keen thinker of the nineteenth century, who had mastered all the systems from Plato to Kant, when he stood at the open grave of his only child, could find no comfort in any philosophical argument, but only in the all-powerful prayer of Christ, "Father, I will that they also whom Thou hast given me be with me where I am" (John xvii., 26); and in the assurance of His beloved disciple, "It doth not yet appear what we shall be; but we know that when He shall appear we shall be like Him, for we shall see Him as He is" (John iii., 2). Supported by these firm assurances, he said, and trusting therein my child's immortal life, I repeat from my heart the words of Holy Writ, "The Lord gave and the Lord hath taken away; blessed be the name of the Lord!" (Job i., 21.)

Faith in Christ who can never die, who is the conqueror of death and the prince of life, gives us the best security for our immortality. In union with Christ the future life is an immortality of bliss; out of Christ it is an immortality of woe.

Let us glance, first, at the notions which prevailed among the heathen and Jews on this subject before the advent of our Lord, that we may see the difference.

1. The heathen ideas of the future life were vague and confused. The Hindoos, Babylonians, and Egyptians had a lively sense of immortality, but mixed with the notion of endless migrations and transformations, through various forms of vegetable and animal life. The Buddhists, starting from the idea that existence is want, and want is suffering, make it the chief end of man to escape such migrations, and by various mortifications to prepare for annihilation or absorption in the unconscious dream-life of Nirwana. The popular belief among the ancient Greeks and Romans was that man passes after death into the Underworld, the Greek *Hades*, the Roman *Orcus*. According to Homer, Hades is a dark abode in the interior of the earth, with an entrance at the western extremity of the ocean, where the rays of the sun do not penetrate. Charon carries the dead over the stream; Acheron and the three-headed dog Cerberus watch the entrance and allow none to pass out. There the spirits exist in a disembodied state and lead a shadowy dream-life. A vague distinction was made between two regions in Hades, an Elysium (also "the Islands of the Blessed") for the good, and Tartarus for the bad.

Socrates, Plato, Cicero, Seneca, and Plutarch rose highest among the ancient philosophers in their views of the future life, but they reached only to belief in its probability, not in its certainty. Socrates, after he was condemned to death, said to his judges: "Death is either an eternal sleep or a transition to a new life; but in neither case is it an evil;" and he drank with playful irony the fatal hemlock. Plato, viewing the human soul as a portion of the eternal, infinite, all-pervading Deity, believed in its pre-existence before this present life, and thus had a strong ground of hope for its continuance after death. All the souls pass into the spirit world, the righteous into the abodes of bliss, where they live forever in a disembodied state, the wicked into Tartarus for punishment and purification, and the incorrigibly bad for eternal punishment. Plutarch, the purest and noblest among the Platonists, thought that immortality was inseparably connected with belief in an all-ruling Providence, and looked to the life beyond as promising a higher knowledge of and closer conformity to God, but only for those few who are here purified by virtue and piety. In such rare cases departure might be called an ascent to the stars, to heaven, to the gods, rather than a descent to Hades. At the death of his daughter, he comforted his wife with the hope in the blissful state of infants who die in infancy. Cicero reflects in classical language "the ignorance, the errors, and the uncertainty of the ancient philosophers with regard to the immortality of the soul." Though strongly leaning to a positive view, he yet found it no superfluous task to quiet the fear of death in case the soul should perish with the body. The Stoics believed only in a limited immortality, or denied it altogether, and justified suicide when life became unendurable. The great men of Greece and Rome were not influenced by the idea of a future world as a motive of action. During the debate on the punishment of Catiline and his fellow conspirators, Julius Cæsar openly declared in the Roman Senate that death dissolves all the ills of mortality, and is the boundary of existence beyond which there is no more care nor joy, no more punishment for sin, nor any reward for virtue. The younger Cato, the model Stoic, agreed with Cæsar; yet before he made an end to his life at Utica he read Plato's *Phædon*. Seneca once dreamed of immortality, and almost approached the Christian hope of the birth-day of eternity, if we are to trust his rhetoric, but afterwards he awoke from the beautiful dream and committed suicide. Marcus Aurelius, in sad resignation, bids nature, "Give what thou wilt, and take back what thou wilt."

Yet the scepticism of the educated and half-educated could not extinguish the popular belief in immortality. The number of cheerless and hopeless materialistic epitaphs is very small as compared with the many thousands which reveal no such doubt, or express belief in some kind of existence beyond the grave.

Of a resurrection of the body the Greeks and Romans had no conception, except in the form of shades and spectral outlines, which were supposed to surround the disembodied spirits, and to make them to some degree recognizable. Heathen philosophers like Celsus ridiculed the resurrection of the body as useless, absurd and impossible.

2. The Jewish doctrine is far in advance of heathen notions and conjectures, but presents different phrases of development.

The Mosaic writings are remarkably silent about the future life, and emphasize the present rather than future consequences of the observance or non-observance of the law (because it has a civil or political as well as spiritual import); and hence the Sadducees denied the resurrection (perhaps also the immortality of the soul). The Pentateuch contains, however, some remote and significant hints of immortality, as in the tree of life with its symbolic import; in the mysterious translation of Enoch as a reward for his piety; in the prohibition of necromancy; in the patriarchal phrase for dying, "to be gathered to his fathers," or "to his people;" and in the self-designation of Jehovah as "the God of Abraham, Isaac and Jacob," which implies their immortality, since "God is not a God of the dead, but of the living." What has an eternal meaning for God must itself be eternal

In the latter writings of the Old Testament, especially during and after the exile, the doctrine of immortality and resurrection comes out plainly. Daniel's vision reaches out even to the final resurrection of "many of them that sleep in the dust of the earth to everlasting life," and of "some to shame and everlasting contempt," and prophesies that "they that are wise shall shine as the brightness of the firmament, and they that turn many to righteousness as the stars for ever and ever."

But before Christ, who first revealed true life, the Hebrew Sheol, the general receptacle of departing souls, remained, like the Greek Hades, a dark and dreary abode, and is so described in the Old Testament. Cases like Enoch's translation and Elijah's ascent are altogether unique and exceptional, and imply the meaning that death is not necessarily the transition to another life.

3. The Christian doctrine of the future life differs

from the heathen, and to a less extent also from the Jewish, in the following important points:

First, it gives to the belief in a future state the absolute certainty of divine revelation, sealed by the fact of Christ's resurrection, and thereby imparts to the present life an immeasurable importance, involving endless issues.

In the next place, it connects the resurrection of the body with the immortality of the soul, and thus saves the whole individuality of man from destruction.

Moreover, Christianity views death as the punishment of sin, and therefore as something terrible, from which nature shrinks. But its terror has been broken, and its sting extracted by Christ.

And finally, Christianity qualifies the idea of a future state by the doctrine of sin and redemption, and thus makes it to the believer a state of absolute holiness and happiness; to the impenitent sinner a state of absolute misery. Death and immortality are a blessing to the one, but a terror to the other; the former can hail them with joy; the latter has reason to tremble. The Bible inseparably connects the future life with the general judgment, which determines the ultimate fate of all men according to their works done in this earthly life.

To the Christian this present life is simply a pilgrimage to a better country and to a city whose builder and maker is God. Every day he moves his tent nearer his true home. His citizenship is in heaven, his thoughts, his hopes, his aspirations, are heavenly. This unworldliness or heavenly-mindedness, far from disqualifying him for the duties of earth, makes him more faithful and conscientious in his calling; for he remembers that he must render an account for every word and deed at a bar of God's judgment. Yea, in proportion as he is heavenly-minded and follows the example of his Lord and Saviour, he brings heaven down to earth and lifts earth up to heaven, and infuses the purity and happiness of heaven into his heart and home. Faith unites us to Christ, who is life itself in its truest, fullest conception; life in God, life eternal. United with Christ, we live indeed, shedding round about us the rays of His purity, goodness, love and peace. Death has lost its terror; it is but a short slumber from which we shall awake in His likeness and enjoy what eye has not seen, nor ear heard, nor ever entered the imagination of man. "Because I live, ye shall live also." John xiv., 19.

CONSOLATION AND WARNING.

REV. JAMES SMITH, D.D.

"We know that all things work together for good to them that love God, to them who are the called according to his purpose."—Rom. viii., 28.

ALL things? Yes; whatever happens to the Christian is directed and overruled by a special providence for his good. It may be very bitter; it may lay him very low; it may try him to the quick; it may keep him in the dust for a long time; but it will do him good, not only in the end, but while it lasts.

Believer, your present trial is for your good; nothing could be better for you. You may not see it now; you may feel as if you never could think so; but the time is coming when you will bless God for it. You love God, though it is but feebly; and that proves that God loves you with an infinite and eternal love. You have come to the cross as a poor sinner, and you look to the Lord Jesus to be your perfect Saviour; and this proves that you have been called according to God's purpose. And it is as one beloved of God, as one of God's called ones, that we may have this assurance respecting you, that *all things*—light and darkness, health and sickness, hatred and love, prosperity and adversity, life and death—will work together for your good. God asserts the fact, and therefore you should believe it. The history of all God's people proves and illustrates it, and therefore you should rejoice in it. Dark clouds bring rich blessings; sharp winters introduce fruitful springs; and sore troubles often precede the sweetest consolations. Your present affliction—be it sickness of body, trouble of mind, bereavements, losses, crosses, or whatever else—is working for your good; not merely will work in the future, but is working now. While your heart is bleeding, while you are tempted to think all is against you, all is working together for your good. "We glory in tribulations also: knowing that tribulation worketh patience; and patience, experience; and experience, hope."—Rom. v., 3, 4.

Unbeliever, "What will ye do in the day of visitation?"—Isa. x., 3.

Troubles, trials, and afflictions are the lot of all; none can finally escape them. It becomes every one, therefore, to be prepared for them. We may soon, we may suddenly, be visited with sickness, bereavement, or death; therefore the Lord kindly asks us what we intend to do when they come. Reader, *what will you do?* Will you bear them with fortitude and patience? Will you look to the Lord for wisdom and strength to enable you to triumph over them? Will you have Jesus to sympathize with you in them, support you under them, and bring you through them? Or will you be left to grapple with them in your native strength? Few sights are more painful than to see a sinner, without a hope in Jesus, without peace with God, without a prospect of glory, sinking into floods of deep affliction.

Reader, *will this be your case?* Is there the least probability of it? If so, let me most earnestly and affectionately beseech you now, before the day of visitation comes, before the storm falls, before the tempest bursts upon you, to seek and find refuge in Jesus. Make personal religion your great object. Seek pardon and peace through Jesus without delay. Set your heart upon union to Christ, and never rest until you enjoy it: it may be realized, and it may be realized by you. *In* Christ, deriving strength *from* Christ, and enjoying communion *with* Christ, you will be prepared for the day of visitation, whether that visitation be temporal losses, soul conflicts, domestic troubles, or even death itself. Seek, oh seek, then, an interest in Christ. Rest not until you know that Christ is yours, and that you are entitled to all the promises of his grace; and then, if asked, "What will you do in the day of visitation?" you will be able to say, "I *will trust in* JESUS."

THE LIGHT IN THE CLOUDS.

Rev. Theodore L. Cuyler, D.D.

I THANK God that never doth He permit a cloud so dark but behind it is the light, and through it streams the mercies, and from it descend plentiful and abounding blessings. Have you not had it, business man, in your experience? When thou wert growing too rich for thy soul's good did not God send to thee that depletion? did not He puncture thee to let the pride and vain-glory run out? When thou wert running at fifty miles an hour along the track of prosperity, did not He, perhaps, dash thee into temporary calamity, in order that He might lower thy pride and put thee on the better track of godliness, humanity and holy living? I am confident that national humiliation, Church trials, and personal adversities are all God's measures for the purification of those with whom He deals, and for the advancement of His own sovereign glory.

Suffering hath many compensations, not only in its influence upon the sufferer in humbling him, bringing him into a sense of dependence, inspiring in him a spirit of prayer, quickening his faith and working out the principles of righteousness, but suffering hath its happy influence on others. Did you ever climb into an attic or thread some back slum with a loaf or medicine or God's Book, and bring cheer to that dark home and heart, and not go home the better man, melted, thankful for your own home and altar, yourself the better for the process through which the suffering of that suffering one had led thee? So it is to-day that philanthropy is one of the blessings that come out of sin and sorrow and suffering. Continually I love to think how

> "Behind the cloud the star-light shines,
> And through the showers the sunbeams fall,
> For God, who loveth all His own,
> Doth send His love on all."

The most transcendent illustration of that in the world was furnished on Golgotha when fiendish spirits were permitted to put to death the Lord of Glory. The most stupendous crime that ever darkened God's heaven was committed between the sixth and ninth hour on Calvary; yet that cloud that darkened the sky, hid the sun, under whose terrible gloom the earth quaked and the dead came forth, is an illustration of the glorious truth that in Him we have the redemption of our sins and the life everlasting. And as long as you and I have Christ, can we not bear all things and endure all things if we have hope of that redemption and that Christ in our hearts and the life everlasting beyond the grave?

In practical application the *first* thing I would have you remember, is that God is often inscrutable, never wrong. Write that with a pen of diamond on a rock: "God is always right when I am wrong." Friend, if on the day of judgment thou goest away condemned into hell for the rejection of the blood of Christ, even there thou wilt stand up and confess, "God is right and I was wrong."

The *second* thought is that on this side of the

cloud, you and I have nothing to do but to receive the truth that comes through and walk by it. I know very often the revealed dispensations, the actual dispensations are very trying. But never get frightened at God's clouds:—

> "Blind unbelief is sure to err,
>   And scan His works in vain;
> God is His own interpreter,
>   And He will make it plain."

Did you not sing—

> "Behind a frowning Providence He hides a smiling face?"

And so it will always be that God is continually making clouds of trials which at first shock and frighten us, but which are to be to us sources of infinite blessing.

One other thought. Clouds of trial often rain down truth to be gathered from no other source. Clouds of trial often rain down truth as the dark cloud in the heavens rains down showers on the thirsty field and lawn. God usually orders it that through penitence come praise and forgiveness, through trial comes triumph; yea, the cloud itself sends down mercy.

I counsel you to gain the utmost benefit of every hard lot, and learn the richest and deepest lesson that God can write on any cloud of trial. There is a great want in all God's people that have ever suffered; there is a great defect in the education of every Christian that has never had a sharp trial. The richest graces grow out of those ploughed fields where God puts the ploughshare of affliction deep into the very subsoil.

And now, last of all, you and I should never be

frightened with adversity as if we were in the path of wrong when it comes upon us, as the Israelites were frightened at the Red Sea, though it lay in their pathway from Egypt, or any more than the disciples were wrong when they crossed the sea at the Master's command, and when a storm came: we never should regard adversity as intended of God to put us back, to hinder us or testify to us that we are in the wrong path; we should learn how to plunge into His sea, and it shall part, and to go out with Him into the storm, and He shall bring us calm.

RETROSPECTION.

ANNA SHIPTON.

"Cast not away, therefore, your confidence, which hath great recompense of reward."—Heb. x., 35.

HE was better to me than all my hopes,
    He was better than all my fears;
  He made a road of my broken works,
    And a rainbow of my tears.
The billows that guarded my sea-girt path,
    But carried my Lord on their crest;
When I dwell on the days of my wilderness march
    I can lean on His love for the rest.

WHEN God afflicts the saints, it is to try their precious faith; afflictions are his spade and mattock, by which He digs into His people's hearts to find out the gold of faith.

REV. W. GURNAL.

TRIALS AND TROUBLES THE LOT OF MANKIND.

John R. Macduff, D.D.

HOW varied are our trials and days of trouble! *Sickness*, with its hours of restlessness and languor. *Bereavement*, with its rifled treasures and aching hearts. *Loss of substance*—the curtailment or forfeiture of worldly possessions—riches taking to themselves wings and fleeing away; or, severer than all, the woundings of friends, abused confidence, withered affections, hopes scattered like the leaves of autumn?

But "God is our refuge and strength, a very present help in trouble." Tried one! He leaves not thy defenceless head unsheltered in the storm— "*Call upon* me!" He invites thee into the pavilion of His own presence! Better the bitter *Marah* waters with His healing, than the purest fountain of the world and *no* God! Better the hottest furnace flames with one there "like the Son of God," than that the dross should be suffered to accumulate, and the soul left to cleave to the dust!

The day of trouble led His saints in all ages to glorify Him. David never could have written his touching Psalms, nor Paul his precious Epistles, had not God cast them both into the crucible. To be the teachers of the Church of the future, they had to graduate in the school of affliction. If He be appointing us similar discipline, let it be our endeavor to glorify Him by active obedience, as well as by passive resignation; not abandoning ourselves to selfish, moody, sentimental grief; but rather going forth on our great mission—our work and warfare—with a vaster estimate of the value of time, and the grandeur of existence.

Remember that the promise respecting these days of trouble is that they shall soon be ended.

"The days of thy mourning shall be ended."—Isa. ix., 20.

The believer has "mourning days." The place of his sojourn is a *valley of tears*. Adam went weeping from *his* paradise, we go weeping on the way to ours. But, pilgrim of grief! thy tears are numbered. A few more aching sighs—a few more gloomy clouds—and the eternal sun shall burst on thee, whose radiance shall never more be obscured! Life may be to thee one long "Valley of Baca"—a protracted scene of "weeping!"—but soon shalt thou hear the sweet chimes wafted from the towers of the new Jerusalem, "Enter into the *joy* of thy Lord!" "*The Lord God shall wipe away all tears from off all faces!*"

"*The* days *of thy mourning!*" It is a consoling thought that all these days are appointed—meted out—numbered. "Unto you it is given," says the apostle, "*to suffer!*" Yes! and if thou art a child of the covenant, thy mourning days are days of special privilege, intended to be fraught with blessing. To the unbeliever, they are earnests of everlasting woe; —to the believer, they are preludes and precursors of eternal glory! Affliction to the one is the cloud without the Bow,—to the other, it is the cloud radiant and lustrous with gospel promise and gospel hope!

Reader! art thou now one of the many members of the family of sorrow? Be comforted! Soon the long night-watch will be over—pain, sickness, weakness, weariness. Soon the windows of the soul will be no more darkened. Soon thou shalt have nothing to be delivered from,—thy present losses and crosses will turn into eternal gains,—the dews of the night of weeping (nature's teardrops) will come to sparkle like beauteous gems in the morning of immortality! Soon the Master's footsteps will be heard, saying, "The days of thy mourning are ended," and thou shalt take off thy sackcloth, and be girded with gladness.

Up to that moment, thy life may have been one long "day" of mourning! but once past the golden portals, and the eye can be dim no more;—the very fountain of weeping will be dried!

"Then, then will be eternal joy."

"For the ransomed of the Lord shall return, and come to Sion with songs, and everlasting joy upon their heads: they shall obtain joy and gladness, and sorrow and sighing shall for ever flee away." —Isa. xxx., 10.

Believer! leave thy "*Bow in the cloud*" behind thee; and with thine eye on the "Rainbow round about the throne" (Rev. iv., 3), think of the gladsome return of God's ransomed ones to Zion—every tear-drop dried, every pang forgotten!

As some seeds require on earth to be steeped in water before they germinate, so is immortal seed ofttimes here steeped in tears. But "*they that sow in tears shall reap in* JOY."

Though "weeping" may endure for the night, "*joy* cometh in the morning!" "You are," says Rutherford, "upon the entry of Heaven's harvest;

the losses that I write of are but summer showers and the Sun of the new Jerusalem shall quickly dry them up." The "song of the night" shall then blend with the song of the skies, and inner glorious meanings will be disclosed to sight, which are now hidden from the eye of faith!

"*Sorrow and sighing shall for ever flee away!*"

"No sickness, no sorrow, no pain," said an aged saint now entered on these glorious realities; "but this is only Thy negative. What, O God! must be Thy positive?" "*Songs,*" "*everlasting joy,*" "*joy and gladness.*" It will be song upon song, joy upon joy, gladness upon gladness! These songs of Heaven will be "songs of *degrees.*" The ransomed will be ever graduating in bliss, mounting "from glory to glory," each song suggesting the keynote of a louder and loftier.

Reader! art thou mourning the loss of those who "are not;" the music of whose voices is hushed for thee forever of time, and who have left thee to travel companionless and alone the wilderness journey? A few more fears, a few more *tears*, and thou shalt meet them in the day-break of glory! Nay, more; they have but anticipated thee in an earlier crown. If they have left thee behind for a little season to continue thy night-song, think with bounding heart of that eternal day, when, looking back on the clouds floating in the far distance in the nether Valley, thou shalt be able to join in the anthem said to be sung by the four-and-twenty elders as they gaze on the throne encircled by the "Rainbow of emerald;" for "*they rest not day and night, saying* Holy, holy, holy, Lord God Almighty" (Rev. iv., 3, 8).

THE SORROWS OF CARE.

Rev. John Philip, M.A.

THE burden of care is the common lot of all. Every one has to carry his knapsack of care.

Many a care-worn countenance do we see; and many an anxious heart beats within the bosom, even when the face may wear a smile. As there are insects that prey upon trees and shrubs, and eat out the pith and scoop out the heart while the rind or bark is left, so there are heart-eating cares that honey-comb the happiness and suck out the sweetness of life, while yet the outward appearance remains much the same. And so swarming cares can penetrate deeper into the heart and scrape it harder than heavier crosses.

More perhaps than the sterner calamities of life, and especially in this fast-driving age, the daily fretting, carking, corroding cares, the little vexations and worries of household management and business affairs, are apt to prey upon the mind and chafe the temper and sour the spirit and wear out the patience. Singly or apart, their influence would be trifling; but recurring so often and multiplying so fast, they form no inconsiderable part of the burdens of life. And as a tree which has been scooped out in the stem is thereby rendered less able to stand the fury of the gale, so by these heart-pecking cares (if no antidote is found for them) our strength is weakened, and we are less able to bear the strain or sustain the heavier burdens of life.

Who now could sustain the pressure and weight of the atmosphere without, if it were not for the pressure of the air within, which creates an equipoise. And as it is by the habitual process of breathing that this equipoise is preserved, so it is by habitual prayer that we get inward strength to balance outward and all other troubles. When the diver is down in the diving-bell, he could not remain any time under the heavy pressure were it not for his constant communication with the atmosphere above, whereby he is provided with a continual supply of fresh air. And so, if we suspend the exercise of prayer, or of that faith which is the very soul of prayer, and thereby cut off our supplies from above, we shall be ready to sink under our burdens, and be submerged in the depths.

But how slow we are to trust! We are too often like one learning to swim, who would fain keep touching the ground with his feet, and fears to trust himself on the buoyant waters, lest he should sink at once. So we would like to feel some good bottom underneath, to have some tangible or sensible ground of comfort, and are reluctant to throw ourselves upon God's bare promise. But we can never know the effectual support He gives unless and until we let go our hold of everything else, and venture our souls solely and wholly upon His sure word of promise. We must break down the bridge of self-will, and fall back on Him alone. So long as we quarrel with His will and wrangle to get our own way, we must remain strangers to peace.

The strength renewed is best displayed in the quiet walk and steady on going of the Christian life. And even the very cares that burden and beset us may prove a blessing in the way of making us more wary and watchful in choosing our steps, and in rendering our foothold firmer, as there is far less risk of sliding on a rough road than on a smooth one.

....

PATIENCE UNDER TRIAL.

WILLIAM R. WILLIAMS, D.D.

LET us consider the motives that should persuade us to be patient as Christians. For as patience includes meekness under wrongs of our fellow-men, we must forgive, or we may not hope ourselves before God to be forgiven. Christ laid the axe where no earthly reformer would have dared to place it, at the root of revengefulness. The Christian law of morals gropes in the heart of every petitioner oft as he prays, and it bids him pray without ceasing. We are warned again that in yielding to impatience and anger we cease to possess our souls; and, as is darkly intimated, Satan takes hold of the deserted rudder and wields the ungoverned helm, and drives before him the infuriated and imbruted man.

Patience includes submission to the divine appointments, and our trials are lessened by serene meekness and resignation. God lightens and removes them more early, and they do not so deeply wound and empoison the soul. But he who frets and fights against God, in the language of ancient prophecy, like a bullock unaccustomed to the yoke, drives the deeper into his own flesh the goad against which he vainly kicks.

We are to remember, too, the necessity of this

grace to success and influence with our fellow-men. It is the patient perseverance in well-doing that builds up consistency, and influence, and weight of character. Nor is it unfitting that we remember how much of mercy and kindness there is in God's allotments; and how, by the general presence of affliction, God has provided in every sphere, the most obscure and secluded even, a scene where He may be glorified, and where the power of His religion and grace may be illustrated; and how, out of such trials meekly borne, He weaves the confessor's wreath and the martyr's crown, and makes the blood of His slain servants the seed of His Church, whilst the wrath of man is forced to praise Him, and the remainder of wrath is restrained.

Are we tempted to impatience and anger with some erring and injurious fellow-mortal? Let us test the old Puritan dilemma in such case. The offender is a Christian or a child of hell. If already or yet to become the first, we shall in heaven not remember with pleasure revengeful and retaliatory wrongs against one of our brethren and of Christ's people. If an enemy of God and an heir of His wrath, he is soon to endure more than man can inflict, and the bar to which he is rushing is one at which strict justice and unforgetting memory preside. Let us dread snatching into our hands the sceptre of Him who has said "Vengeance is mine," and then pronouncing rash and false judgment, rooting up the wheat with the tares, and making sad the heart of the righteous whom God has not made sad. The question of the Judge of all the earth to the over-fretted patriarch has much of dread significance: "Wilt thou also *disannul my judgment*?

Wilt thou condemn Me that thou mayest be righteous?" (Job xi., 8,) Much of our impatience is a virtuous disannulling of God's decisions, and a distinct intimation that His forbearance is wanting in righteousness.

RELIEF IN DARKNESS.

Rev. E. C. Gordon.

THE background of all light is darkness. The background of all knowledge is mystery. In our calculations and forecastings, it would be as unwise to leave out the darkness and the mystery as it would be foolish to ignore the light or despise the knowledge that we have.

There is a disposition in some men, under favorable circumstances, to look only at the light; to rejoice in the knowledge which they have acquired. Others, in adverse circumstances, regard only the darkness and sink beneath the pressure of the mystery. Life is not all clouds and storm. There are times when we feel that mere existence is a luxury. The air is soft; the breeze is balmy; the sunrise is full of hope, even his setting is full of glory; the prospects before us promise blessedness.

And yet there comes to every one a time when men walk in darkness and have no light. Such a time came to Job—not when he was stripped of his property, not when his bones mutinied against him as he sat in dust and ashes. It came when his friends tried to persuade him that he was a rebel against God, and that God was angry with him.

Such a time comes once, it may be twice or oftener, to all men. To the rich as well as to the poor; to those in health as well as those in sickness; to the learned and honored as well as to the ignorant, the obscure, and the despised. A time of darkness and there is no light! When the hard-earned fame is trampled in the dust; when the heart's idol passes into the abyss; when poverty comes like an armed man, when the relentless battle begins with want and shame and woe; when the soul cries from the depths:

"Alas! I have no hope, no rest, nor peace within,
Nor calm of mind, nor passing health, nor contemplation kind!
To me that cup hath been dealt in far other measure."

A time of darkness and there is no light! Sometimes it comes to a man burdened with the consciousness of sin. He must sit down face to face with an accusing conscience. He must give account of wasted opportunities. He must feel the shame of duty neglected; he must bear the weight of evil memories; he must endure the plague of polluting thoughts

Think of the sweep of generations; the populations that have lived and died, numerous as the sands upon the sea-shore, going through life, toiling striving, sinning, suffering, loving, hoping, dying! How can it be that a God of infinite goodness, as well as infinite wisdom and power, should tolerate such a world as this!

Look at that infant child writhing in anguish! See it gasping for breath! See the agony written on every line of its face! Think of the myriads of such cases, and as you contemplate a world where helpless babes are convulsed with pain and die in torture, does not your soul walk in darkness and have no light? Can you not sympathize with the Greek poet who said: "The best thing is not to have been born, and the next best thing is to pass away as soon as possible:" or with the English poet who said:

> "Count all the joys that thou hast seen,
> Count all the tears from anguish keen,
> And know, whatever thou hast seen,
> 'Twere better never to have been."

A time of darkness and there is no light! It is to be observed that this time of darkness comes at times to God's own people. There are some who would have us believe that the Christian life is, or ought to be, a life of unclouded sunshine. They say: "A Christian is the object of God's electing love; he is the subject of God's regenerating grace. He is an heir of Christ's glory. He should bask continually in the light of God's smile."

Beloved, whatever *ought* to be, it is certain that this is not the actual experience of God's people. The Word of God recognizes this; and addresses itself to those who fear God, who obey the voice of his servant, and who, nevertheless walk in darkness. —Isa. i., 10, 11.

To all such, whether they be believers or unbelievers, Christian or infidels, there is only one method by which to dissipate the darkness: one way that may be pursued with success. The way is the way of firm, unquestioning, implicit faith in God. "Let him trust in the name of the Lord, and stay upon his God." Let him commit himself without hesitation or reserve on the infinite wisdom, power, and love of him who is King of kings and Lord of lords.

The bad way is the way of self-trust. It is the attempt to walk by the light of one's own wisdom, to "stay" upon one's own strength. All such kindle a fire for themselves; they compass themselves about with sparks. They walk in the light of their own fire and in the light of the sparks they have kindled. They shall lie down in sorrow.

⁂

WAITING FOR DAY.

H. C. BROWN.

THE night is dark, but God my God
    Is here, and in command;
    And sure am I, when morning breaks
  I shall be "at the land."
And since I know the darkness is
    To Him as sunniest day,
I'll cast the anchor Patience out
    And wish—but wait for day.

Fierce drives the storm, but wind and waves,
    Within His hand are held,
And trusting in Omnipotence,
    My fears are sweetly quelled.
If wrecked, I'm in His faithful grasp,
    I'll trust Him, though He slay;
So, letting go the anchor Faith,
    I'll wish—but wait for day.

Still seem the moments dreary long—
    I rest upon the Lord;
I muse on His "eternal years,"
    And feast upon His word;
His promises so rich and great,
    Are my support and stay;
I'll drop the anchor Hope ahead,
    And wish—but wait for day.

THE BURDENS OF SYMPATHY.

Henry Clay Trumbull, D.D.

IT is only a half-truth to say that "love lightens burdens." Unselfish love, which true friendship is, bears burdens gladly for the loved friend; and if the burden be one of *service*, it is borne as lightly as it is cheerfully. But where the burden is one of *sympathy* with another who is in sorrow or weakness or need, it is all the heavier for the love which prompts its sharing. The term "sympathy" in its broadened meaning includes all close correspondence or sharing of feelings—whether of sorrow or of joy—with another; and with the fact that there is so much of sorrow and trial and bitterness of experience in every human heart, that to feel with another in true and unselfish love is to suffer with another keenly. And this it is that makes sympathy so rare, so costly, and so precious.

If the burden be wholly our own, we have the right, the duty, and the privilege of turning our thoughts away from its weight; of calling in our philosophy to console us under its bearing, or of crushing into subjection the feelings of regret, or of disappointment, or of humiliation, which it engenders. But if the burden is another's, which we bear and share in loving sympathy, we must not try to evade it, or to philosophize away its weight, or to crush out the sense of its bitterness. It must be heavier to us than if it were our own; because it weighs without relief on our other and better self.

There is a beautiful illustration of this truth in the confession of the apostle Paul, when he ventures on what he calls his glory in his weakness. He tells of the trials he has endured in his life of strangely varied experiences, of the toils, the imprisonments, the stripes, the stonings, the shipwrecks, the watchings, the fastings, the shiverings, the desertions, and the betrayals, to which he has been called. And, as the climax of his woes, he adds, as if here was something which was beyond all detail of description, and which transcended his other trials: anxiety for all the churches, which presseth upon me daily. And as it was with Paul, so it is with every truest man everywhere; his weakness, shown in his suffering keenly and constantly with and for those whom he loves, is worthier of honor than his strength over all his personal trials and needs.

The hearts that suffer most in this life are hearts that feel the weight of others' sorrows and needs. A dear, good city missionary, who was hardly less noble and tender and loving than the apostle Paul, was speaking to a young co-worker, of his wakeful, restless nights, after his long days of loving ministry to the poor and the sorrowing. "Why, I should think your good work of the day would make your pillow soft and refreshing at night!" was the surprised response of his young co-worker. "Oh! but the trouble with me is," said the missionary, "I carry a hundred aching hearts to bed with me every night; and I can't sleep, for *their* sorrows!" And that was the burden of true sympathy, a burden which must be borne by any one who feels the sufferings of another.

It costs something to be a friend. It costs more to love than to endure without loving; and although there is a pleasure in the very outlay of love in friendship, that pleasure is inevitably an expensive and painful purchase. This is a truth that we need to have in mind when we find that we are bearing heavier burdens in and through our closest friendships, than in any other sphere. The highest value of a friendship is in what it enables us to be and to do as a friend, not in what it secures to us from a friend. And just in proportion as we are unselfishly loving and true in our friendships, must we be more than sharers in the sufferings of our dearest friends. Not merely in their obvious sorrows and in their manifest needs shall we suffer with them; but in the unexpressed trials of their innermost selves, as recognized by our acuter perceptions in their sense of spiritual loneliness; and in the ceaseless struggles of their sensitively felt contradictions of nature and character. The dearer they are to us and the closer our sympathy with them, the heavier the burdens which we must bear in their behalf.

Nor should we forget what it costs another to be our sympathizing friend. Because he sympathizes with us, he suffers with us; and because he unselfishly gives us a foremost place in his thoughts and feelings, our sorrows and needs burden him more heavily than his own. To sympathize with those who are dear to us is a high privilege in life. This privilege is one of the costliest privileges that is granted to humanity on earth; and it is a privilege worth far more than it costs.

COME YE DISCONSOLATE.*

Thomas Moore (1816).

COME ye disconsolate, where'er you languish,
    Come at God's altar, fervently kneel;
    Here bring your wounded hearts, here tell your anguish,
Earth has no sorrow that heaven cannot heal.

Joy of the desolate, light of the straying
    Hope when all others die, fadeless and pure!
Here speaks the Comforter, in God's name saying,
    Earth has no sorrow that heaven cannot cure.

Go ask the infidel, what boon he brings us,
    What charm for aching hearts *he* can reveal
Sweet as that heavenly promise Hope sings us,
    Earth has no sorrow that God cannot heal.

Here see the bread of life; see waters flowing
    Forth from the throne of God, boundless in love;
Come to the feast prepared; come, ever knowing,
    Earth has no sorrow but heaven can remove.

"Ah, if we only knew it all, we should surely understand
That the balance of sorrow and joy is held with an even hand;
That the scale of success or loss shall never overflow,
And that compensation is twined with the lot of high and low."

F. R. Havergal.

---

* The first three stanzas are as the author wrote them, and not as found in modern Hymn-books.

WHEN THE MISTS HAVE CLEARED AWAY.

ANNIE HERBERT.

WHEN the mists have roll'd in splendor
    From the beauty of the hills,
And the sunshine, warm and tender,
    Falls in kisses on the rills,
We may read love's shining letter
    In the rainbow of the spray,—
We shall know each other better
    When the mists have cleared away.
        We shall know as we are known
          Never more to walk alone,
        In the dawning of the morning,
          When the mists have cleared away.

If we err in human blindness,
    And forget that we are dust;
If we miss the law of kindness
    When we struggle to be just,
Snowy wings of peace shall cover
    All the plain that hides away,—
When the weary watch is over,
    And the mists have cleared away.
        We shall know, etc., etc.

When the mists have risen above us,
    As our Father knows his own,
Face to face with those that love us,
    We shall know as we are known;
Love, beyond the orient meadows
    Floats the golden fringe of day,
Heart to heart, we bide the shadows,
    Till the mists have cleared away.
        We shall know, etc., etc.

AMEN.

F. G. BROWNING.

I can not say,
Beneath the pressure of life's care to-day,
    I joy in these;
    But I can say
That I had rather walk this rugged way,
    If Him it please.

    I can not feel
That all is well, when dark'ning clouds conceal
    The shining sun;
    But then I know
God lives and loves, and say, since it is so,
    Thy will be done.

    I do not see
Why God should e'en permit some things to be,
    When He is love;
    But I can see,
Though dimly, through the mystery,
    His hand above.

    I do not look
Upon the present, nor in Nature's book,
    To read my fate;
    But I do look
For promised blessings in God's Holy Book,
    And I can wait.

    I may not try
To keep the hot tears back; but hush that sigh,
    "It might have been;"
    And try to still
Each rising murmur, and to God's sweet will
    Respond, Amen.—

Consolation for the Aged and Infirm.

Now also when I am Old and Greyheaded, O God, Forsake me not.—*Ps.* lxxi., 18.

With Long Life will I Satisfy him, and Show him My Salvation.—*Ps.* xci., 16.

I'M GROWING OLD.

John Godfrey Saxe.

My days pass pleasantly away;
    My nights are blest with sweetest sleep;
    I feel no symptoms of decay;
    I have no cause to mourn or weep;
My foes are impotent and shy;
    My friends are neither false nor cold;
And yet, of late, I often sigh,
        I'm growing old!

My growing talk of olden times,
    My growing thirst for early news,
My growing apathy to rhymes,
    My growing love of easy shoes,
My growing hate of crowd and noise,
    My growing fear of taking cold,
All whisper in the plainest voice,
        I'm growing old!

I'm growing fonder of my staff;
    I'm growing dimmer in the eyes;
I'm growing fainter in my laugh;
    I'm growing deeper in my sighs;
I'm growing careless of my dress;
    I'm growing frugal of my gold;
I'm growing wise; I'm growing—yes—
        I'm growing old!

I see it in my changing taste;
　　I see it in my changing hair;
I see it in my growing waist;
　　I see it in my growing hair;
A thousand signs proclaim the truth
　　As plain as truth was ever told,
That, even in my vaunted youth,
　　　　I'm growing old!

Ah me! my very laurels breathe
　　The tale in my reluctant ears,
And every boon the hours bequeathe
　　But makes me debtor to the years!
E'en flattery's honeyed words declare
　　The secret she would fain withhold,
And tells me in " How young you are!"
　　　　I'm growing old!

Thanks for the years!—whose rapid flight
　　My sombre muse so sadly sings!
Thanks for the gleams of golden light
　　That tint the darkness of their wings!
The light that beams from out the sky,
　　Those heavenly mansions to unfold,
Where all are blest and none may sigh,
　　　　" I'm growing old."

A COMFORTABLE old age is the reward of a well-spent youth; therefore, instead of introducing dismal and melancholy prospects of decay, it should give us hope of eternal youth in a better world.
　　　　　　　　　　　　RAY PALMER, D.D.

REVERENCE THE AGED.

ELIHU BURRITT.

BOW low the head, boy; do reverence to the old man, once like you; the vicissitudes of life have silvered his hair, and changed the round, merry face to the worn visage before you; once that manly form stalked promptly through the gay scenes of pleasure, the beau ideal of grace; now the hand of time that withers the flowers of yesterday, has bent that figure and destroyed that noble carriage; once, at your age, he possessed the thousand thoughts that pass through your brain, now wishing to accomplish deeds equal to a nook in fame. But he has lived the dream very nearly through; his eye never kindles at old deeds of daring, and the hand takes a firmer grasp of the staff. Bow low the head, boy, as you would in your old age be reverenced.

....

THE complaints of the aged should meet with tenderness rather than censure; the burden under which they labor ought to be viewed with sympathy by those who must bear it in their turn, and who, perhaps, hereafter, may complain of it as bitterly; at the same time, the old should consider that all the seasons of life have their several trials allotted to them; and that to bear the infirmities of age with becoming patience is as much their duty as it is that of the young to resist the temptations of youthful pleasure.

HUGH BLAIR, D.D.

VENERABLE AGE: ITS TRIALS AND CONSOLATIONS.

WILLIAM F. MORGAN, D.D.

ALWAY, and through all generations, the hoary head has been counted a crown of glory to the righteous. Longevity, which in the case of the wicked only aggravates sin, and its attending consequences, affords to the good and faithful child of God a longer term of useful service and holy example, increased proficiency in Christian graces, and a more glorious recompense on high. But more than this: Old age is not to be associated, as a matter of course, with decrepitude or the decays of nature. It has its own appropriate beauty, as well as youth. There is a wonderful attractiveness in its full and golden ripeness, and in the gradual decline of the ancient patriarchs there is a grand dignity and a chastened solemnity which separate them from other men, and compel the utmost homage; and he must be wanting in all proper sentiments, destitute of veneration, and even of common feeling, who can listen to the dialogue between Barzillai the ancient, and David the king, without being irresistibly drawn toward the old man, as he declares his age, and the limitations which fourscore years must necessarily impose upon his movements and the aspirations of an unusually active life. My brethren, I envy not the man, I have little faith in the goodness of his heart, or the elevation of his principles, who can find himself in the presence of the aged—whether it be the honored father trembling on the verge of time, or the infirm and bending mother tarrying meekly for her Master's call—without being stirred by some profound impulse to render honor where it is due, and give expression in some way to holy, dutiful, reverential regard. It is written, "Thou shalt rise up before the hoary head, and honor the face of the old man, and fear thy God." This is a law of divinest sanction, to which even unsanctified nature should bow as by instinct, and which religion should publish throughout the realm of her influence and authority as a law not to be broken. It is broken. It is lamentably and, at times, brutally violated in these advanced days of Christian civilization and refinement. But the law, nevertheless, abides, and he who sets it at naught in cruel hardness and disdain, may expect to be followed by the malediction of Almighty God, and possibly at some coming day to have the chalice of his own abominable selfishness and inconsideration commended to his lips. Undeniably the aged are entitled to our liveliest sympathies and our most sedulous attentions. They have borne the burden and heat of the day. They have reached the border land. They stand hovering between two worlds, and must shortly vanish and be no more seen. Such reflections should quicken, and also make us patient in the discharge of our duties to them. They are going from us, and we in our turn may require the kindness and attention which we bestow.

ITS TRIALS; there are *trials* incident to old age, and which no power of human sympathy can avert or permanently relieve. *Infirmity of body* is one. The vigors of life are failing. The fibre of a constitution which withstood all the assaults of three score years, and promised well for a longer continuance, suddenly gives way. There is a collapse of energies and powers. The functions of the body and the faculties of mind and soul are arrested in their independent life-play, and helplessness is creeping on, and "the keeper of the house begins to tremble, and is afraid of that which is high, and the grasshopper becomes a burden." Infancy is helpless, but its wants are comparatively few, and if these wants multiply with advancing months and years, there comes the needful and corresponding ability to redress them. But with age it is altogether the reverse. Past habits, feelings, pursuits, and enjoyments, have created necessities unknown to infancy—but which are inseparable from age—while the ability to satisfy them is constantly diminishing; and not only so, but this sense of growing helplessness is to the aged a painful, almost an irreconcilable one, in its contrast with the freedom and affluence of physical power which had so long been enjoyed. It is a noble sorrow, it is an heroic cry, deprecating the surrender of a prerogative which has given meaning and power and victory to life. But the struggle is altogether in vain. The surrender is not by the will of man, but of God. I have been deeply moved in the course of my ministry at the lofty spirit with which the aged have sought to hold the ground of earlier and more vigorous days. Many an instance occurs to me when literally "the doors have been shut in the streets" in order that altered aspects might be concealed, and the last terrible ills "which flesh is heir to" might be sequestered from observation. The dread of being burdensome and of wearing out the sympathy of human hearts, is also an oppressive apprehension to the aged. Happily, however, many wants and strong desires perish with the increase of years. The exuberance of life recedes; its activities abate; the glory of the outward world declines.

In this state of dependence and comparative isolation, moreover, change creeps upon everything. The times seem out of joint; the race is degenerate; the former days were better than these. The very elements have undergone a change; the breath of spring, the heat of summer, and winter frosts, are not as in the past, and thus to some life becomes an irritating contrast, and to others an intolerable burden. Nature bends and is breaking beneath the accumulation of years, and seems to beg imploringly for the undisturbed quiet and silence of the grave.

Another trial of the aged is *the altered aspect of society*, the absence of contemporaries and companions, and the deepening loneliness of life. To outlive their generation, even by a little, is to walk a solitary path. The young know little of this, and give it no thought as they hurry on with the multitude of their competitors, and their troops of friends, but age is the era of recollection, and is evermore dwelling upon scenes, events, persons, associates "long since gone and passed away." At length they stand almost alone, looking back; and although Dr. Johnson wisely entreats men, as they advance in years, to keep their friendships in repair, it is unquestionably true that the susceptibility for such attachments diminishes with the decline of life. The past, as a review, a remembrance, a picture, chiefly survives, and is chiefly the centre of thought and conversation. Occasionally we meet one, far advanced in years, who retains that fresh and living spirit which holds him warmly and gracefully to the present, long after he has been detached from those with whom he was familiar, and who walked with him to the House of God, at an earlier period, as friends. But as a rule, the aged retrace their journey and linger upon the place of their birth, and haunt the scenes of their earlier intellectual impressions, their first hopes and most exhilarating joys. The past is with them, covered, it may be, with the "*disjecta membra*" of their exploded schemes; the wrecks of argosies heavy laden with costly ventures, which never came to shore; the past, colored with the hues of disappointment, and the faded tints of long vanished blessings, filled with historic incidents and recollections; the gleam and dying glory of a world whose inhabitants have already joined the company of those who lived before the flood. Their own generation has disappeared; a few may still cling as leaves to the outermost branches of the tree, but the vast concourse have been swept away by the remorseless blasts of mortality, and but very few of all who had known and loved them in the bright morning of their days, can wait upon their funeral solemnities, or follow them to their long home. New voices, faces, plans, new methods of business, new forms and expressions of thought, crowd upon the aged. They are witnesses of changes which astound and bewilder them, and in the busy whirl of things they are more and more alone. The passing age with its rushing tide of invention and reform and splendid development, is more and more a mystery and a blank. And, doubtless, the solitary condition of the aged, in many instances, is aggravated by the disinclination of the young to seek their company. Boys soon spring into manhood; men soon grow old; and the old are soon forgotten. The stripling, with his gold ring and goodly apparel, crowds aside his sire and does despite to the hoary head. It cannot be denied that carrying to extravagance our notion of equality and self-assertion, the young too often exhibit an unfeeling and selfish spirit in their intercourse with those whose age has made them extremely sensitive to neglect. The deference, the helpfulness, the courtesy which youth should extend to age, and which partake not only of duty, but of chivalry, are dying out in this era, and we may well deprecate their decay, and count it as a token of social hardness and declining manhood.

I will mention but one other trial—*the tendency to depression* and the decay of natural spirits. There are those who escape this trial, and preserve to the end of their days a beautiful serenity and cheerfulness. But many an outworn traveller is constrained to say, "I have no pleasure in them." The shadows of a long experience and a varied sorrow have fallen thick around them. They muse and sit apart. They shun the crowd and the gay circle. Shut out from their old haunts of business, and away from general society, they are inclined to brood over their lot and indulge in querulous animadversion upon current follies. Their day is over. The sun of a weary and lengthened life is ready to set. The solemnities of an eternal state, moreover, are distinctly rising into view—and this consideration, when allowed its weight, is sufficient to touch the soul, if not with gloom, at least with thoughtfulness unknown before. Death is at hand. The judge standeth at the door. The world of spirits with its mysteries, and the world of retribution with its adjustments and everlasting decisions—with its boundlessness of glory and of shame, of joy or woe, of life or death—these are not far off; and although we too often find triflers at an advanced point in life, and men who utterly ignore all tokens of their exit, and who even in their dress and conversation affect a period far remote from their own, and simulate the indifference of youth to the concerns of religion, yet there are mutitudes, as we have reason to know, who, trembling on life's verge, are serious as they look forth upon the future, and serious as they look back upon the past, and whisper to their souls "How long have I to live?" They hear the murmurs of the shoreless sea, and are conscious that the time of their departure is at hand. At such a crisis it is sad to be unsupported by the hand of God—sad to be without a Saviour. Human sympathy avails but little. Earthly interests are dead. The tabernacle is falling to pieces. Nothing is left to be desired but the peace which is not of this world, and the sustaining help of the everlasting arms; and if these are wanting, if these have been accounted of no importance, then old age has but little to lighten its darkness, or lift from around it the mists of despondency, irritability and despair.

ITS CONSOLATIONS.—I will endeavor to draw your thoughts away from the trials, toward the *consolations* which attend and comfort the aged believer. The followers of the Redeemer are, doubtless, subject to laws of a physical life, which may hinder and obstruct the spiritual life, and reduce them in old age to a very imperfect enjoyment of Christian hopes and promises. As a rule, however, and as a blessedness often attained, *the last days of the Christian are his best days*, and the end better than the beginning. That portion of his existence which is to be reckoned as probation, and which is to determine the complexion of his eternal state, is about to end for ever. There is but little space left. God alone knoweth its measure. A few more conflicts perhaps—a few more vicissitudes, tears, disappointments, pains, agonies—then will come the end, and all will be over. Rest and recompense will succeed. The beauty and glory of a dawn such as never empurpled our eastern horizon will break upon the emancipated soul; the dawn of peace to the pilgrim who has travelled far through storms and deafening agitations; the dawn of refreshment to the wayfarer whose feet are bleeding and whose strength is spent. Beloved friends, even to the common sentiment of mankind, no one appears so near the threshold of celestial blessedness as the aged saint.

In the course of a long service and experience among all classes and conditions of men, I have learned the full meaning of words which are idly uttered and leave but a faint impression in their ordinary use. Among these, the word Rest has gathered great strength and significance. I have seen men breathless and still toiling—still pressing on—panting—almost despairing, and suddenly, by the visitation of God, stopped, and straightened for the grave. The lines of care were smoothed away, slumber hung upon the eyelids, and the whole countenance regained in death what toil and anxiety and eager aspiration had torn from it in life. But the transfiguration wrought upon the face of age has been even more marked and beautiful, and like the clearing away of mist from the landscape, so have the traces of anxiety and weariness and sickness given place to an aspect of heavenly repose in death, and we have felt the profound meaning of the blessed declaration, "There remaineth a rest for the people of God." And this is the undoubted truth which gilds the closing days of the aged saint. Rest is at hand, and "peace which passeth all understanding."

The aged saint finds *comfort in looking back*, and holding in review the way over which he has passed. It may have been long and rough and crooked, but it is covered with the disclosures of paternal and protecting love. The retrospection of seventy or eighty years presents God continually in forms and ministries of providential care which are only estimated fully at the end.

Then the experience of life is complete, and its range of observation large, and the divine hand is seen moulding the character under the discipline of events and changes, which, regarded singly, seemed strange and untoward, but which in their bearings and relations were in the direction of religious symmetry and elevation. The uses of sorrow are best realized at the last, and the chastening power of those thwartings and special tribulations with which God often tries His dearest children, as in a furnace, heated seven times. So that while the shadows are gathering around him, the aged disciple may stand and gaze at the way-marks of divine love, divine guidance, divine warning, divine support, all along his pilgrimage, and exclaim with accents of trembling exultation, "How patiently has God watched over me, against how many temptations has He fortified me; from how many perils has He rescued me; in how many critical and gloomy hours has He lightened my darkness, and in passing through the water and through the fire how has He held my hand and strengthened my heart." Surely, beloved friends, none can so speak of heavenly and redeeming love, patience, faithfulness, tenderness, compassion, as the aged children of the Father.

Finally, *the past revelation of God's mercy and goodness* is the best pledge of eternal glory. Herein is abounding consolation, and girded by it the veteran soldier and servant waits cheerfully till his change comes. He has his infirmities and temptations, those which especially beset this advanced period, but his Christian principle restrains him from yielding overmuch to the disquietudes and irritations of life. Among younger Christians he sits as a patriarch who has learned sober lessons from a varied allotment, and discovered the emptiness of the world, and is ready to be translated to the city which hath foundations whose Maker and Builder is God. He is not sour or morose. Indeed, there is often a mellowness and childlikeness which are wonderfully beautiful, and a benignancy of aspect and expression which is irresistible; but he is weaned in great measure from the world, and is hearkening for the footsteps of his Beloved Master, as one who has reached a point of transition and must stand ready for the change. Not termination, not annihilation, but a marvellous transformation awaits him; a putting off of defilement, a putting on of light and celestial beauty; an assumption of his true life, an ascension to his true destiny. This is the day-spring about to visit him. This is the dawn about to break. O thou dying saint, thou expiring mother in Israel! the time of thy departure is at hand. Thou hast known suffering; thou shalt know it no more forever. Thou hast tasted the waters of Marah; they were bitter, but thou shalt taste them no more. Thou hast wrestled with temptation, and contended with the powers of darkness, but the adversary shall come near thee no more. Passing within the vail, thou shalt also pass from weakness to strength, from humiliation to glory, from faith to sight, from the arms of mortality to the bosom of God. Behold, I come quickly. Hold that fast which thou hast, that no man take thy crown. Him that overcometh will I make a pillar in the temple of my God, and he shall go no more out, and I will write upon him the name of my God, and the name of the City of my God, which is New Jerusalem.

> Yes, there is golden beauty in decay,
> As autumn's leaves outshine the leaves of May;
> The calm of evening with its roseate light,
> The starry silence of the wintry night;
> The stillness of repose when storms are o'er,
> And the sea murmurs on a peaceful shore;
> The brooding memories of the past that make
> The old man young again for beauty's sake;
> The hope sublime that cheers the lonely road
> Which leads him gently to the hills of God.

I VENERATE old age, and love not the Man who can look without emotion upon the sunset of life, when the dusk of evening begins to gather over the watery eye, and the shadows of twilight grow broader and deeper upon the understanding.

H. W. LONGFELLOW.

WHY MOURN THE OLD?

WM. CULLEN BRYANT.

WHY mourn ye that our aged friend is dead?
   Ye are not sad to see the gathered grain,
   Nor when their mellow fruit the orchards
      cast,
Nor when the yellow woods shake down the ripened
      mast.

Ye sigh not when the sun, his course fulfilled,
His glorious course, rejoicing earth and sky,
In the soft evening when the winds are stilled,
Sinks where his islands of refreshment lie,
And leaves the smile of his departure spread
O'er the warm-colored heaven, and ruddy mountain
      head.

Why weep ye then for him, who, having run
The bound of man's appointed years, at last,
Life's blessings all enjoyed, life's labors done,
Serenely to his final rest has passed;
While the soft memory of his virtues, yet
Lingers like twilight hues when the bright sun is
      set?

THE chamber where the good man takes his flight
Is privileged beyond the common walk
Of virtuous life—quite in the verge of heaven.
                      EDWARD YOUNG.

COMFORT FOR THE AGED AND INFIRM.

REV. JAMES SMITH, D.D.

"Now also, when I am old and gray-headed, O God, forsake me not."—Ps. lxvi., 18.

AGE and its infirmities will creep on us; and with age come weakness, pains, and fears. But an old Christian should be a happy creature; for he has proved the Lord to be faithful so many years, he has had answers to prayer so many times, and the God of his youth stands pledged never to leave nor forsake him. The Lord forsake an old servant!—never. The Father of mercies forsake one of his children when compassed with the infirmities of old age!—impossible. No, no! The Lord, who has borne with us so long, will bear with us to the end. The Lord, who has glorified himself in our life, will get glory to himself in our death. As the God of all comfort, he will comfort us on the bed of languishing, and will make all our bed in our sickness, and when heart and flesh are failing, he will be the strength of our heart, and our portion for ever. Aged believer, doubt not, fear not. God has given you his word; trust it. He has confirmed his word by the death of his Son; therefore exercise confidence in him. He has been a friend and a father to you for many years; and he will be your friend and father to the very last. Be much with him in prayer; and with all the simplicity of a little child. Let your requests be made known unto him. He has grace for old age, as He had for youth; and He has grace for a dying bed as He had grace for all the conflicts of life. Believe his word, rest in his love, expect his blessing to the end, and you shall be more than a conqueror through him that loved you. God never loved you more than he does now in your weakness, pains, and old age; and—sweet thought!—he will never love you less. His love is infinite, everlasting. Having loved, he loveth to the end.

Sighing and sorrow are confined to earth. They are limited by time, and a blessing is pronounced upon them: "Blessed are they that mourn; for they shall be comforted." Every believer is a mourner. We mourn over our imperfect duties, feeble graces, neglected privileges, and many shortcomings. We mourn, because our hearts are unholy and our lives are sinful—because our children are unconverted, and our other relatives love not the Saviour. We mourn because we suffer, but more because we sin. How much there is in the world, in the church, in the family, and in the heart, to make us mourn? We do groan, being burdened.

But soon, very soon, the mourning days of God's people will be ended. All sin and all sorrow will be left on earth when we ascend to heaven. Then our tears will be wiped away; every cause of sorrow will be removed; and joy, peace, and pleasures will be our portion for ever. Then we shall be made perfect in love; then we shall be filled with holiness; then we shall enjoy full satisfaction; then we shall reap in joy who have sown in tears.

Let us, then, look upward and look forward; remembering, when our cup is bitterest, our burden heaviest, and our sorrow greatest, that in a very little time the days of our mourning will be ended—the night of sadness will soon be past, and the morning of joy, everlasting joy, will break upon us. Then there shall be no more pain, neither sorrow nor crying. Then, perfect in knowledge, perfect in holiness, and perfect in happiness, we shall be ever with the Lord. Then we shall see Jesus, be with Jesus, and be like Jesus, and that for ever. Everlasting joy succeeds the sorrows of a day.

"The days of thy mourning shall be ended."—Isa. lx., 20.

A FEW MORE YEARS SHALL ROLL.

Horatius Bonar, D.D.

A FEW more years shall roll,
  A few more seasons come,
    And we shall be with those that rest
Asleep within the tomb.
Then O, my Lord, prepare
My soul for that great day;
Oh, wash me in Thy precious blood,
And take my sins away.

A few more suns shall set
  O'er these dark hills of time,
And we shall be where suns are not,
  A far serener clime:
Then, O my Lord, prepare
My soul for that blest day;
Oh, wash me in Thy precious blood,
And take my sins away.

A few more storms shall beat
  On this wild rocky shore,
And we shall be where tempest cease,
  And surges swell no more:
  Then, O my Lord, prepare
  My soul for that calm day;
Oh, wash me in Thy precious blood,
  And take my sins away.

A few more struggles here,
  A few more partings o'er,
A few more toils, a few more tears,
  And we shall weep no more;
  Then, O my Lord, prepare
  My soul for that bright day;
Oh, wash me in Thy precious blood,
  And take my sins away.

'Tis but a little while
  And He shall come again,
Who died that we might live, who lives
  That we with Him may reign:
  Then O my Lord, prepare
  My soul for that glad day;
Oh, wash me in Thy precious blood,
  And take my sins away.   Amen.

THE TRUE CONSOLER.

O! THERE is never sorrow of heart
  That shall lack a timely end,
If but to God we turn, and ask
  Of Him to be our friend!

WM. WORDSWORTH.

THE BURDENS OF AGE.

Rev. John Philips, M.A.

NOW gradually yet certain these burdens gather about us! The young think they can hardly ever grow old. Yet, year by year, the buoyancy of youth passes into the vigor of manhood, and then green manhood imperceptibly shades off into the sere and yellow leaf. The eye loses its lustre, and the ear its power of distinguishing and appreciating the voice of singing men and singing women, and the palate its relish for dainty food; while the limbs grow rigid, and the hands forget their cunning, and the steps shorten, and the back is bowed down under the weight of years.

There is often a deep feeling of loneliness and weariness and sadness in old age, with all the companions of youth gone, and a busy, bustling world around, intent only on its own interests and aims, and showing so little sympathy, and sometimes so little patience with the aged, as if they had almost outlived their time, and were a hindrance rather than a help to progress.

> "Never again shall I dream such dreams,
> See such meadows and woods and streams,
>   Or carry a heart so glad.
> I have crossed the hill at the turn of life,
> I have borne the burden and heat of strife;
>   I'm tired and a little sad."

And indeed, even long before life reaches this

stage, there is often a weight felt pressing on the spirit, rising out of the remembrance of departed joys, and a deepening sense of this hollowness of all earthly things, the eagle-flight of time, and the fast gathering shadows of eternity.

Life is felt to grow more solemn as it steadily nears the goal and the great apocalypse. Life, too, seems to glide more swiftly as we advance, like the flowing river passing into the rapids, ere it plunge into the boiling cauldron beneath. No doubt there are multitudes that have got into the rapids, and yet don't realise their critical position, because they glide along with such arrowy swiftness, and in such a smooth and noiseless current. But those who do, cannot but feel deeply solemnized at the prospect.

Having the great question of our everlasting future and our final home settled and set at rest, our other cares may well sit less heavily upon us. The infirmities of years may then be viewed as the natural and needful process to ripen the soul for heaven, and to prepare it for being safely gathered into the everlasting garner, like a shock of corn fully ripe.

It is a pleasing sight to see, sometimes, a youthful and almost playful spirit, even in old age. Above all, it is beautiful to see the germ of the everlasting youth shooting up in verdure and in vigor, amid the decays of nature and the infirmities of years. "Although the outward man perish, yet the inward man is renewed day by day."

At times it looks as if the silvery locks were reflecting the sunlight of the celestial city, and as if the withered face were lit up and aglow with the irradiations of the inner glory. As the westering sun, when he descends and nears the horizon, although shorn of his meridian splendor, often looks more full-orbed and ruddy, and bathes with his golden sheen the attendant clouds that hover around and pavilion him at his exit, so the aged Christian often looks more rounded and ripe, more fruitful and mellow, more fair and beautiful, as he goes down into the valley of the shadow, and leaves a trail of glory, a lingering radiance behind. "The hoary head is a crown of glory, if it be found in the way of righteousness." And thus diademed with glory and with beauty, the weary saint is welcomed with the Master's "Well done!" and enters into the Master's joy.

AGE is the heaviest burden man can bear,
Compound of disappointment, pain and care;
For when the mind's experience comes at length,
It comes to mourn the body's loss of strength;
Resigned to ignorance all our better days,
Knowledge just ripens when the man decays.

DEATH is the crown of life.
Were death denied, poor men would live in vain;
Were death denied, even fools would wish to die.
YOUNG.

THERE is not a more repulsive spectacle than the old man who will not forsake the world which has already forsaken him.
AUGUSTUS THOLUCK.

THE BETTER WORLD.

GEORGE D. PRENTICE.

BEYOND the farthest glimmering star
    That twinkles in the arch above,
    There is a world of truth and love
Which earth's vile passions never mar

Oh! could I snatch the eagle's plumes,
    And soar to that bright world above,
Which God's own holy light illumes,
    With glories of eternal love.

How gladly every lingering tie
    That binds me down to earth I'd sever,
And leave for that blest home on high,
    This hollow-hearted world forever?

RELIGION sweetens and sanctifies all the relations of life. It doubly enhances all the ties of nature and kindred, by intertwining them with the more lasting ties of grace. It diffuses a spirit of forbearance and gentleness and brotherly-kindness and charity. It makes home the sanctuary of peace and purity, of love and joy—a model heaven upon earth. It lays the foundation of social order and civil jurisprudence, by inculcating the principles of truth and justice and honor.

REV. JOHN PHILIPS, M.A.

TIME BEARS US AWAY.

CHARLES SPURGEON.

YOU may well conceive how swiftly the mariner flies from a threatening storm, or seeks the port where he will find his home. You have sometimes seen how the ship cuts through the billows, leaving a white furrow behind her, and causing the sea to boil around her. Such is life, says Job, "like the swift ships," when the sails are filled by the wind, and the vessel dashes on, dividing a passage through the crowded water. Swift are the ships but swifter far is life. The wind of time bears me along. I cannot stop its motion. I may direct it with the rudder of God's Holy Spirit. I may, it is true, take in some small sails, of sin, which might hurry my days on faster than otherwise they would go; but, nevertheless, like a swift ship, my life must speed on its way until it reaches its haven. Where is that haven to be? Shall it be found in the land of bitterness and barrenness, that dreary region of the lost? Or shall it be that sweet haven of eternal peace, where not a troubling wave can ruffle the quiescent glory of my spirit? Wherever the haven is to be, that truth is the same, we are "like the swift ships."

THEY only truly mourn the dead who endeavor so to live as to insure a reunion in heaven.

COUNTESS OF BLESSINGTON.

I WOULD NOT LIVE ALWAY.

WM. AUGUSTUS MUHLENBERG, D.D.

I WOULD not live alway—live alway below!
   Oh no, I'll not linger when bidden to go:
   The days of our pilgrimage granted us here
Are enough for life's woes, full enough for its cheer.
Would I shrink from the path which the prophets
        of God,
Apostles, and martyrs, so joyfully trod?
Like a spirit unblest, o'er the earth would I roam,
While brethren and friends are all hastening home?

I would not live alway—I ask not to stay
Where storm after storm rises dark o'er the way;
Where, seeking for rest we but hover around,
Like the patriarch's bird, and no resting is found;
Where Hope, when she paints her gay bow in the
        air,
Leaves its brilliance to fade in the night of despair,
And Joy's fleeting angel ne'er sheds a glad ray,
Save the gleam of the plumage that bears him away.

I would not live alway—thus fettered by sin,
Temptation without and corruption within;
In a moment of strength if I sever the chain,
Scarce the victory is mine, ere I'm captive again;
E'en the rapture of pardon is mingled with fears,
And the cup of thanksgiving with penitent tears:
The festival trump calls for jubilant songs,
But my spirit her own *miserere* prolongs.

I would not live alway—no, welcome the tomb!
Since Jesus hath lain there, I dread not its gloom;
Where He deigned to sleep, I'll too bow my head,
All peaceful to slumber on that hallowed bed.
Then the glorious daybreak, to follow that night,
The orient gleam of the angels of light,
With their clarion call for the sleepers to rise
And chant forth their matins, away to the skies.

Who, who would live alway—away from his God,
Away from yon heaven, that blissful abode,
Where the rivers of pleasure flow o'er the bright
    plains,
And the noontide of glory eternally reigns;
Where the saints of all ages in harmony meet,
Their Saviour and brethren transported to greet,
While the songs of salvation exultingly roll,
And the smile of the Lord is the feast of the soul!

That heavenly music! what is it I hear?
The notes of the harpers ring sweet in mine ear!
And see, soft unfolding those portals of gold,
The King all arrayed in His beauty behold!
Oh, give me, oh, give me the wings of a dove,
To adore Him, be near Him, enrapt with His love;
I but wait for the summons, I list for the word—
Alleluia—Amen—evermore with the Lord.

    GRACE teaches us, in the midst of life's greatest comforts, to be willing to die, and in the midst of its greatest crosses to be willing to live.

                                           MATTHEW HENRY.

DESIRING TO DEPART.

Rev. Abbott E. Kittredge, D.D.

WHILE Death in itself is terrible, Christian faith lifts a man above the thoughts of its terrors; it flashes into the valley the radiance of exultant hope, and then when the feet actually come to the Jordan, the waves always roll back on either side, pain and fear are swallowed up in a river of peace, and "the close of life is the grandest of sunsets."

But Paul in the utterance of our text was not thinking of death; the fact of physical dissolution was only a trifling circumstance to him; for his ecstatic soul had caught a glimpse of the country on the other side, to which Death was only the gateway, like one who from a valley looks in eager longing to the mountain summit and sees not the toilsome steps intervening, takes no note of rocks and precipices, so Paul was gazing on the heavenly Mt. Zion, above the clouds and storms of earth, and his desire for the things which God had prepared for those who love Him bridged over Death so that he did not see it, and in the contemplation of the liberty and rapture of his sanctified soul, he entirely forgot to think about his temporary and crumbling tabernacle. It is not strange, therefore, that he longed to depart, not longed to die, but longed to reach his Home, like one who has been journeying in foreign lands and between whom and the childhood's home thousands of miles of ocean roll. Yet he longed for the voyage, however perilous, however unpleasant with sickness! for all this is forgotten in the thoughts of "Home again," and he desires to depart, and with joyous anticipation steps upon the deck of the vessel whose prow is turned toward his native land.

Now the first essential feature to this condition of mind which is expressed by Paul, is a strong faith in the divine revelation concerning the eternal life. The lack of this faith is the secret of very much of our shrinking from the passage over, for there is an uncertainty clouding the harbor on the other side. To many Christians, Heaven is a dream land; there is no reality to their vision in the paintings of the New Jerusalem. They are skeptical regarding what it is and where it is, what its employments are, concerning the condition of its citizens, and hence naturally they cling to this life, to the things which are seen, and to the riches within their grasp. It would be strange if they did not, for who desires and longs to step from certainty into uncertainty? Said a noted Atheist, not long ago, as he poured out his low blasphemy for the amusement of his audience, "We *know* what this life is—we know nothing at all of the Hereafter—and so we prefer to stay here." From such lips, these words awaken no surprise, but from the lips of a Christian are they not surprising? and yet they find an echo in many a Christian's heart, who, though he sings with the congregation,

> "Jerusalem, my happy home
> Name ever dear to me,"

has not only no desire for the New Jerusalem, but dreads with a positive fear the hour when he shall come in sight of the harbor, for it is unreal and mystical to him. Do you say, "But we have never seen the domes and towers of that City, and we have seen our own land and our abiding city in this world-life." True, but you have never seen Alaska, yet would you say if you planned to go there, "I know what America is, but I know nothing of Alaska, and so I will give up my proposed journey?" No: you would say, "I do know Alaska from the writings of visitors to that land. I have read of its mountains, of its fur trade and its uncultured inhabitants, and I desire to go and see for myself what has been pictured before my mind." Why, I know intimately a gentleman who has never crossed the ocean, and yet has made so thorough a study of the city of London, its buildings and its streets, that it is said he knows the city more perfectly than most of those who live there, and vastly better than the rapid American traveller can. Well, so the Christian may know concerning the city of his eternal residence by a careful study of the description which the King whose throne is there has given to us, so that if Heaven is unreal to you, and only this life real, it is either because you have not read your Bible, or because you do not believe that your Bible states the truth. Why, tell me, how our Father could have added anything more to increase our knowledge of that land? As to its locality, it is where Jesus our risen Lord is. Is not this enough? As to its character, it is a city with twelve gates and every gate a pearl, with walls of burnished gold, with pavement of jasper, sardonyx, and onyx, and the river of life flows through its streets. It is a temple filled with divine glory; it is a palace where the King is arrayed in His beauty of holy love—it is paradise without the serpent and with immortal fruits and fadeless flowers—it is an inheritance incorruptible and of inconceivable wealth—it is a banquet where we shall feed on celestial provisions and be forever satisfied; it is a home sweeter in its joys and affections than our childhood's home, where no one hungers, or thirsts, or sickens, or weeps, or dies; a home without vacant seats, and with the Elder Brother for its richest light and joy. Are more figures needed to make it a reality?

As to its inhabitants, they are the whole family of God from all ages and all lands.

As to their appearance, they are clothed in celestial bodies, all the imperfections of earth are transfigured into a glorious beauty, and yet they are the same persons in traits and character and in their loves, as when here in this life. As to their employments, they praise Him who has redeemed them with His precious blood, and they serve *Him* with unfettered steps and pure hearts. What more can we want to give a reality to Heaven, what more to calm every troubled thought concerning them who have fallen asleep? What more to banish every fear and to quicken our desires to go and taste heavenly joys? Said a gentleman to me not long ago, whose only daughter and child had passed through the gates, "Could you name to me some book that I could read regarding Heaven, for (and his eyes filled with tears) I am studying about it just now." Ah! in the rush of our business cares and the absorbing pleasures of our daily lives, we too often forget that we are pilgrims, and we do not read carefully of the country toward whose confines we are so rapidly journeying. Hence it grows unreal and uninviting. But when God transplants a flower from our own home garden to the richer soil of eternal life, then our hearts follow in a yearning love, and a thousand questions force themselves into our minds, questions concerning that eternal life, and then we read as never before, of the crown, and the harp, and the white robe, and the rest, and the songs, and the tearless service and the fellowship with Christ; and thus Heaven grows real—as real as our own homes to you and me.

TELL me, my secret soul,
   Oh, tell me, Hope and Faith,
Is there no resting-place
   From sorrow, sin and death?
Is there no happy spot
   Where mortals may be blest
Where grief may find a balm
   And weariness a rest?
Faith, Hope and Love, best boons to mortals given,
Waved their bright wings, and whispered, "Yes, in heaven!"

CHARLES MACKAY.

OUR lives are rivers, gliding free
To that unfathomed, boundless sea,
   The silent grave!
Thither all earthly pomp and boast
Roll, to be swallowed up and lost
   In one dark wave.

LONGFELLOW.

THE SEQUEL OF LIFE.

Rev. John Philip, M.A.

LIFE is like a dissolving cloud in the heavens, or a dissolving view in a panorama; as you gaze on it it seems to melt away, until ere long it vanishes entirely out of sight.

When once the spirit is fled, no voice of fond affection, no frantic cry of the bereft and riven heart, no sighs, no sobs, no tears can call forth the smallest response. You may kiss the marble brow or lift the palsied arm, but there is no recognition, no sign of even the faintest spark of life. When the dead body is laid in the grave, the lightnings may flash and the thunders may roll, but they never awaken nor disturb the sleeper.

If the man of business is suddenly struck down by the hand of death, that moment he must ungrasp his hold of all his possessions here, and cease to have the smallest interest in stocks or shares or scrip of any kind. The wheels of business move on as before, the exchange is crowded as ever, and men are speculating as busily on the rise and fall of markets, —but he has no share in all that is done under the sun.

Every life that is lived on earth leaves, and must leave, deep and lasting traces behind it. There is a *sequel* to every life, and that not only in the world to come, but in this present world. There is, so to speak, another life that men live after death, and that in the sphere where they lived before. They call their children, and often their lands, after their own names, or have them emblazoned in heraldic arms, or marble tablet, or granite monument. Or they bequeath some rich legacy for some benevolent purpose, which is thus linked with their memory, and hands down their fame to generations yet unborn.

Indeed there is no one, however humble, that would like to be forgotten. All would naturally wish to live in the memories and hearts of others.

But whether we shall thus live, whether our names shall be cherished to oblivion, must largely depend on the life lived in the body.

Let those winged words of Dr. Chalmers be duly pondered and put in practice: "O man immortal, live for something! Do good, and leave behind you a monument of virtue that the storms of time can never destroy. Write your name by kindness, love and mercy, on the hearts of thousands you come in contact with year by year, and you will never be forgotten. No, your name, your deeds will be legible on the hearts you leave behind you, as the stars on the brow of the morning. Good deeds will shine as brightly on the earth as the stars of heaven."

––––––––––––––––––––––

It is little matter at what hour of the day
The righteous fall asleep. Death cannot come
To him untimely who has learned to die.
The less of this brief life, the more of heaven;
The shorter time, the longer immortality.
DEAN MILMAN.

HOPEFULLY WAITING.

A. D. F. RANDOLPH.

OUR Father's House, I know, is broad and grand;
  In it how many, many mansions are!
  And far beyond the light of sun or star,
Four little ones of mine through that fair land
    Are walking hand in hand!
Think you I love not, or that I forget
  These of my loins? Still this world is fair,
And I am singing while my eyes are wet
  With weeping in this balmy summer air;
Yet I'm not homesick, and the children *here*
Have need of me, and so my way is clear!

I would be joyful as my days go by,
  Counting God's mercies to me. He who bore
  Life's heaviest cross is mine for evermore;
And I, who wait His coming, shall not I
    On His sure word rely?
So if sometimes the way be rough, and sleep
  Be heavy for the grief He sends to me,
Or at my waking I would only weep,
  Let me be mindful that these things must be,
To work his blessed will until He come,
And take my hand and lead me safely home.

"PATIENCE is the key to Paradise."

AL-FARABI.

THE SUNSET OF LIFE.

Bishop Wm. Bacon Stevens, D.D.

THERE is something at once grand and solemn in a setting sun. It is the sinking to rest of the great king of day; the withdrawing from the busy world the light that has called out its activity, and the covering up with the veil of darkness the scenes that glistened with the radiance of noon.

There is, however, in the setting of the sun of life that which is equally grand, still more solemn, and surpassingly sublime. For

> The sun is but a spark of fire—
> A transient meteor in the sky,—
> The Soul, immortal as its Sire,
>   Shall never die.
>
> The Soul, of origin divine,
> God's glorious image, freed from clay,
> In heaven's eternal sphere shall shine,
>   A star of day.

The sun when it sets has run a whole day's circuit; his pathway has apparently traversed an entire arc of the heavens, and slowly, patiently, but surely, it has done its allotted work. And so the aged Christian, when he dies, is described as having "run his race," as having "finished his course." He has perhaps traversed the allotted distance of human life. He has passed each of the three score-

and-ten milestones, and now stands at the verge of the horizon, waiting to sink to rest in the everlasting arms. He has toiled a whole day of life, and has come to his grave in a "good old age," having "finished the work which was given him to do;" and though all his labors have been imperfectly done, though he himself feels more deeply than he can express his unprofitableness before God, yet he looks for acceptance, not to any merits or deservings of his own, but only for Christ Jesus' sake, who of God and by faith is made unto him, "wisdom, and righteousness, and sanctification, and redemption."

The setting of the sun is not always like the day which it closes. The morning may have been bright, and the evening hour dark with tempests; or the rising may have been obscured by clouds and mists, which gradually faded away and left a clear sky at sunset. So the sunset hour of Christian life does not always correspond to his previous day. We have seen the last hours of the believer shrouded in impenetrable gloom, and we have seen them gilded with hope and radiant with the forecast glories of the upper world. The way in which a Christian dies is not always an index of his spiritual condition. He is to be judged by his life, not by his death. The great virtues which make up Christian character are neither developed nor called into action on a dying bed; and it is not in the emotions and feelings manifested there, that we are chiefly to look for evidences of a gracious state.

These varieties of Christian experiences are literally innumerable; but whatever their nature, we must not judge of the validity of one's hope, or the genuineness of one's conversion, by his dying hour.

Yet, when that dying hour accords with a long life of piety, or a true profession maintained in health and strength; when it is but a concentrating within itself of the glories which have been more or less visible in the whole track of his experience, then is it eloquent in its revelations of the riches and peace and joy, which God generally gives to those who are faithful unto death; and though we cannot order when or how our lives shall close upon earth, yet it should be our aim so to live as to secure, if God pleases, a serene, if not a triumphant exit; that our setting sun may, like the sun in the firmament, grow large and more resplendent as it declines, until passing away it shall leave behind it a trail of glory spread all over the place of our departure.

Another interesting thought is, that the sun is not lost or extinguished when it sets. This may seem a very trite remark concerning the natural sun, but it is not so trite when we speak of the soul-set in death.

Our friends have gone from us; the horizon of death shuts them out of view; their light of love, of hope, of piety, shines no more upon us, and we shall never again behold them in the flesh; but they are no more lost than the sun is lost when his red disc rolls down behind the western hills; they are no more extinguished than the burning orb of day is quenched when he sinks beneath the waves of the ocean; for, as the sun, leaving us in darkness, still lights up other lands, so our departed ones shine in another sphere of existence still,—not lost, not extinguished,—but, if the friends of Christ, made to glow with a brighter light and a more enduring glory. When we see the sun set we know that it will rise again; and so when we see the body of our friends borne to the voiceless dwelling of the tomb, we know that they also shall rise again. Every night of death is followed by a resurrection morning. How precious is the thought as connected with God's people that they shall rise from the dead! How rise? With glorified bodies, upon which the second death has no power. Rise by what power? By the mighty power of God. Rise when? When the Lord Jesus shall be revealed from heaven with all his mighty angels, then shall they be caught up to meet him in the air. Rise to what? To glory, honor, and immortality in the presence-chamber of God. How these thoughts light up with brightness every sepulchre of the righteous! How the doctrine of the resurrection throws a halo over every Christian's head-stone, and makes each open grave a little postern-gate leading into glory!

Reader, have you lost a father, mother, brother, sister, wife, husband, child, or lover,—and were they Christ's before they died? Then lift up your heads, wipe away your tears, cheer up your hearts, for they shall come forth again before your face. Their sunset, though it left you in gloom and midnight sorrow, will soon be followed by the dawn of Resurrection day; and when the archangel's trump shall sound out over land and sea, awaking the myriads who slumber in earth's bosom, then shall your beloved ones, who sunk to rest in Jesus, rise again, and go forth to meet and glorify their adorable Redeemer. When that morning of the resurrection dawns, it will usher in a day that has no clouds, a day that has no sunset, and a day that is followed by no night of sorrow or of death.

BEYOND THE SMILING AND THE WEEPING.

Horatius Bonar, D.D.

Beyond the smiling and the weeping,
   I shall be soon, I shall be soon.
   Beyond the waking and the sleeping,
Beyond the sowing and the reaping,
I shall be soon, I shall be soon.
   Love, rest and home! Sweet, sweet hope!
   Lord, tarry not, Lord, tarry not, but come.

Beyond the blooming and the fading,
I shall be soon, I shall be soon;
Beyond the shining and the shading,
Beyond the hoping and the dreading,
I shall be soon, I shall be soon.
        Love, rest, etc.

Beyond the parting and the meeting,
I shall be soon, I shall be soon;
Beyond the farewell and the greeting,
Beyond the pulse's fever beating,
I shall be soon, I shall be soon.
        Love, rest, etc.

Beyond the frost-chain and the fever,
I shall be soon, I shall be soon;
Beyond the rock-waste and the river,
Beyond the ever and the never,
I shall be soon, I shall be soon.
        Love, rest, etc.

HEAVEN AND EARTH.

F. W. Faber.

THERE are no shadows where there is no sun;
　　There is no beauty where there is no shade;
　　And all things in two lines of glory run,
Darkness and light, ebon and gold inlaid.
God comes among us through the shroud of air.
And His dim path is like the silvery wake
Left by your pinnace on the mountain lake,
Fading and reappearing here and there.
The lamps and veils, through heaven and
Earth that move,
Go in and out, as jealous of their light,
Like sailing stars upon a misty night.
Death is the shade of coming life; and Love
Yearns for her dear ones in the holy tomb,
Because bright things are better seen in gloom.

THE DEATH-BED.

Thomas Hood.

WE watched her breathing through the night,—
　　Her breathing soft and low,—
As in her breast the wave of life
Kept heaving to and fro.

So silently we seemed to speak,
So slowly moved about,
As we had lent her half our powers,
To eke her living out.

Our weary hopes belied our fears,
Our fears our hopes belied,—
We thought her dying when she slept,
And sleeping when she died.

For when the morn came, dim and sad,
And chill with early showers,
Her quiet eyelids closed;—she had
Another morn than ours.

THE HOUR OF DEATH.

Mrs. Felicia Hemans.

LEAVES have their time to fall,
    And flowers to wither at the north wind's breath,
And stars to set—but all,
    Thou hast all seasons for thine own, O Death!

Day is for mortal care
    Eve for glad meetings round the joyous hearth,
Night for the dreams of sleep, the voice of prayer,
    But all for thee, thou Mightiest of the earth!

The banquet hath its hour,
    Its feverish hour of mirth, and song, and wine;
There comes a day for grief's o'erwhelming power,
    A time for softer tears—but all are thine!

Youth and the opening rose
  May look like things too glorious for decay,
And smile at thee!—but thou art not of those
  That wait the ripened bloom to seize its prey!

Leaves have their time to fall,
  And flowers to wither at the north-wind's breath.
And stars to set—but all,
  Thou hast all seasons for thine own, O Death.

THE HOME BEYOND THE GRAVE.

Bishop R. S. Foster, D.D.

TO my own mind, when I look in the direction of the future, one picture always rises—a picture of ravishing beauty. Its essence, I believe to be true. Its accidents will be more glorious than all that my imagination puts into it. It is that of a soul forever growing in knowledge, in love, in holy endeavor; that of a vast community of spirits, moving along a pathway of light, of ever-expanding excellence and glory; brightening as they ascend; becoming more and more like the unpicturable pattern of infinite perfection; loving with an ever-deepening love; glowing with an ever-increasing fervor; rejoicing in ever-advancing knowledge; growing in glory and power. They are all immortal. There are no failures or reverses to any of them. Ages fly away; they soar on with tireless wing. Æons and cycles advance toward them and retire behind them; still they soar, and shout, and unfold!

I am one of that immortal host. Death cannot destroy me. I shall live when stars dim with age.

The advancing and retreating æons shall not fade my immortal youth. Thou, Gabriel, that standest near the throne, bright with a brightness that dazzles my earth-born vision, rich with the experience of uncounted ages, first-born of the sons of God, noblest of the archangelic retinue, far on I shall stand where thou standest now; rich with an equal experience, great with an equal growth; thou wilt have passed on, and, from higher summits, wilt gaze back on a still more glorious progress!

Beyond the grave! As the vision rises, how this side dwindles into nothing—a speck—a moment—and its glory and pomp shrink up into the trinkets and baubles that amuse an infant for a day. Only those things, in the glory of this light, which lay hold of immortality seem to have any value. The treasures that consume away or burn up with this perishing world are not treasure. Those only that we carry beyond are worth the saving.

THE memory of the sainted dead hovers, a blessed and purifying influence, over the hearts of men. At the grave of the good, so far from losing heart, the spiritually minded find new strength. They weep, but as they weep they look down into the sepulchre, and behold angels sitting and the dead come nearer, and are united to them by a fellowship more intimate than that of blood.

REV. W. H. FURNESS.

"A HOME in heaven! what a joyful thought
As the poor man toils in his weary lot!"

GRAY.

SHALL WE MEET AGAIN?

GEORGE D. PRENTICE.

THE fiat of death is inexorable. No appeal for relief from that great law which dooms us to die. We flourish and fade as the leaves of the forest; and the flowers that bloom, wither and fade in a day, have no frailer hold upon life than the mightiest monarch that ever shook the earth with his footsteps.

Generations of men will appear and disappear as the grass, and the multitude that throng the world today will disappear as footsteps on the shore. Men seldom think of the great event of death until the shadow falls across their own pathway, hiding from their eyes the faces of loved ones, whose living smile was the sunlight of their existence. Death is the antagonist of life, and the thought of the tomb is the skeleton of all feasts. We do not want to go through the dark valley, although its dark passage may lead to Paradise; we do not want to go down into the damp graves, even with princes for bedfellows. In the beautiful drama of "Ion," the hope of immortality, so eloquently uttered by the death-devoted Greek, finds deep response in every thoughtful soul. When about to yield his life a sacrifice to fate, his Clemanthe asks if they should meet again; to which he responds, "I have asked that dreadful question of the hills that look eternal—of the clear streams that flow forever—of stars among whose fields of azure my raised spirits have walked in glory. All are dumb. But as I gaze on thy living face, I feel that there is something in the love that mantles through its beauty that cannot wholly perish. We shall meet again, Clemanthe."

THE LAST OF EARTH.

KATE PUTNAM OSGOOD.

DEATH—is it Death?
The shadow following still upon the sun,
The one same end of all things yet begun,
After the glory of Life the sudden gloom,
After the strife the inexorable doom,
    The frozen breath?

    Nay, rather see
Where the new grave lies sodden in the rain,
How the bare earth quickens to growth again!
Waiting the wonder-season's lavish dower
Young rootlets creep, a wealth of grass and flower
    Ere long to be.

    When Death has passed
Into the land of silence and of cloud,
The leafless land, wherein no bird is loud,
Life lingers yet with song and blossom rife.
Lo! step for step go ever Death and Life,—
    But Life is last!

"THE true Christian is always young."
SCHLEIERMACHER, *German Theologian.*

REVIEW OF LIFE.

O THOU who, without respect of persons, judgest according to every man's work, have mercy upon me, and blot out the manifold transgressions of my life. It becometh me, O Lord, to take a review of the course in which I have walked; but oh, what a review! Its many talents unimproved, and duties left undone, and sins committed!

I stand before Thee inexcusable—self-condemned; but, blessed be Thy name! not without hope, for there is mercy and forgiveness with Thee. Thou hast provided a sacrifice for sin, a Saviour; to Him would I fly for refuge, and plead that mercy and not judgment may be mine, and that the remainder of my life may be considered a grant of mercy, in order that I may bring forth fruits worthy of repentance. Give me grace, O Lord, not only to repent of past sins and omissions, but to make it much the business of my remaining days to supply the deficiencies of my former ones.

May Thy gracious presence direct and support me. Be thou, O Lord, my light and my strength. Enable me to cast all my cares on Thee. Bless to me both my enjoyments and my sufferings, and whether my remaining days be peaceful or stormy, bright or dark, make me to increase in faith, in holiness, in humility, in patience and charity, that I may be rich towards God and finally gain an abundant entrance to the saint's inheritance.

www.ingramcontent.com/pod-product-compliance
Lightning Source LLC
Chambersburg PA
CBHW022145300426
44115CB00006B/352